NEW YORK HARBOR

NEW YORK HARBOR

A Geographical and Historical Survey

Arthur D. Kellner

McFarland & Company, Inc., Publishers

Jefferson, North Carolina, and London

Library of Congress Cataloguing-in-Publication Data

Kellner, Arthur D., 1925–
New York Harbor : a geographical and
historical survey / Arthur D. Kellner.
p.   cm.
Includes bibliographical references and index.

ISBN-13: 978-0-7864-2400-9
(illustrated case : 50# alkaline paper) ∞

1. New York Harbor (N.Y. and N.J.)—Geography.
2. New York Harbor (N.Y. and N.J.)—History.   I. Title.
F128.63.K45   2006   974.7'1—dc22   2006018560

British Library cataloguing data are available

On the cover: *SS United States*, by Tom Kellner,
oil on canvas, 18" × 24", 2004

Manufactured in the United States of America

*McFarland & Company, Inc., Publishers
Box 611, Jefferson, North Carolina 28640
www.mcfarlandpub.com*

Acknowledgments

This book is the result of a lot of help. My family was a source of continuing encouragement. My wife Rosemae helped immeasurably by providing moral support and many suggestions. My son Tom worked on the art, which was a great boon. His wife Lynne was good enough to read the manuscript, as did my daughter Susan, and they made many improvements. Son Gary sent a host of materials which were of great value. Doug continually reminded of relevant things to read, and looked over the contract (he is a lawyer). Son Steve made many suggestions as well.

The people at the Roseland library helped. Judy Lind, Director, and Reina Jacobowitz were of particular assistance. The personnel at the libraries, societies, and the museum in New York City where part of my research was done proved invaluable.

Lastly, but not the least, my thoughts in writing this book have been of Jim Flynn. "Uncle Jim," although long dead, inspired this effort. He was the captain of the tug I deckhanded on. He was a good man in every respect. He was a charitable man: Every derelict around the harbor owed him money. Smart, he had a shrewd intelligence about him. He could have been a doctor or a lawyer if he had had more education.

This book is dedicated to him. God bless you and keep you, Jim Flynn, for you were the salt of the earth.

My thanks go to all of you.

Table of Contents

Introduction

This is an account of New York Harbor, the way it is now, and the way it used to be. The harbor has changed quite a bit. It was in its heyday in the 1800s and during World War II. It is not that way now, and this book will detail its transformation from a busy, bustling harbor to a more leisurely, quiet port.

In the 1800s, there were several reasons for its being a thriving port. The industrial revolution was in full swing. Factories were growing ever more numerous, and for transportation reasons many of these factories were located on the many waterways that formed the port of New York. Governor Clinton opened up the Erie Canal with great fanfare. The canal connected New York by water with the midwestern and western parts of the United States. Boats and barges could go up the Hudson, connect with the Erie Canal and have access to the Great Lakes, and thus to the Midwest. At that time, waterborne transportation was at the fore. There was no better way to get around or to ship goods. Since that time, land-based transportation and air transportation has taken over for the most part. Shipments are made by rail and people are flown throughout the United States. Since the advent of the automobile, a great road system has been built, and long-haul trucking carries many goods.

People adjust to the changes. Sometimes it takes time. For example, the screw propeller was invented in the early 1800s for use in boats, but it took until the 1900s for it to become widespread in use. At around the same time the steam engine was first applied to boats and ships, but vessels with sails continued to be developed to a very high extent until well into the second half of the century. Human resistance to change is oftentimes great. The people who live in the communities surrounding the harbor have been trying to cope with the changes affecting the waterways, and this book will describe the ways in which the harbor has been transformed.

I sailed many times in New York Harbor, having both a father and an uncle who were tugboat captains. I grew up taking trips with each of them as a boy. My father died when I was seven years old, but my uncle continued to take me out with him for a week at a time. We went all over, wherever we had to deliver a tow: to Eastchester, Newtown Creek, to Port Jefferson on Long Island, to Stamford, Connecticut. Once, we took a garbage scow to the "Acid Waters," the dump area off Sandy Hook. We went to Hoboken for coal. In those days, the tugs were propelled by steam engines. I used to love lying in my bunk, lulled to sleep by the steady "puff puff puff" of the smokestack venting the spent steam. Often, I would go into the engine room. The two cylinders of the engine were above the floor. The "floor" was a steel grating. Through it I could see the rest of the engine extending below, the piston rods connected to the enormous crankshaft. The engine throbbed like a beating heart, moving up and down in steady rhythm. Once it put me to sleep on the engine room bench with its hypnotic reciprocations.

When I became a teenager, my uncle would let me steer. I remember one particular occasion. It was in the late 30s, maybe 1938. We were coming down the East River, running light — without a tow — just passing under the Brooklyn Bridge. There was a lot of traffic on the river: ferry boats crossing the river, car floats scooting in all directions, tugs with tows coming up the river, a petroleum tanker heading for Newtown Creek. My uncle offered to let me steer. I was surprised the captain would allow me to steer with all this traffic around us, although I had asked him many times. I didn't say anything; I just stepped up and took the wheel, which was almost as big as I was. (At that time, the wheel was directly connected by cables to the rudder, so it had to be large to get the leverage to turn it. Later on, as technology caught up, the boats had power-assisted steering, so the steering wheels became smaller, about two feet in diameter instead of five feet. Now, some boats have levers to steer with. Most boats and ships have wheels, although the wheels are much smaller than in former days.) Needless to say, the captain watched very carefully while I steered the boat through the maze of vessels. The first mate came up to the pilot house — it was about twelve-thirty p.m. and he had just had lunch getting ready to go on watch. He was alert to all the boats around us, too. Then he took over the steering and I breathed easily again. I enjoyed steering, but there were a lot of boats on the river.

That harbor of my youth bears little resemblance to the New York Harbor of today.

Later, during college days, I became a deckhand on the boats, sailing mostly with my uncle. I went on to become a professional, but I have had always retained my interest in the harbor. I sailed in the harbor, more recently, on a boat I shared with my oldest son. I have had occasion to observe the harbor and how it has changed over the years. In the 1930s, when my father or my uncle took me on the tugboat with him, I saw a host of vessels in the harbor going every which way. In contrast, later, in my travels around the harbor I noted that there were far fewer vessels on the waters of the harbor. I asked myself, "How can this be?" I determined to find the answer.

I did research. I talked to officials who knew something about the harbor.

Introduction

This book is a result of my search for answers about a changed harbor, and the story of the harbor's changes is one of improvement and growth, of the problems that confront the harbor, and of the changes in the culture and attitudes of the surrounding population.

The reader who is familiar with the harbor will find it discussed from perhaps a different point of view. A reader who is less acquainted with the port of New York (and New Jersey) will find information about the rivers, bays and creeks that make New York Harbor what it is.

New York Harbor is truly a port in transition, but constant change is the nature of any harbor. This story gives a perspective on the changes that have taken place in the port of New York, those that are happening today, and perhaps, those changes, unknown but inevitable, that are the future of New York Harbor.

You could not step twice into the same river
—Heraclitus

1

The Port from a Physical Perspective

A Port in Transition

New York Harbor is a sprawling port. It reaches from Ambrose Light at the entrance, up the Hudson River to the northern tip of Manhattan, out the East River to City Island on the east. It is a magnificent harbor — but grossly underutilized in the present day and age. In the past, New York Harbor was teeming with shipping activity. In the 1850s the Lower East Side of Manhattan was cluttered with ships lined up, one beside the other, the masts reaching to the sky like matchsticks, the rigging a confused mess of seemingly raveled lines. Now, the harbor is less crowded. The New York City parts of the harbor, whose docks and wharves used to be swarming with workers unloading ships, is in many places bare and desolate.

Important Characteristics of New York Harbor

The harbor of New York is one of the largest in the world. It is large not only in size but in diversity. The harbor is not just a protected indentation in the coastline, although it certainly is that to start with. It is more complicated than that, as a glance at the chart will show. The harbor includes bays and rivers, islands, and sandbars as well. Some of the creeks run off the rivers as well as some of the bays. The port of New York is different from other ports in some ways. There are no large ports close by. The beaches of New Jersey stretch for 110 miles until they reach Cape May. To the east, Long Island stretches for 104 miles. There are no ports that a ship can get into along these coasts. In the case of New York Harbor, while it is a large port in area, vessels do not have to go an inordinately long distance to get to sheltered waters. The term *harbor* suggests a compact, protected area right off the ocean, yet this is not true in many cases. Philadelphia is quite a way inland. Ships have to travel through Delaware Bay and the Delaware River to get to Philadelphia. To get close to Houston, Texas, ships have

Numbers show locations of places mentioned in the text.

1. Ambrose Light
2. Sandy Hook Pilots' Boat Station
3. Sandy Hook
4. U.S. Navy Station Earle, NJ
5. Great Kills Harbor
6. Harlem River
7. City Island
8. Hell Gate
9. Ambrose Channel
10. Port Newark & Elizabeth
11. Erie Basin
12. Kill Van Kull
13. Railroads
14. Gowanus Canal
15. Newtown Creek
16. Coast Guard Headquarters
17. World Trade Center
18. Chelsea Piers
19. Morris Canal
20. Sheepshead Bay

to traverse Galveston Bay. The channel is 30 miles in length. New Orleans, while it is a vital port in many respects, is quite a way up the Mississippi River. In New York, the distance is about 10 miles from Ambrose Light to the Narrows. New York is a well-protected harbor, but it does not take unduly long for vessels to get from the mouth of the harbor to their pier or anchorage.

New York harbor has another advantage in that it is mostly free of ice in the winter. The Cunard Steamship Line moved its offices and base of operations from Boston to New York because Boston Harbor was ice-clogged during winter (now Cunard is in Miami to be closer to the cruising area). The Hudson River frequently becomes ice-bound in the winter, but that happens north of New York City where there is less salinity of the water.

The Port Authority of New York and New Jersey states that there is 650 miles of shoreline in New York Harbor. There are estimates running all the way up to 900 miles. That measurement would seem to be a matter of counting every indentation — the finer the measurement is set, the longer the shoreline is. The official measurement is 578 miles for New York City alone.[1] According to the *Gotham Gazette*, Mayor John Lindsay had his staff measure the actual New York City waterfront, and they came up with 578 miles. When the New Jersey parts of the shoreline are added, the figure is close to 900 miles.

Most notable for New York Harbor, and for many harbors for that matter, is the rate of change that characterizes it. It has a remarkable history. Some occurrences were shattering to the people involved. As we look back in broader perspective they seem paler than the earth-shaking impact they had on the people who were involved, but still significant and interesting. Heraclitus said that a man cannot step in the same river twice. The river is always changing, and New York Harbor is in a constant process of change. Changes evolve slowly in some cases; in other instances they happen almost overnight. A harbor depends mostly on the culture of the land around it, the businesses, the nature of the people, their way of life. The harbor is a dynamic entity, seething, bustling, the sum total of the hopes and dreams of thousands of people working in their individual ways to carry out their part of the process of making the harbor function. The harbor changes continually to adapt to the way the people around it choose to live. It is dependent upon the economy of the region that surrounds it, and, increasingly, the economy of the whole world.

Many thousands of people are involved in running the harbor. Some of the people who make the harbor what it is are ships' crews. Others are boatmen. Some are stevedores on the docks. Others are real estate investors planning to renovate one piece or another of the shoreline. In 2002 a total of 228,946 full-time jobs were directly related to New York Harbor activities.[2] Ocean-borne trade and related business comes to $23 billion annually.[3] The harbor remains busy in specific areas, but the pattern has changed from previous years.

In addition to people around it who effect the developments in the harbor, there is another cause of change: Mother Nature. The silting of the upper and

View of Hudson with Manhattan and the East River in the background. The railroad terminals of New Jersey are in the foreground. The picture was taken in the mid–1940s when the Hudson River was busier with commercial traffic than it is today (courtesy South Street Seaport).

lower bays is an example. Some beaches erode and others are built up. Environmental changes take place in the rivers and bays over time. It is said that the harbor is getting cleaner than it has been for centuries, but it still has a way to go to get rid entirely of the pollutants that find their way into the water. Also, technological changes bring new designs of ships and engines.

They bring changes in techniques as well, such as the containers in which cargo is shipped now, bringing on a whole raft of modifications in ship design and cargo-handling processes.

A Quiet Harbor

The port of New York is a different harbor now. Consider this scene.

The time is in the 1960s. A conference is being held in Hoboken, New Jersey, on a bluff above the Hudson River, opposite midtown Manhattan. It is five o'clock in the afternoon on a warm, sunny day. The meeting is coming to a close. The conference

8

leader opens the blinds on a large, wall-to-wall window that overlooks the river. What a brilliant tableau! The liner SS *United States* fills the window as if on cue, moving up the Hudson, approaching her berth on the west side of Manhattan.[4]

Such a scene is not likely to take place in the present day. For one thing, the SS *United States* is not in operation any longer. (The laid-up SS *United States* has been sold to Royal Caribbean International. It will be renovated and put into use as a cruise ship. The foundation that watches out for the SS *United States* is very concerned that the cruise line restore it faithfully.)

Liners that once crossed the Atlantic Ocean have been replaced by modern airplanes that can fly to Europe in six hours, even three and one-half hours on a supersonic transport (SST). As pointed out in an article in *Fortune*, the introduction of the Boeing 707 airplane in 1958 made air flight a popular way to cross the ocean.[5] Before that time, air travel was mainly for the well-to-do or business travelers. In 1978, the federal government deregulated the airlines and then air travel really took off, dealing travel by ocean-going ships yet another blow. Now, ships are almost out of business on that route. (There are exceptions: The liner *Queen Mary II* recently made her debut, sailing to New York Harbor. The proposal was to dock her in Brooklyn.) There are not many ocean liners coming from Europe steaming up the Hudson River these days.

The Hudson River is relatively quiet now compared to the way it used to be. For example, when an automobile full of New Jersey commuters comes down the corkscrew ramp leading to the entrance to the Lincoln Tunnel on the New Jersey side, the travelers are treated to a beautiful view of the Hudson River with a backdrop of the magnificent Manhattan skyline. They are inured to it all from commuting day in and day out; they don't even see it, but if they looked closely they would see only a few boats on the water, a small ferry, a police boat perhaps. No ships. Not much activity at all. Why?

One used to see large transatlantic passenger vessels in their berths on the West Side of Manhattan. No longer. It is true that some cruise ships have been moored at the Passenger Ship Terminal in Manhattan, and the Economic Development Commission of the City of New York wants to invest $250 million in refurbishing the Passenger Ship Terminal. Aside from that, the piers which used to berth the transatlantic ships are largely used for non-marine purposes. Recently, two cruise ships that used to be berthed at Manhattan moved their base of operations to Bayonne.[6]

One series of piers that used to berth the transatlantic ships, called Chelsea Piers, languished and rotted for several years. Strikingly, those piers were recently made into a large recreational area, with a golf driving range, tennis courts, and a host of other recreational facilities.

Technological change has had its effect. In the 1800s, sailing vessels reached proudly into New York Harbor. They were replaced by steam-driven vessels toward the latter part of the 19th century. Now, the modern jet airplane has replaced the ocean liner. In addition, recreational use of the harbor has increased quite a bit, as evidenced by the marinas that have replaced the commercial piers. Times change. Driven by the many forces that act upon it, the harbor adjusts to keep up — sometimes slowly as piers fall into decay, sometimes rapidly as new construction takes place.

CHANGES THAT HAD AN IMPACT ON THE HARBOR

As one looks back in the history of the development of the harbor, there are several events that stand out in their effect on the movement of vessels on the water. The dredging of Ambrose Channel was a great step forward. Also, the clearing of Hell Gate made the passage through that area much safer for the steamboats and ships that came into New York Harbor through Long Island Sound. During recent decades, the demise of many tugboat companies has had a large impact on the harbor. One sees far fewer tugs on the water than previously. Tows are few and far between. Also, changes in patterns of rail transportation have resulted in a decrease in rail float activity. In addition, during the 1800s and 1900s there were many ferryboats on the rivers. They were operating because they were needed — they were the only way to get across the rivers. The Brooklyn Bridge was opened in 1873. That put one of the ferry companies out of business. Today, there are eight bridges across the East River (one of them, Hell Gate Bridge, is a railroad bridge). Also, in the 1930s, the Lincoln and Holland tunnels were constructed beneath the Hudson River. Before that time, ferry traffic was heavy across the Hudson River. Now, there are ferries but they are completely different. They are much smaller because they are not designed to carry vehicles, and they are much faster. The new ferries are coming more and more into use these days, especially after the World Trade Center disaster of 2001. The reasons for these changes will be described in greater detail as the story of the harbor unfolds.

New York Harbor has changed. It is grand, glorious, the most magnificent harbor in the whole world. It is without a doubt the port that has the most potential as a shipping center. Its potential is not reached, however, at the present time nor will it be in the near future. Historically, it was the greatest shipping port. In the early 21st century, it is not the greatest shipping center. Many of its docks are rotting or have been converted into recreational uses. Much of the waterfront now consists of parks and esplanades. Civic groups want access to the waterfront. They want to use it for recreation, for pleasure boating, and most of all, they want it cleaned up. As shipping and industry has moved out, these groups are speaking in a louder voice. Much of the waterfront has been converted to parks, tourist attractions, museums and other similar uses. Gone are the days when the harbor belonged to the harbor people, the people who owed their livelihoods to the rivers and the bays.

The Waterfront Transformed

NEW YORK HARBOR BECOMES A SHIPPING PORT

When the Dutch settled New Amsterdam, the harbor still consisted of a waterway virtually untouched by human existence, unsullied by man's drive to make it into something he could use. At first, ships anchored out in the rivers or the bays and used small boats to come into shore. Little by little, the residents constructed docks to moor the vessels and seawalls to contain the erosion that threatened the water's edge. By the time the British took over from the Dutch in the 1700s, docks and piers had become commonplace. After the American Revolution, a building boom followed.

In the 1800s, when New York Harbor was becoming one of the great ports of the world, the need for piers and docks to moor the many ships that came into port was particularly great. These ships were berthed in piers on the Lower East Side of Manhattan and in Brooklyn for the most part. Later in the century, and on into the 1900s, Manhattan's West Side became built up with piers as the great ocean liners were berthed there after their ocean-spanning passages. The New Jersey shore of the Hudson River also began to be built up as the shipping companies and the railroads expanded into areas such as Bayonne, Jersey City and Hoboken.

PLANNING FOR WATERFRONT CONSTRUCTION

During the industrial age, many factories were built along the waterfront. The docks teemed with many components of the shipping industry at work there. Development of the waterfront was completely geared to the commercial interests until about the middle of the 1900s, resulting in helter-skelter development, a dock built here, a pier constructed there, a factory here. There was no overall plan. The start of comprehensive planning began with the establishment in 1870 of the Department of Docks (DOD). The DOD took part in the design of significant docks and piers, several of which still stand today, like Pier A in lower Manhattan.[7]

Pier A was occupied by the Department of Marine and Aviation of the City of New York, the new name for the former Department of Docks. The sign for the department was still prominently displayed for a long time after the department no longer occupied the building. It was on the river end of the building for all ships and boats to see as they passed by. However, the department was quietly disbanded when its functions were taken over by the Port Authority of New York and New Jersey. The police department Harbor Unit was also based there, but now it is located in the Brooklyn Army Terminal.

Pier A is located at the north end of the Battery, close to Battery Park City. When it was built, at a time when the Department of Docks was endeavoring to utilize the most sophisticated methods in their designs, Pier A represented an advance in construction techniques. Expensive materials went into the under-pinnings of the pier structure; the foundation was constructed upon bedrock. Some persons criticized the design of the building itself, much as other struc-tures built in the same era were criticized. The buildings were constructed of flimsy materials, sheet metal in many cases. The buildings had fancy architec-tural details pressed into the surface metal. The thinking was that the buildings should look nice, but they did not have to be of solid construction in view of their intended use — to store materials in transit, for the most part.

Pier A was built in the period 1884–86. The clock tower was added in 1919. It was designated as a war memorial of World War I — the first permanent memorial to that war. It was at the time the only clock striking time in ship's hours other than the one at the Naval Academy at Annapolis on the east coast.[8] Pier A is now in the hands of developers who want to turn it into restaurants and a visitors' center.[9, 10] The National Park Service is involved. The National Park Service wants to use it as a screening center for passengers scheduled to go on the boats to the Statue of Lib-erty and Ellis Island. It will be settled eventually, but the local citizens are impatient.

The piers, built in the late 1800s, particularly on the west side of Manhat-tan, extended from the land like fingers. They were built longer and longer until the authorities became concerned with their effect on the rivers. In 1855 the New York Harbor Commission was set up to forestall further encroachments on the harbor. Of course, as longer ships were built, the drive to build longer piers increased, and much petitioning and lobbying went on. Eventually, the Federal Rivers and Harbors Act of 1888 passed the responsibility for controlling pier length to the U.S. Army Corps of Engineers.

NEW YORK CITY DEPARTMENT OF DOCKS

When the Department of Docks (DOD) was established after the Civil War, in 1870, there were great expectations for the department. It was set up to coor-dinate the growth of the waterfront of New York Harbor, at least the New York City part of it, where most of the shipping installations at the time were located. DOD made many contributions to the development of the waterfront at a time when New York Harbor was coming into its own as a world shipping port. To show the importance of this newly established department, General George McClellan, a noted civil war figure, was appointed as head.

One of McClellan's significant accomplishments as head of this department was the construction of seawalls around the harbor, especially around Manhat-tan Island. Called the Riverwall, it was carefully planned, made of stone and con-crete, the latest design of the time. Much of the way we see the waterfront in the present day was constructed at this time. It consisted of large blocks of stone or concrete placed one upon the other parallel to shore. It was built up to about six feet above the waterline. Then, earth, refuse or rubble was filled in behind it. Begun in 1871, the Riverwall project was largely complete by 1916. The Department of Docks had built close to 62,000 feet of bulkhead. Other departments had built 32,000 feet and private parties 12,000 feet.

FILLING IN THE WATERFRONT

During the latter part of the 1800s, while building or improving the docks around New York Harbor was taking place, marshes and tidelands were filled in. In other cases, bulkheads were constructed along the river and earth and rubble filled in behind them, many of them part of the Riverwall project. The result was that the waters were encroached upon and the land area became larger. It has been estimated that Manhattan Island is now 30% larger than it was when the early settlers came. The rivers—the North River (Hudson) and the East River—are fairly wide, so it was tempting to the pier owners to lobby for longer piers. However, it was a questionable practice. It became illegal to encroach upon the rivers, and it still is illegal, although along came the plan for Battery Park City in the 1990s and the authorities made an exception. Battery Park City stands

Lower Manhattan in the 1880s. Governor's Island can be seen across the East River (Library of Congress).

13

as one of the modern developments on the waterfront of the Lower West Side. The constructors filled in 62 acres in all, including Pier 1. Pier A, adjacent to Pier 1, was untouched. (The fill came from the excavation for the World Trade Center). Waterside, on the East River at 30th Street, is another example of condominiums built out onto the waters of the harbor.

CHELSEA PIERS

Another accomplishment of the Department of Docks, although General McClellan was long gone by then, was the construction of the Chelsea Piers on the West Side of Manhattan. The Chelsea-Gansevoort Plan was proposed in 1880. The plan was to develop the waterfront in the Chelsea and Gansevoort sections of Manhattan by building very modern and impressive structures on piers built out into the waters of the Hudson. At that time the waterfront was a seedy, rat-infested, dirty area that provided little welcome for transatlantic passengers. The ships were palaces of ornate luxury, but on departing from the ship in New York, the passenger was faced with the desolation of the dock area. The Chelsea Piers development intended to correct that impression by offering the arriving and departing passengers a comfortable, clean, well-designed terminal.

The planning for the project lasted for decades. Applications for approval went on while the officials debated the issues involved. One of the issues was the length of the piers. Ships were being built in England that were longer than ever before. The new ships *Luciana* and *Campania* were 600 feet long. New York officials applied for longer piers, and they were finally able to build to 728 feet in pier length.

After the legal issues had been resolved, funding of the project became a problem. Half the project was approved and in 1894 work began. The five Gansevoort piers were the first to open, in 1902. Then, work was initiated on the Chelsea parts of the project. It was finally finished in 1910. For 30 years the project had been under discussion, and now New York Harbor could be proud of its transatlantic terminals. Extending for about three-quarters of a mile along the shore on the West Side of Manhattan, the Chelsea Piers were generally considered to be good-looking. They had been planned as a unified set of piers, rather than the hodgepodge of design that individual pier owners built. For many decades they served well as terminals for the transatlantic ships, until the inexorable process of change caught up with them and they fell into disuse.

Entering Port: The Lower Bay

AMBROSE LIGHT

One of the first things a ship sees as it approaches New York Harbor is Ambrose Light. It used to be a lightship, the *Ambrose*, last of a long line of lightships that were stationed outside New York. The first one was put in place in 1823.

Sandy Hook lightship in about 1900. Lightships have been replaced by fixed automatic beacons. A schooner can be seen behind the ship, probably a pilot boat (Library of Congress).

The *Ambrose* is now on exhibition at the South Street Seaport, which is on the lower East River in Manhattan. The Coast Guard built a steel tower to replace the lightship in 1967, which served as a beacon to many ships as they approached the harbor. The crew was removed from the light tower in 1988 and it became an automated light. Ships approaching New York frequently set the location of Ambrose Light in their GPS navigation equipment* as a waypoint to steer to. This practice created a problem when in 1995 a ship, the *Aegeo*, on automatic steering, crashed into the light, doing quite a bit of damage to the structure. Shortly after the ship struck the light tower, the Coast Guard polled the commercial shipping industry and the boating public about their need for the light. Opinions were to keep the light, but the Coast Guard constructed a new tower about a mile to the northwest of where it had been. The old tower has been dismantled.

GPS: Global Positioning System, a system of 24 satellites, completed in 1994, for finding position on Earth.

The new tower was damaged again by the freighter *Kouros V* in January 2001. The light was repaired, however, and continues to light the way to the entrance to New York Harbor. (Earlier, in 1908, *Relief*, a temporary replacement for the regular lightship, was hit by the *Green Bay*, a freighter. It was sunk, but the crew was rescued.) It is evident that the beacon light, in the center of all the ship traffic coming into New York, is a vulnerable target for ships.

ENTERING NEW YORK HARBOR

Almost all ships enter New York Harbor through the Ambrose Channel. A few ships, under special circumstances, enter the port via Long Island Sound. The Long Island Sound entrance/exit is used mostly by tugs with tows, such as an unloaded oil barge being towed from Bridgeport or New Haven.

Ships entering New York Harbor usually wait in the vicinity of Ambrose Light to pick up a pilot. A pilot will come from the waiting pilot boat in a pilot launch, a fast motor cruiser that will come alongside the ship while the ship is under way. Then there is a moment of excitement while the pilot makes the jump from the pilot boat to the ship's ladder. That can be a relatively calm moment or it can be sheer adventure depending on the sea conditions.

The pilot will then guide the ship up Ambrose Channel, into the Lower Bay, through the Narrows between Staten Island and Brooklyn, into the Upper Bay. From there, depending on where the ship is bound, it may go through Kill Van Kull into Newark Bay, somewhere on the East River, or maybe the Hudson River (called the North River by boatmen in the harbor).

Here is an example of how a pilot would guide a ship to an anchorage. It is excerpted from a description in *Ocean Navigator*.[11] The ship was the 830-foot *Eagle Baltimore*, entering the harbor through the Narrows. The pilot called VTS (Vessel Traffic Service — to be described in greater detail in the Coast Guard section) to advise them where he was going, in this instance, to the Stapleton anchorage off Staten Island. After the pilot had slowed the ship, he looked at the chart to check on the depths in the anchorage. He wanted to be close enough to the shore so that he would not be extending out into the channel, but he did not want to get so close to the shore that he would drag aground. The article describes how the pilot lined the ship up with a tractor on the shore, using the tractor, in effect, as a range marker. In this case the pilot had grown up on Staten Island and used his knowledge of every inch of the shore.

An alternative route into New York Harbor is used by some vessels and tows going into the Raritan River or Kill Van Kull. In this case, ships would pick up their pilot just off Sandy Hook. The pilot would guide the vessel through ship channels across the Lower Bay to the Southeast corner of Staten Island, past Perth Amboy, into Arthur Kill, the eastward end of Kill Van Kull. Naval vessels going to and from the long pier at Earle Ammunition Depot use the Sandy Hook Channel.

If the weather is good, ships will occasionally anchor outside the harbor, awaiting a favorable tide, or perhaps waiting for docking instructions from their headquarters in port.

SANDY HOOK

Sandy Hook reaches out like a long sandbar. It is like an arm that closes off the Lower Bay from the open ocean. Many times have I sailed around the point to go from the choppy waters of the ocean to the relative calm of the bay. The difference in sea conditions always amazed me, but it was welcome relief from the sometimes roiling waters of the ocean. Lower New York Bay is called Sandy Hook Bay in the part closest to the arm of Sandy Hook. Sandy Hook is an extension of the shoreline of the state of New Jersey. On Sandy Hook near the end of the point, but not right on the point, is the oldest lighthouse in the United States, built by the Dutch settlers in 1689. It used to be on the end of Sandy Hook but now it is some distance south of Sandy Hook Point. That is part of the change created by nature: The tidal current over the years has deposited sand at the end of the point.

At the end of Sandy Hook, just inside the channel, there is usually a large number of fishing party boats anchored. There must be good fishing in that location because the boats are always there when the weather is good and the tide is right.

People sailing in Sandy Hook Bay can see the clamdiggers out in their open boats, raking their share of clams, filling their baskets, building up their muscles by working the long rakes which reach to the bottom. They can work far into the bay because the water is not very deep. Unfortunately, the coliform bacteria content of the waters in the Lower Bay is high, so the waters of the bay are not open to the general public for clamming. The reason they are open for commercial clamming is that the law requires commercial clammers to take their clams to local processing centers where the clams are treated.

THE LOWER BAY

The entrance to New York Harbor consists of the beginning of the Lower Bay, between Sandy Hook and Rockaway Point (Breezy Point). The waters around the end of Sandy Hook are relatively shallow, as they are all across the Lower Bay. They shift in depth from year to year as winter storms pile up sand in some areas and take it away in others. A number of channels have been dredged over the years in the Lower Bay and they are marked by buoys. The main channel used by ships as they enter and leave New York Harbor is Ambrose Channel which was dredged from 1901 to 1908. It runs straight into the Narrows. In the early 1900s, bigger ships, of much greater draft, created a requirement for dredging this channel. It is interesting to note that a similar requirement exists in the present day. Later, we will explore the steps that are being taken at present to accommodate the new, deep-draft container ships that are coming into use.

Although it is protected by Sandy Hook and the Rockaways, the Lower Bay can get rough at times, especially if the wind surpasses 15 knots in speed. One of the reasons that the Lower Bay is so violent in high winds is that there is not much depth to the water there. The waves are closer together and steeper compared to the ocean, where the waves are farther apart. The Lower Bay, just like the Upper Bay, is fairly shallow given its wide dimensions. It's only about 20 feet deep on average (except for the channels). It is interesting that when a person stands on the shore and looks out at all that water, he naturally has the impression that it is all deep water. Not so, as far as New York Harbor is concerned. There are many areas in which the water is relatively shallow, even only a few feet deep at low water in some places. There are many places mariners simply cannot go with their boats, and they have learned to stay in the channels for the most part. The big ships are even more constrained. They have to stay in the middle of the channels, and at high tide for some of them. That is one reason why it is so important for a ship to have a pilot on board who knows the waters like the back of his hand.

Eons ago the area that constitutes New York Harbor was considerably above sea level. The Hudson River scoured out what is now called the Hudson Canyon offshore of the harbor entrance, lying presently deep under fathoms of water. One of the causes of the shallowness on the Lower Bay is the silt which is brought down by the Hudson River, and to a lesser extent by the East River. The tides run strongly in the rivers and the bays. The hydraulic effect is to deposit large quantities of sand and silt on the bottom, usually where one wants it least from a navigation point of view. The result is that the Lower Bay as well as the Upper Bay is criss-crossed with dredged channels, especially the Lower Bay, where we find the Sandy Hook Channel, Swash Channel, Chapel Hill Channel, to name a few. Centuries ago, ships used to go by way of Sandy Hook, past Romer Shoal, to the right of West Bank to get to the Narrows. The ships were of relatively shallow draft by present-day standards and even then they scraped bottom or had to wait for high water to go into or out of the harbor.

To the South in the Lower Bay, is the shoreline of the New Jersey Highlands, a relatively undeveloped shoreline, a few houses here and there, a marina behind the Atlantic Highlands stone jetty that forms a good anchorage for pleasure boats. A fast, modern ferry to New York travels from Atlantic Highlands. Nearby is the navy installation at Earle Ammunition Depot with its long pier that stretches out into the bay for two miles, dominating the surroundings. Navy ships dock there to load up with ammunition.

Another harbor in the Lower Bay worth mentioning is Great Kills Harbor on Staten Island.[12] It is a fine port for pleasure boaters. However, except for the local sailors, it is not well known among the boating gentry. Too bad. It gets little attention from the sailors who go south in the winter and north in the summer. It is like a New England port in that it is still essentially undeveloped, right here in New York Harbor, part of New York City.

Ever-changing Harbor

The story of New York Harbor is a story of pluses and minuses. There is still pollution in the Lower Bay, as in the harbor overall. Sailing in the Lower Bay, one can on occasion still see solid material floating on the surface of the water. Sometimes, the water in the Lower Bay has a reddish-brown color. Back in time, there existed a plan for developing Great Kills into a large beach complex. The time of the plan was 1937. It never came to fruition. The economic conditions of the time probably killed the plan, but the waters of the Lower Bay are not the best to swim in. They are becoming cleaner, but there is still room for improvement because of the pollution.

When one views the harbor from any vantage point, the harbor seems to be in a state of flux. Until the middle of the 20th century, the harbor was bustling. There were boats and ships going every which way. There were tugs with barges in tow, ferries criss-crossing the rivers, railroad car floats going back and forth. Now, when one sails through the harbor one sees that many docks are abandoned and derelict. The harbor has changed. Shifts have been made in the areas of prime activity. That's how the harbor is: ever changing.

The Sound of the Harbor

The harbor sends a different message to each individual experiencing it. To the recreational fisherman it means a day on the boat near Sandy Hook. To the ship captain it means approaching a perhaps unknown harbor, waiting for a pilot to guide the ship in. To the tugboat captain it means taking a tow into New York Harbor and docking at Staten Island. To get the flavor of this experience, let's listen to the communications between ships, or between boats and shore stations.

> "This is the tug *Catherine McAllister* (to shore station in Staten Island). We're just passing St. George. We expect to be in in one hour. Have your dock crew ready to unload cargo."
> "This is Pilot Boat No. 3. We'll be at Ambrose Light at 1330 hours." (Pilot boat radioing to ship awaiting pilot to arrange a rendezvous).
> "Coast Guard, this is the ship *Merriweather*. We are a 600 foot tanker. We just passed through the Narrows heading toward Governor's Island. We're headed for the East River." (To the Vessel Traffic Service (VTS))

Each communication is stated in a matter-of-fact voice, flat, unemotional. It is routine, part of the job, but extremely important to each person involved. It is the sound of the harbor.

The Narrows and Upper Bay

The Real Harbor

When most people think of New York Harbor they think of the part around Manhattan. For the general public, this is the real harbor. When a ship comes into the harbor, it usually passes through the Narrows, unless it enters the harbor through the Long Island Sound entrance, which is less frequently used nowadays. The Narrows is a mile-wide body of water where Brooklyn and Staten Island almost touch. A bridge was built across the Narrows in 1965, a long span of a suspension bridge. The bridge is an important road link between Brooklyn and Staten Island. The bridge is named Verrazano after the explorer who was the first sailor to come to New York Harbor more than 300 years ago.

The Lower Bay and the Upper Bay are two relatively large bodies of water, although a glance at the chart will show that the Lower Bay is much the larger of the two. The Upper Bay and Lower Bay shrink down to an hourglass shape at The Narrows. As a ship comes through the Narrows, it enters the Upper Bay. Staten Island is on the left; Brooklyn is on the right. The buildings of downtown Manhattan are starting to come into view, off in the distance, a gradually growing spectacle of sparkling edifices.

Closer at hand is the Bay Ridge neighborhood in Brooklyn; then Erie Basin and the Red Hook section of Brooklyn appear. The docks begin after passing through the Narrows; before that, esplanades line the Brooklyn shore. The water of the Upper Bay becomes relatively shallow off Bay Ridge, so that area has been

The Narrows in an old print, looking toward the Lower Bay. Brooklyn is on the left, Staten Island to the right (Library of Congress).

set aside as an anchorage. Many ships can be seen anchored there, waiting for a lighter to load or unload them, or waiting for their turn at the docks of Brooklyn. There is deeper water to both sides of the anchorage, but the main channel is to the left, proceeding right up the middle of the Upper Bay.

The Staten Island ferry, which travels between the Battery of Manhattan and St. George, Staten Island, plies its route entirely in the Upper Bay. Even so, it is a fairly long ferry ride. It leaves the ferry slip at the Lower East Side of Manhattan, where the East River flows into the Upper Bay, wends its way past Governor's Island, then heads for St. George on the northeastern end of Staten Island. There is almost always one ferry under way on the Upper Bay, plodding its way determinedly to its destination. For a long time the fare was only a nickel. Now the passage on the ferry is free of charge, a gesture to the Staten Island com-

Upper Bay. Staten Island ferry (foreground) wends its way to Manhattan. The *Constitution* (left) and the *Olympia* (right) are leaving port. The Statue of Liberty is in the distant center. The view is toward New Jersey. December 1, 1955. (Museum of the City of New York).

muters who work in Manhattan. The trip is also a treat to the many sightseers who get to see the harbor in all its glory, passengers who care to look have a breathtaking view of downtown Manhattan. Governor's Island, the Statue of Liberty, the historic buildings of Ellis Island, the tall buildings of Jersey City, the piers of Brooklyn are all in view.

At the Narrows, on the Staten Island side of the bay there is Fort Wadsworth. One of the towers for the Verrazano Bridge stands near the fort, which is on the water's edge. In days gone by, the guns of the fort deterred enemy ships from passing through The Narrows. Now, the U.S. Coast Guard has its headquarters for New York Harbor on this post, not right in the fort, but nearby in a contemporary building.

As one goes further into the harbor, Kill Van Kull is on the left, curving around Staten Island and separating it from New Jersey. Approaching the Battery, the southern tip of Manhattan, Liberty Island is encountered, with the Statue of Liberty welcoming visitors into the harbor. Past Liberty Island, also toward the Jersey shore, is the slightly larger Ellis Island, the well-known immigrant landing place. Since 1954, it has ceased being a processing place for immigrants but some the buildings have been designated as national historic sites. The ownership of Ellis Island has been a matter of contention between New York and New Jersey for many years. Among other things, New Jersey was disturbed by the fact that the island was much closer to its shore than to New York yet was not considered part of the state of New Jersey. The court case was recently decided with a Solomon-like decree that gave most of the land to New Jersey, but some land to New York.[13]

Kill Van Kull and Arthur Kill

KILL VAN KULL: A CRUCIAL WATERWAY

The Kill Van Kull is only about four miles long, but it is very important to the port. The Kull is an offshoot of the Upper Bay of New York Harbor. It separates Staten Island from New Jersey and is the lead-in to Newark Bay for ships wanting to reach the container docks of Elizabeth and Newark. Reaching off the Upper Bay, it stretches only a few miles to the south, to the entrance to Newark Bay; then, it connects with the Arthur Kill to complete the separation of Staten Island from New Jersey.

The most notable aspect of Kill Van Kull is that the container ships take this route into Newark Bay to the container piers, where the giant cranes can unload their containers with relative ease (not to neglect Howland Hook, for which Kill Van Kull is also a link to the Upper Bay). These cranes unload the containers right onto waiting trucks in some cases. Otherwise, the cranes unload them on the ground. These large ships, loaded to bursting with containers, in their short trip up the Kill Van Kull to Newark Bay go under the Bayonne Bridge, an enormous arch bridge which spans Kill Van Kull, connecting Staten Island with New Jersey. Kill Van Kull is currently dredged to 40 feet at mean low water. The U.S. Congress has approved dredging to 50 feet and the Corps of Engineers has undertaken the project.[14, 15] Some of the larger container ships are reportedly coming into the harbor not fully loaded because of the depth of the water, since the more fully loaded they are, the deeper the ships are in the water. There is potential for more shipping into New York Harbor, the New Jersey parts at least, and that is why the dredging of Kill Van Kull is taking place now.

West of Constable Hook is an indentation on the shore called Johnson's Cove. It is filled with the remains of old sailing vessels, deposited there long ago to waste away, washed by the comings and goings of the tide.[16] Most people see these old ships as an eyesore. Others who are more sentimental think these hulks should be restored to their former glory. At the very least, the area that they occupy is undeveloped waterfront that has the potential to be utilized in one way or another.

The container revolution has had a great effect on New York Harbor, shifting the major part of the port activity to New Jersey. This fact has great implications for the future of New York. New York and New Jersey, which constitute the Port Authority, have a sort of *entente cordial* at present, although New York is asking for a bigger piece of the pie at Howland Hook. It is part of the interplay between New York and New Jersey. Their respective influence on the Port Authority has great impact on what happens in the port of New York.

STATEN ISLAND SHORE

Boats and ships going from the Narrows into the Upper Bay pass St. George, Staten Island, on their left. St. George is where the ferryboat terminal is located. Officials have recently renovated the ferry terminal so the commuters to Manhattan have a comfortable beginning to their trip. Further up into Kill Van Kull, several tug companies have their base of operations. It is a scene of shipyards and other marine-related enterprises. Eventually, Shooters Island is passed, opposite the entrance to Newark Bay. Shooter's Island is a pristine, very natural setting. It is now a wildlife sanctuary, but unfortunately it is also home to many old, derelict boats left to rot their lives away.

ARTHUR KILL

The first major installation on the Arthur Kill as one leaves the Kill Van Kull going eastward is the Howland Hook Terminal (recently renamed the New York Container Terminal; see later section on the Port Authority). The Howland Hook Terminal is very active. It is located where the waterway separating Staten Island from New Jersey turns east. It is not as large as the terminals at Newark and Elizabeth, and some people have complained about the fact that there is no 50-foot dredged depth in its future. The plan was to dredge only to 41 feet in the waters around Howland Hook Terminal, but terminal authorities want to participate in the growth of trade beneficial to New Jersey and the management of the terminal and local community organizations want the channels to be dredged deeper. (The Army Corps of Engineers apparently plans to dredge to a 50-foot depth at Howland Hook, according to the project manager.)[17]

The terminal at Howland Hook is operated by the Port Authority of New York and New Jersey. It is on a tract of 187 acres.[18] It is a short way from the Staten Island end of the Goethals Bridge, which is of some advantage because of the accessibility of trucks to the bridge (although the traffic is high). The Howland Hook Terminal has the capacity to handle containers, and that is why the terminal wants to capitalize on future growth by having the channel leading to their docks as deep as it is in the Kill Van Kull. As with terminals of Newark and Elizabeth, most of the transportation is by trucks, but the Arlington railroad yard is nearby, so some of the containers are shipped by rail after they are unloaded off the ships at the terminal. However, the proportion of cargo shipped by rail is still small and the management of the terminal is pressing to make it larger.

Located on the New Jersey shore of the Arthur Kill are several petroleum companies. Tankers and oil barges towed by tugs are seen in these waters. There are many tank farms, and there at least one tank farm located on the Staten Island side of the river as well. However, the Staten Island side of the Arthur Kill is surprisingly undeveloped for the most part. Community groups and government agencies want to keep it that way. The authorities are constantly making improvements in the ecology of Arthur Kill. An example of that care is the Fresh Kills project. Situated in Staten Island, Fresh Kills used to be a major dumping ground for the garbage that was generated in other parts of New York City. The garbage was loaded on scows in various parts of the city.[19] The loaded scows were then towed by tugs to Fresh Kills. Pressured by the Environmental Protection Agency (EPA), New York City decided to close the landfill in 2001, although it was reopened to process the rubble from the 2001 World Trade Center disaster. Since that time elaborate plans have been drawn up to make the landfill into a public park including a golf course. If it is finished according to the plan, Fresh Kills will be a pretty picture of grassy hills and trees for the residents to use and enjoy.

Like Kill Van Kull, Arthur Kill is home to many derelict ships and boats; in fact, Staten Island's relatively natural shores seem to attract them. On the Arthur Kill, barges, scows and many old tugboats are scattered about the waters near the shore.

Part of Arthur Kill is Prall Island, 80 acres of pristine close-to-the-shore land. Taken with Shooter's Island, this island is the pride of government agencies and community organizations because of the regrowth of the natural habitat. It is the hunting ground of herons and other wading birds, among other birds and animals that proliferate there. The water quality has been improving in Arthur Kill. It is still polluted by the commercial activity of the boats and ships and the runoff from land installations, but to a lesser extent than before.

The Waterways That Separate Staten Island from New Jersey

Kill Van Kull and Arthur Kill are very much a part of New York Harbor. They are located at the extreme end of the harbor — Arthur Kill, particularly, is at the southern end. (Newark Bay, which is home to the container ports of Newark and Elizabeth and thus so important to New York Harbor, is at the southern end of the harbor also.) Ships and tows that have destinations in the Arthur Kill coming from ports to the south would use the Lower Bay to gain access to the port. The channels there are deep and well marked. Coming from the Long Island Sound, they would go through the Kill Van Kull to the Arthur Kill.

The Staten Island shoreline is relatively undeveloped. There is much potential there for future development. The community organizations have emphasized access to the water by the residential population, and government agencies such as the EPA are interested in restoration of the waterfront to its natural condition. To the commercial interests, the waterfront areas represent potential for business purposes. Which will win out? It depends, as with the whole harbor,

The Jersey Central Terminal. No longer used, it is on the waterfront of Liberty Park, site of the former Jersey Central classification yard.

25

Above: Lackawanna Ferry Slips. Hoboken is being revitalized now. The ferry slips are a waterfront attraction. *Below:* The *Santa Maria* at New York Grace Line Terminal. (Charles Evers painting, undated. Museum of the City of New York. Gift of the Grace Line).

upon how the surrounding culture evolves. In the near term, it appears that the trend is for the waterways to become more natural and ecologically pristine.

The Hudson River

The river that runs down the west side of Manhattan Island and flows into the Upper Bay at the Battery is called "the Hudson" by most people who live around New York Harbor; not Hudson River, not the Henry Hudson, just "the Hudson." It is called the North River by the boatmen who work in the harbor. Probably, they call it by that name because it originates toward the northern part of the state of New York, at a romantically named lake called "Tear of the Clouds."[20]

The Hudson is a picturesque river in many ways. Even as it flows in New York Harbor, and that is a very small extent of its overall length, it is very scenic. In the harbor, the river is flanked by the buildings of Manhattan on one side and, above Hoboken, it has the high-rising Palisades to enfold it with their beauty. It is a relatively wide river (the Hudson is wider than the East River). North of New York City, the contours of the land surrounding it become more mountainous. The river snakes through these hills like a magical ribbon. Starting out as the product of many streams and rivulets that flow into it, plus the strong outflow from the lake from whence it originates, the Hudson flows southward through a sizable part of New York State. Toward the north it is a natural freshwater stream. However, it is connected to the ocean at its lower end. So, the river meets the flow of salt water somewhere on its southward course. It varies with the time of the year: In the spring there is more fresh water pouring into the river. Usually it is salt all the way to Poughkeepsie, about 50 miles north of New York City.

The Hudson River Day Line used to take passengers on trips up and down the Hudson. That was in the day of the steamboat, like the *Alexander Hamilton*, a large paddle wheel steamer with a triple expansion steam engine that made trips between New York and Albany. Trips are still made up the Hudson — the scenery is very pleasant — but the boats are smaller now, and they do not have the panache of the old boats. (When last heard of, the *Alexander Hamilton* was rotting at a New Jersey pier on the Lower Bay. A group was trying to raise money to restore it but not having much success.)

In nature's inexorable process, the flow of the river from the north brings silt and other sedimentary deposits with it, much of which finds its way to the bottom of New York Harbor. Whereas the strong current makes the river rather deep in the middle, shoaling toward the shore has been problematic at times. Some New Jersey piers have become silted up so that they have had to be dredged. Also, parts of the Upper Bay are not very deep, especially toward the New Jersey side of the harbor. The Army Corps of Engineers has a constant problem with the Hudson in New York Harbor, and frequent dredging is necessary.

Jersey City waterfront on the Hudson River. There now are tall buildings to match Manhattan's skyline.

There are a number of bridges along the full length of the Hudson. The only one that pertains to New York Harbor is the George Washington, built by the Port Authority in 1931. The bridge goes from Fort Lee in New Jersey to the northern part of Manhattan. It connects to the Cross-Bronx Expressway (which has been called a long parking lot) and then over the Throgs Neck Bridge to Long Island. When one drives through New York City one becomes acutely aware that the city is a series of islands; there are so many bridges and tunnels to negotiate.

JERSEY SHORE OF THE HUDSON: THE "GOLD COAST"

Some people have called the Jersey shore of the Hudson the "Gold Coast."[21, 22] The reason it has been called the gold coast is that there are so many new buildings there, and real estate has been flourishing. The communities along the Hudson have changed a great deal in recent years. They used to be seedy waterfront operations, rat-infested areas of decay and dereliction. Now, they are becoming office and bedroom complexes right down to the water's edge.

Jersey City is a good example. Beside Liberty State Park, the old Jersey Central Yard on the peninsula adjacent to the Hudson, developers have built New-

West Side of Manhattan when transatlantic passenger ships occupied the Hudson River piers. The linner S.S. *Constitution* is just departing. Shown also, left to right are the **Queen Elizabeth, Olympia, United States** and **America** (South Street Seaport).

port City, a group of high-rise buildings that have changed the scene from the river. What used to be wharves and ferry slips is now a panorama of tall buildings that overlook the harbor. Also developed further south is Port Liberté, a condominium community built on the water.

Ironically, the World Trade Center disaster had a beneficial effect on the growth of the Hudson River shoreline of New Jersey. A few companies moved to New Jersey after the attack. Other companies were attracted by the lower rents and better style of life for their employees, a shorter commute for New Jerseyans being one consideration.[23] This is not to say that all has been rosy for New Jersey, or that there has been a mass exodus of companies from Manhattan across the river to New Jersey. The Port Liberté development, referred to above, had its share of economic difficulties before they eventually were straightened out. The problem with the New Jersey shoreline of the Hudson is the same as that which affects the entire harbor of New York: Economic cycles play their part.

Nevertheless, the New Jersey shoreline of the Hudson has changed considerably in the last few years. From Bayonne on the south to Fort Lee on the north the waterfront has been revitalized. Shopping malls, office buildings, and residential condominiums have replaced the factories, shipyards and railroad facilities. These changes have taken place because the factories have moved south (or gone out of business). The railroads have been replaced by the interstate road network, and shipping has been concentrated in other parts of the harbor, notably Port Newark and Elizabeth. A new light rail system has been built, going from Bayonne to Hoboken, which should improve the transportation infrastructure. Some stock market firms have announced plans to move across the river to New Jersey.

Mariners on the waters of the Upper Bay or the Hudson see not only the skyline of Manhattan but now they take in the ever-increasing tall buildings of Jersey City on the west side of the river.

Military Ocean Terminal

At Bayonne, just before Kill Van Kull, are the two enormous piers of the Military Ocean Terminal. It used to belong to the U.S. Navy, which had some very large ships moored there. Several years ago the Port Authority of New York and New Jersey took it over. Recently, Royal Caribbean International adopted part of it as their New York Harbor base of operations.[24] Specifically, the cruise line wanted the marine terminal for its new ship, the *Voyager of the Seas*, but moved one other ship to Bayonne as well.

The view of Manhattan, across the river, is spectacular from this vantage point, as it is all up and down the Jersey shore of the Hudson River.

Officials have announced a federal grant of $3 million to refurbish the Military Ocean Terminal. It will be called Peninsula at Bayonne Harbor. Proposals call for, in addition to marine usage, residential, industrial, cultural and open-space facilities, and an office complex. The harbor is changing. The Military Ocean Terminal, which used to berth mammoth naval vessels and which saw a great deal of men and materials shipped overseas during the wars, now will become the scene of activity of a different kind.

The East River

New York's Link with Long Island Sound

The East River is very important in the overall operation of the harbor. Every day boats and ships traverse its waters because it is the connection between the harbor and Long Island Sound. That fact makes the East River what it is—a tidal strait. It is also a body of water that separates the borough of Manhattan from Long Island. It is a long river that snakes its way past Manhattan, through Hell Gate, going by Flushing Bay, turning left at Throgs Neck, then feeding into Long Island Sound. Twice each day, waters flood through the narrow banks of Hell Gate to connect the sound to the Upper Bay. That is why the tidal current runs so strong in the East River. The water of the wide Long Island Sound squeezes through Hell Gate and then down through the narrow river. At times, the current reaches six knots in velocity, particularly where the river becomes narrow, such as at the infamous Hell Gate or where it splits to surround Roosevelt Island.

The river has an overall length of 14 miles, going well past Hell Gate to connect to the sound near Stepping Stones Light and City Island. City Island is at the extreme end of the harbor, where Long Island Sound begins. (City Island is described in the section dealing with recreational use of the harbor.)

EAST RIVER IN THE 1800S

The East River has a grand history. During the 1800s, it was the busiest part of the harbor; in fact, the port of New York was then the busiest port in the world. (It is no longest the busiest harbor. In the United States, Long Beach in California and Seattle-Tacoma, in Washington, surpass it). At the beginning of the 1800s, ships found it easy to anchor in the East River, just off the Lower East Side or off downtown Brooklyn. As piers were built, ships tied up at the Lower East Side of Manhattan. South Street and the neighborhood around it became the maritime center for New York. Shipping companies located here, and the U.S. Customs House was built at the Battery. In addition to the wharves which were built on Manhattan at the lower East River, Corlears Hook was the site of many shipbuilding companies. These shipyards were on the East River, on the bulge of Manhattan where the Manhattan tower of the Williamsburg Bridge now stands.

Many ships were built in the shipyards of Corlears Hook. Shipping companies were eager to have the magnificent sailing ships built because the demand for trade between nations was great. These ships carried such cargoes as manufactured goods from England and cotton to Europe. The ships even went to the Orient. These were fast-sailing ships, great clippers, full-rigged ships with three masts, and square sails on all three masts and a spanker sail on the mizzen. Built primarily for speed, they cut through the water, throwing up great plumes at their bows, leaving a wake behind them that stretched far. The clippers had studding sails in light winds to catch every whisper of a breeze. They were strongly built as well, to weather the storms that they inevitably encountered.

In 1818, the Black Ball Line initiated scheduled service to Liverpool, England.[25] (It was to become one of the leading shipping lines of its time.) Merchants were eager to have their cargoes on these scheduled runs because the ships crossed the ocean fast, and they did it on schedule. Because of the prevailing winds the eastbound passage was faster, and some of the packet ships sailing east-

South Ferry at the Battery on the East River. A Staten Island ferry is leaving the terminal. In the foreground, a destroyer is seen headed for the Upper Bay (South Street Seaport).

ward to England reached their destination in 37 days, which was good time in those days.

The wharves at that time hummed with activity. The docks were packed with produce. Stevedores loaded ships. The East River was in great prominence — the Hudson River had not yet found its place for transatlantic ships. That would wait for the steamship to replace the great sailing vessels, toward the latter part of the 19th century. In the meantime, the great packet ships made their passages in the shortest times in history. Records were set for sailing great distances in a minimum amount of time.

From the early 1800s until the Civil War, Manhattan's South Street was the center of much maritime activity. The vessels were tall sailing ships — the main-

South Street, on the Lower East Side of Manhattan, was once filled with ships as seen in *View in South Street*, drawn by I. Pranishnikoff. *Harper's Weekly* Illustrated Newspaper, 1878 (Museum of the City of New York).

mast of the William H. Webb–built ship *Challenger* rose to 200 feet above the water. The bowsprits of the vessels overhung the street to reach almost to the buildings. Masts and rigging dominated the area. Ships lined up one after the other, waiting to be loaded or unloaded.

The packet ships were the source of news from Europe. At that time, the wireless had not been invented and the transatlantic cable had not yet been lain. The ships would come past Sandy Hook, some carrying the familiar black ball on their fore topsail or some other similar marking that designated the shipowner. A sloop would go out to the ship to obtain some advance news, such as the price of grain on the London exchange, monetary exchange rates, or some similar information that had profit potential. Eventually, a semaphore signal was set up on Staten Island to relay the information. It was sent to the Battery, to a firm that could use the information to advantage.

In Robert Greenhalgh Albion's book, *The Rise of the New York Port*, about the port of New York during the 1800s, he describes the situations that made New York so successful during this stage of history. One of the issues he talks about

Aerial view taken over Brooklyn looking northwest. Governor's Island is in the center. Gowanus Canal is at the bottom, and Erie Basin is shown just above the entrance to Gowanus. The Hudson stretches up to the left and the East River to the right (South Street Seaport).

Schooner moored at Pier 11, Lower East Side in the East River. Tall buildings of Manhattan appear in background. Berenice Abbott, April 9, 1936 (Museum of the City of New York).

New York Harbor from the Brooklyn Bridge. View of piers of the East River in the 1800s. N.Y. Recorder Souvenir, undated (Museum of the City of New York).

is the cotton triangle.[26] New York was the central leg in the cotton triangle. The other legs were the southern ports of the United States and Liverpool, England. While the southern ports transported some of their cotton directly to England, they sent a good part of their cotton to New York to be forwarded to England. England at that time was a leading processor of textiles, a great deal of which was imported through New York from the United States. Albion points out that it was not necessary for New York to be involved in this trade, and when the Civil War started, the cotton triangle diminished. However, the cotton triangle did exist over many decades. England bought its cotton through brokers in New York even though it was not completely necessary to do so.

EAST RIVER—GOVERNOR'S ISLAND

On the east of the island of Manhattan, opposite the Battery, at the very beginning of the East River, is an island called Governor's Island. The Dutch purchased it from the Indians in 1637.[27] An island of 173 acres, it is situated a half-mile south of the Battery. Its shape has been likened to an ice cream cone, with the ice cream being the northern part. As with many islands in New York Harbor, it has been made larger by extending its area with dirt fill. The southernmost area, the cone in the ice cream cone analogy, was filled in with dirt taken from the digging of the Lexington Avenue subway.

Buttermilk Channel is to the east of Governor's Island, separating the island from Brooklyn. The wharves of Brooklyn's Red Hook section and Gowanus Bay curve around from the Upper Bay into the East River.

In Revolutionary War days, Governor's Island was occupied by the British, but it was later used for an American army base. The island has belonged to the federal government. Fort Jay and Castle William were built in the early part of the 19th century to protect the harbor. The army left in 1966 and the U.S. Coast Guard moved in, using the island as a headquarters until 1996, at which time it was vacated as a cost-saving measure. From 1996 to 2003, the federal government tried to decide what to do with the island. In January 2003, possession of the island was turned over to New York State by the federal government. The proposal currently is to use the island for a recreational, educational and cultural center.

Most people from communities around the harbor have never set foot upon Governor's Island. Although it has been a part of the city geographically, it has long been a government operation and was not accessible to the community, even though the island is only a short ferry ride from downtown Manhattan. Officials are hoping the island will be used differently in the future, with people visiting the island for sightseeing and other cultural activities. The forts are now national historic sites and there are several fine historic residences on the island. The fact that President Reagan met with Mikhail Gorbachev in 1988 on Governor's Island gives the site additional historic interest.

The harbor is changing and Governor's Island is part of that change.

BROOKLYN NAVY YARD

A short way up the East River, just beyond the Brooklyn Bridge on the Brooklyn side, is a slight indentation in the shoreline called Wallabout Bay. It is the site of the former New York Naval Shipyard, informally referred to as the Brooklyn Navy Yard. The U.S. Government closed it in 1966. Prior to that time it contributed significantly to the busy pace of New York Harbor. Among the many features of this amazing shipyard, famous vessels were built in the Brooklyn Navy Yard. Included are the *Fulton*, Robert Fulton's steam frigate; the ironclad *Monitor*; the *U.S.S. Maine* of Spanish-American War fame; and the *U.S.S. Arizona*.[28]

Some of the ships built at the Brooklyn Navy Yard were quite large. Fortunately, there is 40 feet of depth in the East River for the two miles to the Upper

Bay of New York Harbor, and deep channels extend from there out of the harbor.[29] The Brooklyn Bridge, under which ships built at the Navy Yard must pass, has a clearance of 127 feet. While the East River is deeper at its southern end, it has at least a 35-foot depth for its full length, which means the river will accommodate fairly large ships. What happened to the Brooklyn Navy Yard when the government closed it down after more than 150 years as a busy navy facility? Now it is an industrial complex spread out over 300 acres along the Brooklyn waterfront. Included is a film studio along with other businesses—jewelry making, electronics, furniture design, architectural services and so forth. There are shipbuilding operations to take advantage of the huge drydocks, long wharves, and other maritime facilities left over from the Brooklyn Navy Yard.[30] However, the business activities include many operations that are not marine-related. That is the trend now for waterfront properties. It is realistic in terms of today's economics.

ROOSEVELT ISLAND

Ships going up or down the East River have to pass Roosevelt Island. A two-mile sliver of an island, its southern end lies opposite midtown Manhattan at about East 42nd Street. The island parallels the river, extending up to about East

Consolidated Edison power plant on the East River in midtown Manhattan. The power plant supplies light and heat for many of the buildings in the surrounding area. The Empire State Building can be seen in the background.

Domino Sugar plant, now closed. There are not too many commercial installations remaining on the East River.

86th Street, just before the entrance to Hell Gate. A prominent feature, the Queensboro Bridge, has two of its towers on Roosevelt Island. The bridge is of cantilever design and crosses the East River from Manhattan to the borough of Queens. It was built in 1926. Another unique feature is the tramway that takes residents and visitors to the island. The tramway goes from Manhattan along the northern side of the bridge to the island. Riders get a good view of the river and the island from more than 200 feet up as they cross on the tramway. There is also a subway station at the island as it goes from Queens to Manhattan and back again.

The history of Roosevelt Island goes back to the Dutch. In the nineteenth century, institutions were built there for mentally disturbed people. Hospitals were also built on the island. For part of the time it was a site for a prison. From 1921 until 1973, the island was called Welfare Island and nobody lived on the island except the people who worked at the various institutions. Since the late 1960s, condominiums have been built the island and many people now live there.[31]

Roosevelt Island's location in the middle of the river causes the river to split into two channels, one to the west of the island, one to the east of the island. For ships, the preferred channel has always been to pass to the west side of the island.

Occasionally boats and tows would go to the east side of the island, but not any longer. Only the smallest of boats can go to the east side of the island now. That is because a lift bridge was built in 1956 going from the island to Queens, and Queens has been supplying the island with police and fire protection since that time. The lift for the bridge is so infrequently raised these days that the authorities have proposed leaving it down permanently as a cost-saving measure.[32]

EAST RIVER: THE WAY TO THE SOUND

As a vessel or a tow negotiates its way through Hell Gate it passes North and South Brother Islands, then Rikers Island. It still has two bridges to go under, the Bronx-Whitestone Bridge and the Throgs Neck Bridge. At Throgs Neck it makes a radical turn to port and heads toward Stepping Stones Light. At this point in its journey it is almost in the Sound. The vessel has used the "back door" to exit from New York Harbor.

The Harlem River

A RIVER BETWEEN RIVERS

The Harlem River connects the East River and the Hudson River, which was an important reason for its development as a waterway. It is located at the northern end of Manhattan. It separates Manhattan Island from the Bronx. It is north and east of Manhattan, a narrow, curvy waterway that connects with the East River at Hell Gate, then runs almost north for most of its 2.8 miles, The Harlem River causes the Washington Heights area of Manhattan, and the parks north of it, to be relatively narrow compared to the rest of Manhattan. Part of the Harlem River, early in the history of the city, was rather shallow, and it wound around quite a bit with deep bends, especially at the northern extreme where it meets the Hudson River, a place called Spuyten Duyvil. This aspect of the river was to be changed.

A WATERFRONT COMES ALIVE

As the population of New York City increased, the Harlem River waterfront began to be developed. Bridges were built when the need for transportation across the river increased. Also, it was necessary for the city's supply of drinking water coming from the Croton Reservoir in Westchester County to cross the river, so a large aqueduct was constructed. This structure was called High Bridge, and it still stands today, although it was rebuilt in the 1920s. Originally it was like a Roman aqueduct, with many arches going across the Harlem River. It was rebuilt as a steel structure with one major arch spanning the river instead of small stone arches, the pillars of which impeded navigation on the river.

Top: High Bridge. The metal portion shows how it was rebuilt so as to remove the stone columns which were obstructing the river. *Bottom:* Macombs Dam Bridge. A dam once stood here. It was taken down by members of the community.

Although it provided good fishing and clamming, the Harlem River was not navigable all the way through from the Hudson to the East Rivers. In the early 1800s there were numerous impediments to navigation. One entrepreneurial gentleman of the time built a dam across the river. There was a bit of consternation among the local residents about the dam's blocking the river. Finally, after many years of legal wrangling, a group of citizens took it upon themselves to literally tear a hole in the dam and let the water flow in its natural course. The citizens were dragged into court but, unbelievable though it may sound, the court ruled in their favor, saying it was high time the river was made navigable again. The dam builder, Robert Macomb, built a bridge where he had built the dam. The latest version of this bridge, still standing, was built in 1895. It is a swing-type bridge, constructed of iron, of truss design. It was declared a city landmark in 1992. To this day and age, it is called the Macombs Dam Bridge.[33]

THE MOVE TOWARD MAKING THE
HARLEM RIVER COMPLETELY NAVIGABLE

The Harlem River area has quite a history behind it. The urge to make it a completely navigable river was very strong. The Erie Canal had been built in the period 1817–25. The canal connected the transportation network to the central part of the continent, and toward the middle of the 1800s it helped make New York Harbor into a leading port of the world. At that time most produce and other cargo moved by water. The trucks came later, after the highway system was built.

There were some who thought the Harlem River should be open to shipping, a shortcut, so to speak, from the Hudson to the East River and Long Island Sound. This would benefit the vessels heading east, out of the Sound. (Contrary to the general perception, the coast lies in roughly an eastward direction by compass in this part of the continent. It lies more north to south from New Jersey onward.) The waterfront of the Harlem River, and there were about three miles of it on each side, was thought to have potential for development in any number of ways. After it was opened in 1825, the Erie Canal was heavily used. The port of New York was an important link to the Erie Canal. From the port of New York cargoes were shipped through the canals to the Great Lakes and thence to the Midwest and the rest of the North American continent. Waterborne transportation was at its zenith: The road system had not been built yet and the technology of the trucking industry had not yet arrived. It was said by some officials that the construction of the Erie Canal had enabled the port of New York to become in the second half of the 19th century the greatest port in the world. For this reason, the pressure to construct the Harlem River Ship Canal began to build up.[34]

The main problem in considering the Harlem River safe to navigate was the area around Spuyten Duyvil. There was a severe bend in the river at this point and the river at this portion was not very deep. The plan was to make a cut to straighten out the bend; the question was where to make the cut. Three different routes were considered. The officials selected one of them, Dyckmans Creek, a narrow, shallow body of water. A contract was awarded in 1884. Progress was slow, though. Even by 1886 the construction firm had not done much on the project. The state of New York petitioned the federal government to take over the job, and in 1888 the Corps of Engineers started work.[35] Their plan was to dredge a channel 400 feet wide and 15 to 18 feet deep through Dyckmans Meadow. The workmen had to blast through a large piece of rock to make the cut. The distance of the cut-through was only 1,000 feet, but it was difficult to blast it piece by piece as they contended with one problem after another. Then came the famous blizzard of 1888. It dealt a devastating blow to the Harlem River project just as it did to everyone else in the Northeast. The engineers had built a cofferdam to keep the river water from coming in where they were digging. The cofferdam collapsed, and to add to their problems the storm caused the river's waters to go over the dam and flood the place where they were working. It took a while for them to get the repairs accomplished. Finally, in 1895, the construction firm finished its work. The Harlem Ship Canal was opened. Speeches were made. There was a procession of boats. Great expectations were voiced for the new Harlem River.[36]

A Busy Waterfront

For a while the Harlem River flourished. The river was busy with shipping activity.[37] Brick was brought from upstate New York. Lime and cement came from overseas. There was a need to increase the wharf space. For a short time, wharf space became so scarce that vessels had a pay a bonus to obtain space at the docks. In contrast, at the present time the Harlem River is hardly used at all for shipping purposes. The commercial waterfront has mostly disappeared. The New York City Department of Planning considers only the southeastern part of the river to be zoned for working waterfront development, a small portion bordering on Port Morris. Most of the waterfront along the Harlem River consists of public parks and esplanades for the use of community residents, along with a few railroad facilities. Much of the former commercial docks has fallen into ruins, seemingly abandoned. There are now 15 bridges across the river. Four of them are fixed bridges, with a minimum clearance of about 100 feet, high enough for a large ship to go through. That's not the problem. The problem is that the Harlem River is only 20 feet deep, and that limits the size of vessels that can go through the river. In fact, there are several problems. There are 11 lift or swing bridges that a ship or a tug with a tow would have to go through. Imagine the captain having to contact each of these bridges to request an opening. It would be easier to go around the Battery and up the East River. Now, it is used mostly by the Circle Line cruises to take tourists around Manhattan Island. Their boats are

The railroad bridge at Spuyten Duyvil looking north from Inwood Hill Park. This site is where the Harlem River connects with the Hudson River.

deliberately designed so as to fit under the many bridges that they have to go through.

The officials had good intentions when they exhibited a drive for closure: to make Manhattan completely an "island" by deepening the Harlem River. The public has a strong demand for closure, to finish things off, to complete the pattern. It's a positive process in most instances; it causes us to complete a task, to finish a report, to see things through to the end. The Harlem River had been a thriving waterfront in the 1800s, accessible from the East River side. In contrast to the thinking of the officials who wanted to make the river completely navigable, many citizens thought the Harlem River "improvement" a useless exercise. The *New York Times* actually advocated filling it in.[38]

A PROMISE UNFULFILLED

History has shown the improvements in New York Harbor to be worth the initial investment of time, effort and money. Most of the projects that were accomplished over time, such as the clearing of Hell Gate, the dredging of Ambrose Channel, the dredging of Newtown Creek, Gowanus Canal and the many creeks of New York Harbor, proved to be worthwhile. The improvement of the Harlem River as completed in 1895 was not as clear-cut in effect over the long run. It is doubtful if many vessels, wanting to go from the Hudson River to the Long Island Sound and then east (or the reverse), used the Harlem River.

If the officials who lobbied for the making of the Harlem River completely navigable had not done so, onlookers nowadays would see a completely different picture of the Harlem River. The low railroad bridge at Spuyten Duyvil would still be seen from the Hudson. The High Bridge with it its aqueduct bringing water to New York City would still be there, with its water tower close by. But the cut across Dyckmans Meadow would not be there, and Dyckmans Creek would wind slowly from Spuyten Duyvil. It was filled in in 1910. Marble Hill, which was geographically made part of the Bronx by the cut, would still be physically connected to Manhattan. As a matter of fact it is still administered by Manhattan. Much has changed with the Harlem River.

The Gowanus Canal

EARLY HISTORY OF THE CANAL

Gowanus Canal grew up with the development of New York Harbor. At one time, until the 1950s, it was a busy waterway. It is not busy now.

The entrance to the Gowanus Canal is an inlet off Upper New York Bay, adjacent to Erie Basin, below the Red Hook section of Brooklyn. In the early history of the harbor, Gowanus was a natural creek going two miles into the heartland of Brooklyn. As time went on and the area became settled, the stream was widened and docks were built. It was in 1849 that New York State, spurred by the creek's commercial potential, enacted legislation to excavate the creek and make it into a canal. Industry was attracted to the waterfront and by the late 1800s the Gowanus Canal thrived with marine activity. That was when waterborne transportation was in its heyday, before trucking became the main form of transport for industry.

Boats, barges and scows brought loads of bricks and lumber into Gowanus. There was a strong market for such products because a great deal of building was going on in Brooklyn at the time. Later, in the 1940s, the Gowanus Canal was a bustling area. The Ira S. Bushey shipyard, for example, was well occupied turning out tankers. Tugboats were going in and out of the canal with barges in tow. The Bushey fleet of Red Star tugboats kept the drydock busy with repairs and maintenance.

DRYDOCK AT IRA S. BUSHEY YARD

As an example of marine activity on the Gowanus Canal, the tugboat *Takana* went into drydock at the Ira S. Bushey yard in the 1940s. The *Takana* was an old wooden tug, originally steam, that had been refitted with a low-horsepower diesel engine. To "go into drydock" means, at the shipyard, to maneuver the boat between wooden "walls" that are connected below the surface of the water in a three-dimensional u shape. The boat was positioned over wooden blocks set up to conform to the shape of the hull. As the drydock is pumped out, it rises until the boat is completely out of the water.

The *Takana* was in the drydock to put ballast in the water tank, which took up the whole stern area of the vessel. This tank had provided water for the steam engine; the boat had a separate tank for drinking water. The yard workmen loaded what seemed to be an enormous amount of Belgium blocks into the steam water tank. The purpose was to achieve better trim of the boat; the stern had been too high out of the water.

The Ira S. Bushey yard was a busy place. Shipyard workers, hundreds of them, labored on their various chores. Ships, boats, barges and scows were being built by the dozens. Although by then ships were made of steel and welders were in great demand, there was still a lot of wood used in marine construction. Scows and barges, in particular, were made of wood and the Ira S. Bushey yard had its

Sand scow at the Gowanus Canal. In the background high subway station and a lift bridge over canal.

share of such vessels to construct. Woodworking skills for shipbuilding are rare now except for construction of museum ships, and the workers in those situations oftentimes have to learn the skills from scratch.

GROWTH OF INDUSTRY ALONG THE CANAL

The growth of industry was in full sway in the 1800s and 1900s. Spurred on by the industrial revolution, our culture was geared to maximize growth. Whatever industry wanted, it could have. With all the commercial activity that was going on in the Gowanus Canal, pollution of the waterway became rampant. The citizens lacked present-day sewerage facilities. Factories were pouring their waste into the canal. There was no governmental control of the environment. In fact, the populace did not seem to care. The emphasis was on commercial activity. The waterway was there as a receptacle for whatever waste there was, and the people used it that way, until the Gowanus Canal became an open sewer. By 1900, even before, the stench was horrible. People became used to the smell of Gowanus. It was part of living in that area. The odor of Gowanus became identified with Brooklyn. Ellen Snyder-Grenier in *Brooklyn: An Illustrated History* quoted a

Benson Scrap Metal Company, a small business on the Gowanus Canal.

Local businesses beside the Gowanus Canal.

Brooklyn politician of days gone by: he said, in effect, for a man having grown up in this area, having smelled Newtown Creek or Gowanus, there is no place like Brooklyn.[39]

PUMPING STATION INSTALLED

Among other problems, the waters of the Gowanus Canal were relatively stagnant. There was not enough tidal flow to create a flushing effect. The authorities finally tried to do something about the situation, and in 1911 a flushing tunnel was built.[40, 41] The idea behind this project was sound, to a point. The authorities laid a pipeline going from Buttermilk Channel, at the beginning of the East River opposite Governor's Island, to the head of the Gowanus Canal. The idea was to bring in relatively clean water from the East River to flush out the canal, ending the stagnation by introducing a flow of water from the head of the canal to the outlet of the canal on the Upper Bay.

The authorities built a pumping station near the head of the canal. They installed a motor and a large propeller to move the water and create a flow through the canal. It did not completely solve the problem, but apparently it helped; until 1960, that is, when a workman dropped a manhole cover onto the propeller and the mechanical malfunction was not repaired. In 1994, the Department of Environmental Protection became involved, with some urging by community groups, and it began a project to reactivate the flushing tunnel. The project included dredging a portion of the Gowanus where sediment had gathered at the outlet section. A new motor and propeller were installed. Inaugurated in 1999, the new tunnel reportedly is pumping 200–300,000 gallons a day through the canal. It helps, but based on an on-site inspection made recently by the author, Gowanus Canal is still polluted. Its waters are cleaner than they used to be, but there is still flotsam on the surface in the corners of the creek where there is not good circulation. The water still looks gray and dirty. It is reported that the oxygen level is still below standard.

COMMUNITY INVOLVEMENT

One of the reasons for the improvements in the Gowanus Canal is that the community is becoming more involved. Local organizations have sprung up. These organizations are evaluating the status of the canal, planning improvements, communicating their impressions, and lobbying to get things done. An example is the Gowanus Canal Community Development Corporation. That organization has been interested in the development of the canal and the adjacent Red Hook and Carroll Gardens sections of Brooklyn. To some extent gentrification of the surrounding residences has occurred. Close to the canal are a number of small businesses, hundreds of them, attracted no doubt by the low cost of this run-down area. There are storm and sash operations, lumber sellers, dealers in other construction items, electronics and the like. They are not marine-related and have no connection with the canal itself. It is as though the canal has been subsumed by the surrounding non-marine culture.

Gowanus Canal is no longer important as a waterway. The bridges over the canal are an example. There are five bridges, yet with only two operators.[42] The few boats that use the canal have to schedule in advance to get an opening. Many of the streets surrounding the canal are one-way streets. Some of the avenues crossing the bridges are one way. Like Newtown Creek, Gowanus is considered by some people as a liability that blocks the way for efficient car and truck transportation in the area. The streets around the Gowanus Canal are a hodge-podge of traffic lights. Automobiles and trucks dominate the area.

CURRENT CONDITION OF THE AREA

Although the general area is very industrialized, these operations are not heavy manufacturing operations. Those businesses have long gone. What has grown up is the light manufacturing businesses or operations such as wholesalers, storage places, and trucking operations. Community groups have planned restaurants, recreational piers, esplanades, a place where tourists would come — as one group has said, a place like the "Riverwalk" in San Antonio, Texas. In support of that thinking, Joseph Seebode, Manager of Harbor Projects for the Corps of Engineers, said that they had begun a project to dredge Gowanus Canal.[43] The only businesses seen on a tour of the area that are marine-related are several sand and gravel operations and a petroleum depot. One sand and gravel installation had a scow moored alongside the dock. It would seem that the sand and gravel business, as well as the petroleum business, would lend themselves to the kind of bulk transportation that could be carried on scows and barges. In fact, during this tour a tug brought in a scow and dropped it off at a sand and gravel installation nearer the mouth of the canal. It was a large diesel tug from the Buchanan line. After the tug had landed the scow, the deckhand wanted to go up to the nearby supermarket to get a pack of cigarettes. The tug landed him at the dock. The deckhand had to climb the fence which ran along the edge of the dock to get access to the land side.

There were no places where the public could get access to the water. It was fenced off for the most part, with forbidding-looking chains and locks on the gates. Many of the fences had razor-wire on the top, making it look like a high-crime area. There was a surprising growth of trees along the waterway, but they were the kind of weedy trees that flourish in urban areas. There were several places where the water's edge was natural, where no docks had been constructed. They give hope to what is a generally seedy area. There were no restaurants, no recreational piers, no new condominiums. It certainly does not look like the "Venice of New York," as it has been called by some.[44]

While the future plans are for the upgrading of the Gowanus Canal area, that condition does not exist at present. It is nowhere near it. True, the authorities have made great strides on the environmental condition of the water. The anticipated dredging would help considerably to remove the contaminants on the bottom. Changes in the surrounding neighborhood will only occur slowly. Several newspaper articles have stated that the area around Gowanus is in transition, that it is on its way to becoming a more attractive location for the local citizens. This impression is only partially true. It still has a long way to go. What has to happen is the many small businesses have to change, the culture has to change. It will take many years, perhaps generations. However, the community groups are everlastingly optimistic.

Newtown Creek

The entrance to Newtown Creek is on the East River, opposite midtown Manhattan. The waterfront on Newtown Creek at the entrance offers a breathtaking view of the tall buildings across the East River on Manhattan Island. Newtown Creek has its own tall buildings to boast of — a few of them. Near the

1. The Port from a Physical Perspective

Above: Entrance to Newtown Creek from the East River. The tall building toward the left is the Citibank Building in Queens. *Below:* Bayside Petroleum Products from the Grand Avenue Bridge over Newtown Creek. Oil barges still go to the end of the creek.

entrance are the two multistory condominiums of Queens West, a condominium development recently built in the borough of Queens overlooking the East River. The new buildings of Queens West present a sharp contrast to the oldness and tawdriness of the general Newtown Creek area. In Long Island City, not too far from Newtown Creek, is the Citibank Building, a multistory building that stands out from its surroundings as a true skyscraper.

Newtown Creek runs for about three and a half miles into Brooklyn and Queens, including two tributaries with the historical names of Dutch Kill and English Kill, which run off to the north and south. The main branch of the creek forms the dividing line between the boroughs of Brooklyn and Queens.[45]

THE CREEK IN THE EARLY DAYS

When New York City was settled, Newtown Creek was a tidal waterway in a very natural state, with clear streams that flowed through rolling hills.[46] Many of the tidal marshes were long ago filled in to create land for people who were anxious to settle in the area. At first the commerce along the waterway was agricultural. The entrepreneurs occupied land along the waterfront and shipped their wares along the creek in barges and other boats. Then, in the 1800s, the industrial revolution took over and plants and factories grew plentiful along the waterway. Oil refineries were set up. Other companies included a kerosene treatment plant, fertilizer plants, glue makers and varnish manufacturers. With the factories came pollution, as in so much of the rest of New York Harbor. The plants operated without environmental controls. The people who reveled in the industrial growth did not even think of the environment in the 1800s and early 1900s.

PRESENT CONDITIONS

Now the industrial plants are abandoned or have been torn down. The Laurel Hill Chemical Works, a company owned by Phelps Dodge, was recently demolished.[47] All that remains is an empty lot. Officials are mulling over what to do with the space. The ground is severely polluted by many years of chemicals leaching into the soil.

Like the Gowanus Canal, Newtown Creek is surrounded by a host of small businesses, not marine related. Along the creek, there are several marine-related businesses, petroleum installations for the most part. New York Harbor is the most active petroleum port on the East Coast. Most of the petroleum installations are on the Arthur Kill in Staten Island or in New Jersey, but some of them are on Newtown Creek. It is a wider creek than Gowanus, spanning 200 to 300 feet in some places. It is more like a small river. The opportunities for installations along the creek are many, although they are few and far between at present. Abandoned factories and warehouses occupy many of the waterfront sites. The old Brooklyn

Derelict building on Newtown Creek. Former Marlyn Warehousing Corporation.

Eastern District Railroad, which served the Newtown Creek businesses, was dissolved some time ago, done in by the rapidly growing trucking industry.

In contrast to this desolate condition, isolated bits of the shoreline are in a natural state. Surprisingly enough for this urban environment, some marshes or wetlands are still to be found toward the entrance to Newtown Creek on the east side of the creek.

ROLE OF COMMUNITY ORGANIZATIONS

Community groups have been watching out for Newtown Creek's interests. It seems there is a potential conflict here, however. While the New York City Planning Department has Newtown Creek zoned for industrial use, the community organizations are lobbying for more community-oriented use. Meetings have been held and discussions of what to do with the Newtown Creek waterfront have taken place. Many of the goals of the respective parties are in common. Like most community groups that have to do with the waterfront, the community groups associated with Newtown Creek are interested in such things as access to the water. There is very little access to the waterfront in the Newtown Creek area. Naturally, the community boards are also interested in converting unused waterfront property to parks and other community uses. Those groups are banding with governmental groups to clean up the pollution in Newtown Creek, and they have had some positive results, although the water is far from clean at present. With federal funding, a processing plant was built on Newtown Creek that filters the water and returns clean water to the creek. Some waterfowl have been seen on the waters. Kayakers use the creek, and other recreational boats are seen from time to time. Some people fish in the waters but the environmental and health authorities recommend against eating too much of the sea life that is taken from the creek. They are concerned about the mercury content, among other contaminants.

SIMILARITIES AND DIFFERENCES BETWEEN NEWTOWN CREEK AND GOWANUS

It is natural to consider Newtown Creek and Gowanus Canal as being in the same category of waterways. They are both offshoots of the East River, extending into what is basically a heavily urbanized area. (Gowanus's inlet is located at the turn of Brooklyn where the Upper Bay and the East River come together.) The two waterways are similar also in that they are much improved environmentally. Both waterways were severely polluted, as was much of New York Harbor. But Gowanus Canal and Newtown Creek were especially contaminated because they were creeks dead-ending in densely populated areas, with no flow-through of water to clean them. Also, they are similar in that part of the improvement in water quality is a result of industry's leaving and a cessation of the pollution that it was pouring into the waterways.

The essential difference between Gowanus and Newtown Creek is that the whole of Newtown Creek is designated by the New York City Department of Planning as a *Significant Maritime and Industrial Area* (SMIA). There are six areas designated as SMIAs in the waterfront of New York City.[48] Only the beginning parts of the Gowanus Canal, Red Hook and Erie Basin, are zoned commercially. The difference mainly lies in the future plans for the two areas.

FUTURE DEVELOPMENT FOR NEWTOWN CREEK

The future of Newtown Creek is dubious. Whereas New York City has the area zoned for commercial development, it is doubtful whether much of the unused property on the waterfront will be used for that purpose. Perhaps it is a sign of the economic times. More likely it is that the culture has changed. Whereas the economy of the past was manufacturing oriented, there is now a more service-oriented economy, an economy in which being located on the water provides no particular advantage. (For that matter, manufacturing companies no longer have to locate on the water — they have the trucking industry to provide their transportation needs.) Urban planning organizations are looking for ways to entice more businesses to locate on the waterfront of Newtown Creek.

Pipe discharging fluid into Newtown Creek. It is questionable whether the liquid is clean.

It remains to be seen whether New York City will get industry to come back to the Newtown Creek waterfront. Much of that waterfront is unused at the present time, and Newtown Creek has lost its significance for transportation purposes. In fact, like Gowanus, the creek is considered by some people to be a liability — a barrier which has to be crossed via a bridge. The U.S. Department of Transportation (DOT) is proposing that the Grand Street Bridge remain closed for river traffic. The DOT says the bridge does not see enough use and it would be an advantage not to have to maintain it so it can be opened. Some people think that policy will signify the end of economic and community development for Newtown Creek. It is evident that changing times have caught up with Newtown Creek.

Notable Bridges of New York Harbor

There are eight bridges across the East River. There is only one across the Hudson River in New York City, the George Washington Bridge; and then there is the Verrazano Bridge linking Brooklyn with Staten Island across the Narrows. In addition to the bridges, there are tunnels which link up the land sections of the harbor. The first bridge in the harbor was the Brooklyn Bridge, begun in 1869. Others were constructed soon after the Brooklyn Bridge was opened: the Williamsburg Bridge, the Manhattan Bridge and the Queensboro Bridge. Eventually, as road transportation built up, a whole network of highways around New York Harbor developed. Bridges were part of this network, and other bridges were added, including the Triborough Bridge, the Bronx-Whitestone Bridge and the Throgs Neck Bridge.

First Bridge on New York Harbor

Brooklyn Bridge — what a beautiful bridge. With the sculpted arches in its towers and delicate, spider-like cables radiating out from its pedestals, it stands grandly over the East River, beckoning to the ships and tows and lighters to pass under its span. It was built in the latter part of the 19th century. New York Harbor was a busy port at that time. There were no bridges in the harbor then. There were ferries to bring the people and their horses and buggies across the waterways that made New York Harbor a group of islands, but the ferries were not enough. What was needed was a bridge to connect the city of New York, which consisted of Manhattan at the time, with the city of Brooklyn. Among other things, connecting these two cities would allow the population of Manhattan to spill over into Brooklyn, which was still relatively rural.

The first bridge to be built on New York Harbor, the Brooklyn Bridge was a product of its time. Aesthetically, it was Victorian in nature. Its towers were of traditional design, built of granite, with pointed arches molded into them by the careful arrangement of the stones. And still, it was of the latest technology. Creator John Roebling had experience building suspension bridges. [49, 50] It was built of steel, a new alloy at that time. Roebling had his own company that made wire rope products. He was an imaginative man and was instrumental in getting the politicians to put their stamp of approval on the project. An organization was formed, the New York Bridge Company, to build and maintain the bridge. Roebling not only designed the bridge, he oversaw its construction — until his accident. He was injured while looking for a specific location for the Brooklyn tower site. A ferryboat crushed his foot. He died of tetanus shortly afterward as a result of his wounds, and his son, Washington Roebling, succeeded him as chief engineer on the project. It was a sad affair. Washington became deeply involved in the project. He lived in Brooklyn, a few blocks away from the construction site. When he succumbed to compression sickness after supervising the work in the caissons for the towers, he watched from his bed through the bedroom window. Undaunted, he still supervised the workers by writing notes about the project and having his wife carry them to the men.

Top: The Brooklyn Bridge links Brooklyn and Manhattan. Designed by John Roebling, it was New York Harbor's first bridge. Construction began in 1869. *Bottom:* Manhattan tower of the Brooklyn Bridge. Pier 17, South Street Seaport, is beyond the bridge. Background: buildings of downtown Manhattan.

CAISSONS

The caissons were wooden containers, large enough in which to build the foundations of the towers. The caissons were built nearby on the East River and floated down the river to the site. Since the towers were in the river, near the shore, these caissons were designed to hold out the water and sink into the riverbed as the excavation inside the caisson took place, six inches a day. Because they were designed to be waterproof, a key feature of these caissons was that they were pressurized. That led the workers, including Washington Roebling, to suffer from the agonies of decompression sickness, a newly discovered ailment. At that time, no one knew how to treat it. It was caused by nitrogen bubbles forming in the bloodstream, painful and very debilitating. Some of the workers died from it.

MISFORTUNES

Other misfortunes occurred during the construction of the Brooklyn Bridge. A number of accidents occurred during the rigging of the cables. In 1878, a strand of cable broke. The cable flew back, fatally injuring one worker and knocking another worker off the tower. Another worker got his foot caught in the drum which was involved in the cable work. He was killed instantly. Along with workers who were affected by the caisson disease, more than 20 workers were killed in accidents that occurred during construction.

CABLES OF THE BROOKLYN BRIDGE

The cables of the bridge had to be strong to stand the strain of the roadway they were to hold up, especially since the bridge was designed to have subway cars and trolleys go over it. (The subway over the bridge was discontinued in 1944 and the trolleys shortly afterward.) There are a total of four weight-bearing cables spanning the river in the Brooklyn Bridge. They are 153/4 inches thick. A scandal broke out when the contractor who supplied the wire used inferior metals to make the wire. However, Roebling had computed that even with the inferior wire the cables were still many times the strength required. So, rather than bearing the time and cost of replacing the inferior wire, he accepted the situation. The New York newspapers made a big fuss, nevertheless.

SPANNING THE RIVER

The Brooklyn Bridge is typical of suspension bridges, although at the time it was built it was a fairly new idea. The two towers are built close to the shoreline on each side of the river. The roadway is suspended from four large cables slung over the tower on each side and anchored at both ends of the structure by large stone bulwarks. It was in 1876 that the two towers were first joined by a

Workmen removing the footbridge during construction of the Brooklyn Bridge (Library of Congress).

wire rope. Then the cables were spun from wires about size of a pencil in thickness. The vertical cables were secured to the beginnings of the roadway, and then the real roadway was constructed. The cables radiating from the towers on each side were than added. An elevated promenade was built for pedestrians and bicycles. The outer lanes were for horse-drawn vehicles.

OPENING DAY OF THE BROOKLYN BRIDGE

Opening Day was on May 23, 1883. President Chester Arthur and Governor Grover Cleveland dedicated the bridge among cheering attendees. The bridge was a wonderful sight to behold, and New Yorkers and Brooklynites were proud of their bridge. The charge was one cent to go over the bridge on that illustrious day, and the bridge was filled with people. The completed bridge was a tribute to John Roebling, whose courage and creativity had so much to do with its completion. It was a tribute as well to his son Washington, who gave so much of himself to the project. His wife participated in the ceremony. There was much gaiety, and the affair ended with fireworks that lit the skies.

The centennial for the Brooklyn Bridge was celebrated in 1983. The Brooklyn Bridge has seen many changes since that opening day: The horse and buggy has been replaced by the car, and trucks now rumble across the bridge taking their cargoes into the crowded streets of Manhattan. The Brooklyn Bridge is a symbol of the harbor, old yet beautiful. It has experienced a lot of changes and it has survived.

QUEENSBORO BRIDGE

When John Roebling first conceived the idea of a bridge across the East River, his first choice was the location at which the Queensboro Bridge was eventually built. The river was narrower at that point and had a long, narrow island in the center of it on which to put two of the supporting piers. However, the city fathers wanted a bridge built to Brooklyn at that time. Eventually, the need to link to Long Island through the borough of Queens became compelling, and the legislature gave the go-ahead to the Long Island Bridge Company in 1867. There

The Queensboro Bridge an excellent example of the cantilever design. The towers are on Roosevelt Island in the middle of the East River.

Top: Hell Gate Bridge. Only the lower cord of the arch is load-bearing. The towers on each side of the East River were built high for aesthetic reasons. *Bottom:* Queensboro Bridge in 1932. Schooner at the dock. The view is to the west, to Manhattan.

were many delays, however. The contract to start work on the construction of the bridge was not awarded until 1881. There were still more delays. The expansion of the city of New York to five boroughs in 1898 helped get things started again, but it was only in 1902 that the mayor appointed Gustav Lindenthal as bridge commissioner. (Lindenthal subsequently built the Hell Gate Bridge, also.)

Because the East River had an island in the middle of it, the individual spans of the bridge did not have to be great. Therefore, it was possible to use a cantilever design even though the bridge was 7,000 feet long. First the supporting masonry piers were constructed. There were six of them: two on Blackwell's Island (later renamed Roosevelt Island), two in Manhattan, and two in Queens. From the masonry piers, the trusses were built out to connect in the middle of the span. Pennsylvania Steel Company did the metal work.

The Queensboro Bridge has a unique feature to it that was not built into the original design of the bridge but added more recently. That feature is the tramway going from Manhattan Island to Roosevelt Island. It was constructed to take the residents of Roosevelt Island to and from Manhattan. Many condominiums have been built on Roosevelt Island during recent times. The character of that island is becoming more cosmopolitan these days. The community group has more of a voice now than it ever had before.

THE HELL GATE BRIDGE

Farther up the East River is the Hell Gate Bridge. The river is quite narrow at that point. That is why the waters rush through at that portion of the river when the current is at its fullest. Because of the narrowness of the river it was possible to construct an arch bridge, the longest and strongest arch bridge at the time it was opened, which was 1917. It was a railroad bridge, built by the Pennsylvania Railroad. The Pennsylvania Railroad was a big, profitable corporation when the Hell Gate Bridge was constructed, but it came upon hard times because of the changes in modes of transportation. To solve its problems the Pennsy, as it was known, merged with the New York Central and the New Haven in 1968. The merged corporation went bankrupt in 1970. The government took it over under the name Amtrak. (Much of this information comes from an article that appeared in *The New Yorker* magazine in 1991.[51] The article is thought by some people to have influenced the Congress to approve a bill appropriating money to maintain the bridge when it sorely needed it in the 1990s.)

The architect of the Hell Gate Bridge was well known at the time: Gustav Lindenthal. Lindenthal's first desire was to build a bridge for the Pennsylvania Railroad across the Hudson River, to bring trains into midtown Manhattan. It is hard to believe, but the Pennsylvania Railroad, as big as it was, had no terminal in Manhattan before Penn Station was built. The railroad chose to build a tunnel under the Hudson River instead of the bridge.

Brooklyn tower of Brooklyn Bridge. River Café at base of tower. Manhattan Bridge in background.

The Hell Gate Bridge was constructed with the intent to link up with the New Haven Railroad to carry passengers to the northeastern United States, notably Boston. The idea was to bring passengers into Manhattan, then under the East River to Queens, then across Hell Gate Bridge to meet the New Haven Railroad in the Bronx. If the Pennsylvania Railroad had known what the future held for it at the time the Hell Gate Bridge was built, it would probably not have built the bridge; but it had grandiose plans.

An interesting point in the construction of the bridge: Only the lower cord in the arch is designed to bear the load of the roadway (tracks). The upper cord is merely to add strength to the lower cord; it stiffens the lower cord by the lattice-work of girders connecting to it. For this reason the towers on each side of the river would have had to be only high enough to support the lower cord. Instead, the towers of the Hell Gate Bridge were built tall enough to accommodate the upper cord as well as the lower cord. The towers were built so high only for aesthetic reasons. In addition, since it was not necessary to have the upper cord of the arch actually connected to the towers, there is a six-inch gap between the upper cord and the tower on each side of the river, a gap which is not visible to the naked eye.

Hell Gate Bridge showing tower on Wards Island. Triboro Bridge, Manhattan is in background.

The Bayonne Bridge over the Kill Van Kull is, similarly, an arch bridge and its concrete abutments are designed low enough to accommodate only the lower cord of the arch. There are steel towers built on top of the concrete, presumably for aesthetic reasons. This is not to take anything away from the Bayonne Bridge—the Hell Gate Bridge is considered more beautiful, but the Bayonne Bridge was the longest arch bridge when it was opened in 1931. The overall effect of the Hell Gate Bridge constitutes a brilliant design that has lasted to this day. It is one of the landmark bridges of New York Harbor.

Waterfront Diversions

RESTAURANTS ON THE WATER

New York Harbor is changing, and evidence of that fact is the number of places close to the water whose purpose is to feed, entertain or inform the populace. The harbor is no longer a place to work. No longer, in most places, do sweating stevedores labor to unload a ship; no longer are sacks of potatoes cluttering the docks as they wait for a ship to carry them away. The harbor has become a diversion for many people, local residents and tourists both.

There are restaurants by the water now. There are such establishments as the River Café on the East River at the foot of the Brooklyn tower of the Brooklyn Bridge. It is built on a barge moored at the dock. Its main selling point is a view of the river and the boats going by. (Boats are not allowed to tie to their dock, though, according to Kornblum in his book *At Sea in the City*.[52]) South Street Seaport is right across the East River. The many restaurants there are reported to provide a good night out dining.

Another restaurant by the water is the Chart House (in the former location of *Shanghai Red's*). This one is in New Jersey, in Weehawken, near the New Jersey side of the Lincoln Tunnel. It is situated at the very end of a long pier jutting out into the water. Patrons can see a grand view of Manhattan across the Hudson River through the picture windows of this restaurant.

There is another restaurant on the water; in fact, it is called the Water Club. Like the River Café, it is built upon a barge, only the water club spans two barges. It is located on the East River, in Manhattan, on 30th Street.

South Street Seaport

On the Lower East Side of Manhattan, almost at the Battery, is the South Street Seaport.[53] The seaport has a museum and several restored ships and boats to excite the eye of anyone who wants to get a nautical look at New York Harbor. It opened in 1967. Before, the docks and shore of South Street were teeming with nautical life. Now there are visitors to the South Street Seaport anxious to see the sights. As described in the section of this book on the East River, South Street was the hub of shipping activity in Manhattan in the latter part of the 19th century. The seaport has done a good job of duplicating bygone days. Much of the area consists of restored buildings and docks. Some of the restored buildings, like the old and venerable Fulton Fish Market (recently moved to the Bronx) is now a place of mostly non-nautical shops. (However, there is an extensive library which is very nautical, but it is not used much by visitors.)

Alongside the pier, you will find ships like *Wavertree*. *Wavertree* is a rather large sailing vessel, methodically restored, a ship that once went to China to bring back tea for the American appetite. Other in-water boats are also in that area on display. Some boats take people on cruises around the harbor, like the *Lettie G. Howard*, a seagoing schooner from bygone days.

South Street Seaport covers a wide area. The complex includes many old buildings, some from the 1800s. A good number of people frequent the shopping area at Pier 17. A chapter in *The New York Waterfront*, by Kevin Bone,[54] was critical of South Street Seaport because the writer of the chapter thought shops in the seaport should be nautical in nature. Most of the shops in the seaport are

Top: South Street Seaport entrance. The tower is dedicated to the *Titanic.* It came from the old Seaman's Institute. *Bottom:* The old Fulton Fish Market after it was renovated. A restaurant and shops are in it now.

Top: Pier 17, South Street Seaport seen from the East River. The buildings in the background are in lower Manhattan. *Bottom:* The *Peking* in the water at South Street. The ship is quite large, as one can tell by the size of the yards and bowsprit.

more typical of the ones seen at an inland mall, it is true. Be that as it may, the casual visitor can get a good dose of salt air when he or she visits.

LIBERTY STATE PARK

On the New Jersey side of the Hudson River, not far from the Statue of Liberty, stands the Liberty State Park. It was established in 1976. The site, 1,122 acres, was previously owned by the Central Railroad of New Jersey, in the days when railroads were in ascendance. The peninsula on which the park was built used to be bustling with railroad cars and steam engines. There was a terminal on the river at the end of the peninsula, which still stands. It is the pride and joy of the park, a stately Victorian building overlooking the Hudson. When you come up the Hudson River the main thing that you see, aside from the buildings of Manhattan, is the Jersey Central Terminal. As mentioned in another part of this book, this terminal is where the immigrants who had come through Ellis Island first set foot on the mainland to depart on trains to their new life in the United States.

One of the main attractions in the park is the Science Museum. It is a large building consisting of all kinds of exhibits, biology, physics; all this, and a gorgeous view of downtown Manhattan across the river as well. The park has hiking trails and fishing along the water. There is no problem with access to the water by the public in this case.

INTREPID MUSEUM

At Pier 86 on the West Side of Manhattan at about the center of the island is the Intrepid Museum. The *Intrepid* is an aircraft carrier of World War II vintage. The *Intrepid* fought in many battles in the Pacific and was involved actively in the space program as a recovery ship in the Mercury and Gemini programs. It was decommissioned in 1974.

There are other sights to see there as well. The submarine *Growler* is moored nearby, open for inspection by any curious onlooker. The British Airways supersonic transport Concorde airplane is also on display. Too heavy to rest upon the deck of the aircraft carrier, the Concorde is on a barge moored just across from the carrier.

The *Intrepid* museum includes all kinds of wartime airplanes on its deck or in its hangar. There is a host of other exhibits on the ship as well.

STATUE OF LIBERTY

No book about New York Harbor could overlook the Statue of Liberty. It is so much a part of the harbor. The statue has been around for a long time and it never seems to change, although it has, just as with everything else — it was renovated in 1986, just in time for the celebration of its 100th anniversary.[55]

Liberty Island is a part of the National Park Service. There are many rea-

Top: The *Jewel* ready to depart from West 42nd Street. Enthusiastic passengers are looking forward to a tour of New York Harbor. *Bottom:* Circle Line boat going south past Jersey City on the Hudson River.

Top: U.S.S. *Intrepid.* This World War II vessel was decommissioned and now serves as a museum. *Bottom: Lettie G. Howard* on cruise on the Hudson River.

The Statue of Liberty was renovated in 1986. The lamp in the torch still lights, although it was reconfigured during the renovation.

sons why the Statue of Liberty is popular. Maybe the foremost is its location at the center of the harbor. (The Waterfront Commission measures its jurisdiction as 25 miles from the Statue of Liberty in all directions).[56]

A gift from the French, the Statue of Liberty was inaugurated on July 4, 1886. It was designed by Frederic-Auguste Bartholdi. It has been from the start of its life a symbol of liberty and freedom and has welcomed immigrants to the shores of the United States. The statue's location in the Upper Bay, near the southern end of the Hudson River (close to Ellis Island) makes it especially suitable to welcome immigrants, although not many of them come by ship nowadays. Yet its torch shines brightly for all who are in the harbor to see.

ELLIS ISLAND

Slightly to the north of the Statue of Liberty is Ellis Island. Ellis Island was for many years a place for processing immigrants to the United States. Many of our forefathers passed through Ellis Island. According to the National Park Service website, 12 million immigrants who came into New York came through Ellis Island in the period 1892–1954.[57]

Ellis Island, a welcoming place for immigrants. Now, no longer used for immigration, it is open to visitors as a National Park.

Sketch made in 1887 of immigrants on a ship entering New York Harbor. The immigrants are getting their first glimpse of the Statue of Liberty (Library of Congress).

Ellis Island was established as an immigrant station in 1892 and served as such until 1954. After it was retired as an immigrant station, the buildings fell into disrepair. After being restored, the main building was established as a museum in 1990. Not all the buildings have been restored, however. The island is open to visitors, who also enjoy a short cruise from the Battery.

2

Port Management and Operations

Who Controls New York Harbor?

The question of who controls New York Harbor is not easily answered. The harbor region is composed of several political entities, the states of New York and New Jersey being the main ones. The many cities and municipalities bordering on the waters of the port have their interests to protect. The departments of New York City certainly become involved in what is going on in the harbor. The New York City Police Department has a harbor unit based in the Brooklyn Army Terminal. It has 25 boats at various locations throughout the harbor. As an example of the relationships between communities which have properties on the waterfront, Captain Kenneth Kelleher, head of the NYC Harbor Unit, mentioned that the NYC police have an agreement with the communities on the New Jersey side of the Hudson that the NYC police have authority to the water's edge.[1]

"New York Harbor" is a misnomer of sorts. Actually, sections of New Jersey make up an important part of the port. When reference is made to New York Harbor, which is done for the sake of simplicity, they will implicitly include the New Jersey areas that make up a key part of the port. New York Harbor covers a *region* and it is a very vital region. It makes the port of New York and New Jersey a functioning whole. The economy, the political forces, the culture of the area play an important role. Since New York Harbor is in the Northeast, the most heavily populated area in the United States, it has the businesses, the transportation links, the manpower pool, the financial resources, all the assets to generate the processes that make a port operate. These assets do not always work to best advantage, particularly the political power relationships, which may result in delays while frictions between power structures are worked out.[2]

ORGANIZATIONS THAT HAVE AN IMPACT ON THE HARBOR

The mayor's office of the city of New York takes part in transactions having to do with the harbor from time to time, but not as much as one might think. This is especially true when one considers that the harbor, from a geographical point of view, is so important to the city. (New York City has 578 miles of waterfront.) The mayor's office limits its involvement to matters of broad political concern.

An organization that has a major impact on the development of the port is the Port Authority of New York and New Jersey. It controls the airports, bridges and other installations around the harbor. The Port Authority, a bi-state agency, invests billions of dollars in port improvements. Needless to say, those investments give it a lot of influence in what is going on in the port. The Port Authority included New Jersey in its name in 1972 to recognize that New Jersey played a significant role in the operation of the port. It is apparent that New Jersey has come more and more into the forefront of the harbor operations, particularly since the growth of the containership operations in Port Newark and Elizabeth and the development of the "Gold Coast" on the New Jersey side of the Hudson River.

Another active player is the Environmental Protection Agency, which has control over actions that affect the ecological, biological and chemical status of the waters of New York Harbor. Right now, that agency is significantly involved in dredging considerations, a matter that is extremely important to the development of the port. Similarly, the U.S. Army Corps of Engineers is an important organization. It maintains the navigation channels in the port and in doing so it is responsible for conducting the dredging activities, a continual challenge in New York Harbor because of the tendency of the Lower and Upper Bays to silt up. (This narrative will go into the dredging in greater detail in later sections since it is so important to the history of New York Harbor and its future.)

Probably the most important influence to ships and boats operating in New York Harbor is the U.S. Coast Guard based on Staten Island at Fort Wadsworth, at the foot of the Verrazano Bridge. The Coast Guard sets the rules for everything that moves on the water. Coast Guard personnel are the protectors of both pleasure and commercial mariners, ready to come to the rescue of all those who venture on the water. However, they also serve as stern parents who enforce the maritime rules and regulations. In addition, the Coast Guard establishes anchorages, takes care of navigation aids such as channel buoys, inspects ships, and performs a host of other functions that have to do with the operation of vessels. After the 2001 attacks on the World Trade Center, the Coast Guard became especially important to the port because of security considerations.

The Waterfront Commission of New York Harbor was set up in 1953 to regulate the loading and unloading of the ships that come and go in the harbor. It functions as an instrument of the states of New York and New Jersey. Before the Waterfront Commission came into being, there was a strong criminal element on the waterfront. The Waterfront Commission is the watchdog agency to keep crime off the waterfront, and it has made a number of improvements in the working conditions of the stevedores since its inception.

A number of other organizations have an interest in the status of the port in one way or another. They include organizations such as the New York Shipping Association, the Maritime Association of the Port of New York and New Jersey, and others. Included in these organizations is a group dedicated to helping the crewmen who come into the harbor on ships from all over the world: the Seamen's Institute, a body set up in 1834. A church-based service, it provides recreational and other services to the seamen who come into the port.

So who controls New York Harbor? It depends on what location and what operation is being talked about. In his book, *Empire on the Hudson*, Jameson Doig talks in great detail about events at the Port Authority.[3] The Port Authority undoubtedly is directly related to what goes on in the harbor. Another important organization is the Coast Guard, especially at this time of great emphasis on security against terrorism.

The question of who controls New York Harbor depends upon whether we are focusing on the water, or the land around it. The system for controlling the operation in the harbor evolved over time to meet one perceived need, then another. That system is important to the theme of this book. The focus will be on the water and the waterfront in later chapters, particularly the changes that have taken place over the years.

There are many pieces to the intricate mechanism that is the port of New York.

The Role of the Port Authority

The Port Authority of New York and New Jersey is probably the organization with the most influence on developments in the harbor. The Port Authority was set up in 1921 to bring a regional approach to planning for the port. A complicating fact for New York Harbor is that there are two sovereign states involved. There are 219 municipalities related to the harbor, not to mention the five boroughs of New York City, each of which is more populated than some of the municipalities. All of these entities have parochial interests. The one thing that they have in common is the waterways that constitute New York Harbor. The Port Authority was one of the first regional organizations set up to cut across such political boundary lines.

The Port Authority has been eminently successful in some respects. It built the George Washington Bridge over the Hudson and the Lincoln and Holland Tunnels under the Hudson. In doing so it had a tremendous effect on transportation in and around the harbor. It also built John F. Kennedy Airport in Queens and Newark Airport in New Jersey (recently renamed Newark Liberty International, although that name has not caught on with the public as yet). The Port Authority also manages LaGuardia Airport in Queens. One of its notable achievements was building the World Trade Center, where it had its headquarters until the 9/11 disaster. It developed marine terminals at Red Hook in Brooklyn. Probably the biggest effect on New York Harbor was the development of the Port

Newark and Port Elizabeth terminals in New Jersey in the 1960s. The Port Authority had great foresight to make that move.

The Port Authority's influence touches the infrastructure for the trade and transportation of this region. The port serves a regional market of some 18 million people. It serves as an access link to the hinterland of the United States, and to all of North America as well.

THE PORT AUTHORITY'S INFLUENCE BRINGS CONTROVERSY

During its history, the Port Authority has had to grapple with many divided interests, and it still finds itself embroiled in all kinds of conflicts. An example of how the Port Authority gets involved in controversy goes back all the way to when the organization was first founded.[4] It happened that the railroads followed the procedure of transporting railroad cars on car floats across the harbor from New Jersey, where the railroads ended, to points (mostly) in Manhattan, Bronx and Brooklyn. The railroad tugs with car floats were the very essence of harbor traffic. The railroads had to do it that way because the terminals were on the mainland of New Jersey, a condition that exists to the present time (although the railroads are now much less of a force). The Port Authority criticized this practice as adding to the cost of shipping to New York City destinations. For years, the Port Authority tried to persuade the railroads to band together, to form a common group that would transport the railroad cars across the harbor. The Port Authority felt that outcome would make the best of a situation that was cumbersome at the very least. To the contrary, the railroads thought that alternative would hurt the spirit of free enterprise and competition on which they were founded. Each railroad felt the touch of competition with the other railroads and none was of a mind to band together. The Port Authority fought a losing battle on this issue. However, the railroads lost out in the long run; they lost out to the trucking industry.

This issue became a source of tension between the railroads and the Port Authority. In the 1920s and the 1930s when the Port Authority was just getting started, the state of New Jersey filed a suit contending that it cost much less to ship a product to New Jersey terminals than to New York City, where the cargoes had, additionally, to be transported on railroad floats ("lightered") to the New York parts of the harbor, and that the state of New Jersey should be charged less, accordingly. The lighterage case went on for many years. It was finally settled in 1934. That year the Interstate Commerce Commission made its decision: to deny New Jersey's suit. One of the effects of that decision was to hold the Port of New York (and New Jersey) parts together in a unified fashion.[5]

DREDGING AND THE ENVIRONMENT

A conflict that the Port Authority is involved with has to do with environmental issues. Dredging is a particularly nagging concern, one that the Port

Authority is tussling with at the present time. The Port Authority forges ahead with its plans nevertheless, using its great deal of influence. "They have tonnage," as is said in the Navy, and the reason the authority has this tonnage is that the governors of each state are co-heads of the board, and the states receive income from rents and leases of state-owned properties as well as the tolls from the tunnels and the bridges. The states are in a position to invest hundreds of millions of dollars per year. Over a five-year period the Port Authority planned to invest $9.5 billion in port improvement projects. However, that was reduced in the 2003 budget by $1 billion because of the World Trade Center attacks of 2001 and the consequent diminution in renevue.[6, 7]

In any event, the Port Authority continues to announce great investments in projects under its auspices. It represents a harbor that is very important to the commerce of the nation and the global economy as well.

PORT AUTHORITY SET UP TO PROVIDE REGIONAL APPROACH

The Port Authority was set up to coordinate the separate interests of the region. Has it done that well? There are still squabbles between New York and New Jersey, yet they manage, after some time, to work the problems out. The outcome is not always optimal; it is usually a compromise. In a recent disagreement, the New York governor's office thought that New Jersey was getting too, much subsidies to keep the giant shipping company with Maersk-Sealand in New Jersey amounting to many millions of dollars. Governor Pataki felt the Port Authority was subsidizing the PATH trains, the subway system that operates between Jersey City and downtown Manhattan, resulting in the fares being too low. Of course, the New Jersey commuters were happy with the fares. Eventually, it was worked out.[8, 9]

Perhaps more important to the settlement of the agreement was New Jersey governor Christine Whitman's willingness to go along with the inclusion of projects for New York's sake: selling or leasing the World Trade Center, leasing air rights over the Port Authority Bus Terminal, and $250 million for transportation projects in New York.[10] Of course, after the 9/11 tragedy the World Trade Center deal is no longer an issue.

SHIFT OF SHIPPING OPERATIONS FROM
NEW YORK TO NEW JERSEY

A key part of the plan for developing the shipping terminals has been deepening the channels for the containership operations at Port Newark and Port Elizabeth. These operations had become the major shipping areas of the port of New York, and they represent one of the key changes in the harbor as a whole. The focus of shipping operations has clearly moved to New Jersey. The New York portions of the harbor, notably Manhattan and Brooklyn, have become relatively dormant as far as import/export shipping is concerned. The Red Hook section of Brooklyn, in addition to container operations, which are much smaller than in New Jersey, still handles the importation of coffee and cocoa. Manhattan is almost out of the shipping business for all practical purposes.

Why did this change occur? There are several reasons. New Jersey had the land; container operations require a lot of open space. Containers do not need to be housed in a warehouse. They can be stored in the open. Much space is needed: There are a great number of containers processed every year, and the number is getting larger every year.

Significantly, New Jersey's location on the mainland side of the port provides access to the rest of the country, the land transportation links, the trucks, the roads, the turnpikes. Although not perfect (there is concern about the clutter of traffic), these routes are thought better by most persons than those located in Manhattan or Brooklyn. New York City consists of various islands, such as Manhattan and Brooklyn (Long Island) that can be accessed only through the bridges and tunnels, by air or by boat. The traffic through these facilities is terrific. It is difficult for a truck to get through Manhattan. It seems like all day long there is constant rush hour, and trucks loaded with cargoes picked up in Red Hook are hard pressed to get to New Jersey, headed for the inland states.

Another issue is dredging, although that is proceeding according to schedule. The Port Authority's plan to dredge the channels in Kill Van Kull and Newark Bay generated a number of hearings by the state legislatures and the U.S. Congress. Actually, dredging has been going on for many years. In 2002, Congress passed a bill to allow dredging to a 50-foot depth in Kill Van Kull and Newark Bay.[11] Environmentalists continue to object. For example, dumping the dredged materials in the "Mud Dump," a 15-square-mile area five miles from Sandy Hook, has been questioned repeatedly. In the current situation, one of the problems was where to put the material dredged from the Kill Van Kull and Newark Bay, some of which was considered to be contaminated. Several alternatives were considered. The obvious one was to dump it in the Mud Dump (called "Acid Waters" by local boaters and fishermen). The state of New Jersey had a problem with that alternative and the environmentalists became involved as well. The site, now renamed the Historic Area Remediation Site or HARS, has been the subject of seemingly endless hearings and studies.

DREDGING INVOLVES CONTROVERSY

One alternative to the question of where to put the dredged material was a "borrow area" in Newark Bay — an area in which the dredgers would dig a hole beneath the waters of the bay and put the dredged spoil in it. Then they would cover up the contaminated material with a layer of clean fill. Implementation of the project has proceeded, and they have in fact put some of the material in the "borrow pit" in Newark Bay. The authorities also considered making an island in Newark Bay with the dredged spoil. That idea did not get very far, but they did send some of the material they have dredged so far (the dredging has been under way for several years; it is a long-term project) to fill an abandoned coal mine in Pennsylvania. Also, some of the material was used to pave a mall parking lot in New Jersey. Only a relatively small amount was utilized in these ways, however. They are expensive alternatives to sea-dumping. One estimate has it that the cost to transport fill to "upland areas" is $35–$50 per cubic yard versus $5–$10 to dump it nearby in the ocean.[12] At the present time, the dredging company is disposing of the dredged spoil in HARS, the offshore dumping site that was formerly called the Mud Dump. The environmental organizations do not like it one bit.

THE COMING OF CONTAINERIZATION

The Port Authority owes a debt of gratitude to Malcom McLean. He is the shipping magnate who came up with the idea of using containers to ship cargo.[13] In 1956, McLean, whose shipping line was based in Port Newark at the Port Authority docks, took the step of loading a trailer truck directly onto the deck of a merchant vessel. Later, special containers for cargo were constructed. Containers were advantageous as all the cargo could be stored in locked containers, which could be unloaded by dockside cranes directly onto waiting trucks or railroad cars. This was a tremendous step forward from the days in which stevedores had to unload the breakbulk cargo piece by piece from the bowels of the ship. Under the old method, the cargo frequently was then placed in a warehouse. Later, it had to be transferred to a truck or railroad car. This technique was cumbersome, to say the least.

The container approach caught on and mushroomed. New York became the first container port in the world. Now, every large port throughout the world is geared for handling container ships, and some of them have surpassed New York in efficiency — Hong Kong and Singapore, for example. About 95 percent of cargo is transported in this way. It proved to work exceedingly well. As a result, the Port Authority has expanded its development of the Newark and Elizabeth sections of the harbor area, and it continues to develop the Howland Hook terminal, although to a lesser extent.

Containerization led to the present proposal to deepen the channels leading to the Newark and Elizabeth ports, which are on Newark Bay, just a five-mile run from the Upper Bay through the Kill Van Kull. The reason for the push to deepen the channels is that some of the new container ships require 50 feet of depth to come into the harbor. It is an attempt to keep up with technological developments. The Port Authority had approval from the U.S. Congress (and some contributing funds) to dredge to 45 feet. The Port Authority then came up with the proposal to dredge to 50 feet all at once. The proposal estimated that the overall savings from the one-time dredging would be $800 million. The plan is to complete the project by 2009.

PLANNED IMPROVEMENTS IN THE INFRASTRUCTURE

The Port Authority, in typical entrepreneurial spirit, is thinking ahead. It is making improvements in the infrastructure. It is improving railroad connections to the container operations. It is making some improvements to the container-processing operations. There is still a lot of concern about the ability of the roads to carry the traffic envisioned in the future. The railroad operations must be beefed up, but the railroads are reluctant to make the investment. The Port Authority has investigated the possibility of having tugs tow barges holding containers to regional distribution centers as a way of alleviating the stress on road transportation. It remains to be seen whether this proposal will work out.

The United States has an insatiable appetite for automobiles and the Port Authority has large operations of this sort under its auspices. The Auto Marine Terminal, along the Jersey City/Bayonne waterfront, claims 143 acres. Also, automobiles are handled in the Port Newark/Elizabeth Auto Facilities.

A 2004 article presents a rather upbeat picture of the future of New York Harbor. It is mostly based on the increase projected for Port Newark, Elizabeth, and Howland Hook Terminals. It makes no mention of the Brooklyn and Manhattan waterfront areas, except to say that there has been a shift in import operations from the New York part of the port to New Jersey (and Howland Hook Terminal in Staten Island).[14]

HOWLAND HOOK TERMINAL

How does Howland Hook Terminal fit into this picture? It is smaller than the Port Newark and Port Elizabeth terminals, but it is growing, too. The author visited there recently.[15] There was a container ship docked at the pier, a large ship called the *Repulse Bay* out of London, loaded above the gunwales with containers, as container ships normally are. There were 10 gantry cranes facing the pier. One of them was in the process of unloading the *Repulse Bay*. There were four new cranes included, just built, impressive in their height. They were much larger than the older cranes. Brad Winfree, a terminal official, said they were going through the testing stage. He mentioned that one of the older cranes (not the one unloading the *Repulse Bay*) was damaged and would be scrapped. That would leave nine cranes to unload the two ships that would fit at the pier.

Brad Winfree described the ships that often dock there to unload their cargoes of bananas. The ships unload the bananas into a warehouse on the grounds. There, they await trucks to cart them elsewhere in the region.

Trailer trucks were everywhere. They had come to pick up the containers, which were stacked up outdoors all over the terminal. It seemed like thousands

Top: Containership *Repulse Bay* at pier in Howland Hook Terminal. Containers are stacked up on the deck. Gantry cranes are poised to unload her. *Bottom:* New gantry cranes for Howland Hook. These gantry cranes have been assembled at the terminal. Here, they are going through a testing stage before being put to use.

Top: Fork-lift truck for handling containers. Trucks such as this one can stack containers three-high. *Bottom:* Stern of *Repulse Bay.* The ship has many containers stacked on the deck which cranes are in the process of unloading.

of them, tended by forklift trucks which piled the containers two high or even higher, or lifted them onto waiting tractor-trailers. Mr. Winfree said that because of the trade imbalance, there being much more imports than exports, the ships had to carry empty containers as they sailed away from the United States. (There is a large pile of empty containers on the New Jersey Turnpike near Newark Liberty Airport. The problem of how to deal with the empty containers is a very real one.)

Mr. Winfree also commented that the name of the container terminal was changed in 2005. Henceforth, the name would be New York Container Terminal instead of Howland Hook Terminal. Mr. Winfree said the change in the name of the terminal would identify it more closely with New York Harbor. It will still be under the auspices of the Port Authority.

KEY TENANT THREATENS TO LEAVE PORT NEWARK

With reference to the Port Authority investment plan for developing the harbor, Governor Whitman of New Jersey had reservations about the disposal of the dredged materials. Eventually, she became head of the EPA. (She has long since left this post.) Meanwhile, the U.S. Congress approved the digging of the channel to 50 feet, so the Port Authority embarked on that project (through the Corps of Engineers) and has been so occupied for a number of years. All the while, one of the leading transportation companies in the container operations in Port Newark, the Maersk-Sealand Company, threatened to leave New York Harbor for Halifax, Nova Scotia, or Charleston, South Carolina, ports that are in contention as leading container ports. With the approval of the dredging operations and the other improvements that are in the plan, they agreed to stay in Port Newark.

POLITICAL RELATIONSHIPS ARE INHERENT IN THE PORT AUTHORITY'S STRUCTURE

The Port Authority by its nature is clearly deep into the politics of the two states that it represents. By tradition, the governor of New Jersey chooses the chairman and the governor of New York chooses the executive director. The regional planning concept has proceeded on a relatively sophisticated level. The Port Authority is rife with political relationships but it also is a very entrepreneurial organization. The organization sees other ports as competitors and it is determined to do well by comparison. The authority is investing billions on the future of imports into the United States. The Port Authority has had to scale back its ambitious plans to some extent, partly because of the World Trade Center disaster of 2001. One estimate is that it will cut planned capital improvements by $2 billion, from an originally planned $9.5 billion.

The World Trade Center attacks struck an undeniably strong blow to the Port Authority. There are some who feel the Port Authority has proved extremely resilient in the faces of such events as the loss of the World Trade Center and the loss of income from the bridge and tunnel tolls and the PATH ridership which was a direct result of the attacks. However, there are others who are critical of the Port Authority, saying it should be more steadfast in its plans.

An issue which has plagued the Port Authority for some time is the implication that it has favored New Jersey development of the port. It is understandable that most of the container operations were put in New Jersey. After all, New Jersey had the land, and that was what it takes, large amounts of space to store the containers after they are unloaded from the ships. The Red Hook container operations in Brooklyn are nowhere near as large as Port Newark/Elizabeth, nor is the Howland Hook container operation on Staten Island. The Port Authority has made some gestures to expand the latter operations. Congressman Jerrold Nadler has long pushed for a rail tunnel from Brooklyn to Staten Island. Several appropriations for studies of this tunnel plan have been made, and the Port Authority gave a low-key endorsement to the plan. The proposed tunnel seems to be more of an issue all the time. Proponents of the rail tunnel say the promise was made in 1921, when the Port Authority was formed.

THE FUTURE OF THE PORT AUTHORITY
IS THE FUTURE OF THE PORT

It is certain that the Port Authority of New York and New Jersey is very much a part of New York Harbor. It would be difficult for anyone to go through the harbor without seeing some evidence of its influence. Its influence is mostly economic, which is very important. The Port Authority is investing billions in the future of imports in the United States. There is a good probability that this investment will pay off, given the trends that have materialized thus far.

The United States Coast Guard

COAST GUARD FUNCTIONS

Since the World Trade Center disaster of 2001, the U.S. Coast Guard has received a great deal of favorable publicity. Some recreational boaters see Coast Guard personnel as stern policemen who enforce the rules on the waterways. Fortunately, most boatmen perceive them as a source of help, people who make it possible to sail safely and enjoyably. Some boatmen are in the Coast Guard Auxiliary and they go out in their boats on weekends and patrol the local waters.

Frequently, the Coast Guard has occasion to board ships and boats in the harbor. One of its purposes is to carry out inspections to see whether the vessel has the proper equipment on board and whether the equipment is in shipshape condition. The Coast Guard also renders assistance to vessels that find themselves in an emergency situation. Frequently, Coast Guard boats used to be found assisting boats that ran aground for one reason or another. However, the Coast Guard does not do that so much anymore. Nowadays, unless there is serious danger, the Coast Guard leaves that kind of rescue business to the many commercial tow operators who have sprung up in each harbor. The change in Coast Guard policy was partially due to cutbacks in funding — until the September 11th attacks, that is.

Coast Guard operations in New York Harbor are now based at Fort Wadsworth, at the base of the Verrazano Bridge in Staten Island. For many years they were based on Governor's Island. In a relatively new building, they administer the operation of the Coast Guard in the New York area, and they monitor the shipping operations in New York Harbor from their Vessel Traffic Service.

Vessel Traffic Service

The Vessel Traffic Service (VTS) is an activity that reaches throughout the harbor. The network is controlled from a large room at the Coast Guard headquarters, perhaps 30 feet square. It is darkened a bit so the colored lights from the screens seem to jump out from the scopes. The sailors seated at the scope use hushed tones when talking. The radar screens are arrayed around the walls. In addition, video screens sit above the radar consoles, on which can be viewed all the key areas in the harbor, Kill Van Kull, the Lower Bay, the Narrows, Hell Gate

The U.S. Coast Guard on the East River. This boat is a buoy tender (note the crane on deck.)

Coast Guard boat on the Hudson River. Security is tight in the harbor. U.S.S. *Intrepid* and the Concorde are in the background.

and so on; it is all laid out before the operators. The full-color radar screens show all the vessels in the area. The layout is similar to what one would find in an air traffic control center. The operators conduct transmissions with the ships and boats in the harbor, exchanging information on such matters as heading, speed and destination. Typically, a ship gives an operator information on where it is headed. A tug pilot describes tow, that it is a cargo of cement, that he has it alongside (on the side of the tug as opposed to towing it astern on a hawser). The tug pilot talks about going to Erie Basin. With this system, especially now that security is such an issue, the Coast Guard is well informed on what is going on in the harbor.

THE COAST GUARD'S ROLE IN THE PORT

Commander Dan Ronan is the Director of Waterways Management, which includes the VTS operation.[16] The author met with him, and he talked about the Coast Guard functions and the challenges it faces; for example, the clearing of the ice in the Hudson River to get the oil barges to upstate New York.[17] He described it as a "catch-22. When we have a mild winter the river is free of ice, but the citizens do not need as much oil for heating their homes. When the winter is more severe, and there is more oil required, the river is blocked with ice." (He was talking about the Hudson River north of New York City which gets iced up in the cold weather because of the lower salinity in the water. Commander Ronan has additional responsibility part way up the Hudson even though it is not considered part of New York Harbor.) When it is necessary, a big Coast Guard vessel goes up there and clears the ice so the tows can get through, and that is a load off Commander Ronan's mind.

Commander Ronan cited New York as the busiest port on the East Coast for petroleum products. The refineries and tank farms are located mostly on Staten Island and some in New Jersey, along the Kill Van Kull. There are smaller operations in Queens, accessible from the East River. When the VTS system handles a tanker or a tow with an oil barge, they are usually headed to or from the Kill Van Kull.

Coast Guard Reaction to the World Trade Center Attacks of 2001

The Coast Guard was actively engaged in the aftermath of the September 11, 2001, attacks. When the first plane hit the World Trade Center, the Coast Guard officers, like most people, did not know what to make of it. Then, as the full implication of the disaster became clear, the Coast Guard was among the many organizations that went into action. One of the first actions the Coast Guard took was to forward-deploy the VTS personnel on a borrowed pilot boat to the Battery area. There, they coordinated the evacuation of the survivors by boat across the harbor to areas such as New Jersey or Brooklyn. Automatically, the Coast Guard put into effect what amounted to the OpSail Plan. That plan dated back to 2000, the year that New York Harbor had entertained a large number of sailing ships. The Coast Guard called the plan to coordinate the gathering the OpSail Plan on September 11. The Coast Guard just implemented it because it made sense to do so.

As Commander Ronan and others have pointed out, the marine companies responded to the situation by providing boats to evacuate people from downtown Manhattan. The bridges had been closed. The PATH trains which go from Jersey City under the Hudson River to the World Trade Center were not operating—the train station at the WTC was completely buried under rubble. The Holland and Lincoln Tunnels were closed. There was no way for people to get off lower Manhattan Island except by boat, and the marine community responded beautifully. Ferry companies supplied boats, as did dinner cruise companies. Tugs carried people across the rivers and across the Upper Bay to other places in the harbor. All this activity was coordinated by the Coast Guard. (This evacuation is discussed in greater detail in the section on the World Trade Center attacks).

The Coast Guard was of course very concerned about security. At the time of the disaster the officials did not know the scope of the attacks, whether more were coming, or where they would come from. They knew that New York Harbor was vulnerable. They took steps to bar ships from entering the harbor. The Coast Guard did not do this lightly. The Port Authority estimated it would cost $20 million per day in lost revenue to shut down the harbor. But it had to be done. For two days, it seemed like all shipping stopped. Actually, a few crucial shipments were carried out, such as New York City sewage disposal ships, which had to dump their sludge out at sea as they routinely do. The ships are based near Hell Gate. A few oil barges with essential shipments of petroleum products moved in the harbor, also. Recreational boats had to wait considerable time before they could enter the harbor. Overall, there was not much activity in the harbor immediately after the World Trade Center disaster.

After the two-day delay, when the ships were again allowed to enter the harbor, the Coast Guard inspected every one beforehand to make sure there was no security risk. About 40 ships per day enter New York Harbor, so this was no easy task. A few ships were detained while various questions were investigated. In the end, no ships were completely barred from entering the harbor during this period.

It has been said that the harbor is very vulnerable to terrorist attack. Among the many responsibilities of the U.S. Coast Guard is the security of New York Harbor. One of the potential problems is the many containers that are brought into the harbor on ships during the year. In 2001 Senator Charles Schumer of New York State wanted to x-ray all the containers.[18] In 2004 the authorities reportedly looked at only 2 percent of them. Apparently, the authorities increased that to 6 percent according to a TV news broadcast in 2004, but it is still a small number,[19] still not enough inspection. It is difficult to investigate a cargo container. Among the problems is that if a container has explosives in it it might blow up when the door is opened. Inspecting all the containers is physically impossible. Even inspecting a large number of containers is very manpower intensive. The containers have to be unloaded by hand and then loaded again. The idea of x-ray inspection is better, but not without its drawbacks. Meanwhile, the subject of the security of the containers entering the port is getting increased attention from the media.

While such issues are being thrashed out at a higher level, the Coast Guard goes on with its job. The Coast Guard has implemented the Qualship 21 initiative, an approach to inspecting ships.[20] Under this program, the Coast Guard concentrates its efforts on inspecting lesser-quality vessels according to a matrix of information it gathers about each ship. The known "quality" vessels get lesser inspection in their program. That way, the Coast Guard uses its time and manpower most effectively, and that is important because the Coast Guard has undergone continual cutbacks in its budget. With the security threat after 9/11, the Coast Guard was beefed up considerably in order to carry out its security role.

Presumably, it will receive longer-term increases in manpower and equipment; Commander Ronan says the Coast Guard will grow by 15percent to meet port security in New York Harbor.

COAST GUARD HAS BEEN OVERSTRETCHED

The Coast Guard has so many functions and responsibilities that one may wonder how it has the manpower and equipment to carry out all of them.[21, 22, 23, 24] In the aftermath of the September 11 attacks, the U.S. Coast Guard was moved organizationally into the Homeland Security Department (formed 2002). Until the passage of this bill, late in 2002, some people thought the Coast Guard should be part of the Defense Department. Previously, under the Transportation Department, it was in some respects "lost" in the many functions and activities of that department. Its budget had been severely cut back. A few congressmen are supporters, and that helps, and the Coast Guard gets good support from members of the boating public who see it as a protector. Every year, some Coast Guard station is proposed as a candidate to close down as a cost-saving measure. The boating public makes an outcry and the station ends up continuing in operation.

While the security threat is being dealt with, the Coast Guard in New York continues to carry out its more routine functions. It maintains the navigation aids (aids to navigation, known as ATON, are coordinated by Boston authorities, as Boston is the headquarters for the First District, of which New York Harbor is a part). Also, the Coast Guard coordinates the many events that take place in the harbor, such as the aforementioned OpSail 2000. These events include sailboat races, yacht regattas, fireworks displays, and so on. While they are fun events in many respects, the Coast Guard takes them very seriously. They are important to the Coast Guard from the point of view of navigational safety. With the current threat of terrorism, New York Harbor is a potential target. The Coast Guard in New York Harbor has been reinforced by vessels and manpower from other ports, such as Boston. This author believes the whole Coast Guard budget should be increased.

The United States Army Corps of Engineers

EARLY ACTIVITIES OF THE CORPS OF ENGINEERS

The U.S. Army Corps of Engineers has served the maritime interests of the country since the early history of the Colonies. One of its earliest exploits was during the Revolutionary War. The Corps of Engineers was called on to place a heavy chain across the Hudson River. The chain was designed to deny British warships access to the upper part of the river. The Corps of Engineers received this assignment because of its engineering expertise, which was exercised quite well. The location of the chain was near where West Point is today. Perhaps because of the Corps of Engineers' identification with the West Point area, the head of the Corps of Engineers was named as the first commandant of the newly established military academy at West Point. The first class graduated in 1802.[25]

The corps went on to accomplish many engineering projects during the Civil War. After that war, they became involved in dredging. The dredging technology was in its infancy in those days, consisting of what was essentially a steam shovel mounted on a barge. It worked fine as long as the water was not too deep and the weather was good. The corps worked on the inland waterways at that time. Later in the century, when they dredged the Gedney Channel and what was to be called the Ambrose Channel in New York Harbor, the engineers ran into technical problems, especially problems caused by the weather in the exposed ocean locations. Eventually, they were able to work these problems out and they were successful with their dredging operations. The accomplishments of the Corps of Engineers in completing Ambrose Channel and the clearing of Hell Gate will be discussed in detail in other sections of this book.

THE CORPS OF ENGINEERS IN NEW YORK HARBOR

As the 19th century wore on, the harbor of New York thrived as a leading port of the nation, and the Corps of Engineers was deeply involved in what was going on at the time. From mid-century on, the length of piers in the harbor became an issue. It had become common practice to dump refuse in the water between the piers. Ashes, cinders, rainwater runoff—all went into the harbor. Eventually, the slips became shallow and the owners were motivated to build the piers farther out in the river to get into deeper water. The authorities had to gain control over the situation because, among other things, the tidal flow was being impeded and shoaling of the Hudson River was occurring. The city of New York passed a law limiting dumping. However, strangely enough, there was no penalty for violation of the law. Dumping in the river and between the slips went on until 1888, when Congress passed a law giving the supervisor of the harbor (then a navy captain) the power to set limits and to prosecute offenders. It was called the Harbor Delineation Act.[26]

Another issue had developed during this time. The issue was the dumping of material into the channels themselves. The Corps of Engineers had a difficult time with this practice. In *The Cradle of the Corps*, an excellent history of the corps in the New York District, the author talks about a particularly irksome problem caused by the dumping of stone into what was then called the East Channel.[27] This dumping was particularly troublesome for the corps because the dredges could not scoop up the stones as they could the mud and sand. Additionally, it was very expensive to dredge up the stones. The corps had to employ special contractors to raise the stones with bucket cranes.

The Corps of Engineers became involved in remedying the constriction and the shoaling of the rivers. This situation was especially grave in the Hudson River in the latter part of the 19th century. Several transatlantic shipping lines had piers at Jersey City, and those piers extended into the river beyond the legal limit. The piers on the Manhattan side of the river extended far out also and the river was somewhat constricted at this point. A shoal had developed off Jersey City as a result. Hearings were held. A long, drawn-out process ensued. The legislation of 1888 helped to control the problem, and finally the Corps of Engineers dredged the shoal. By the end of the century the river flowed in a more normal manner.

After 1900, the Corps of Engineers supervised the dredging of the Hackensack River and the Passaic River in New Jersey. At that time, there were more industrial plants along those rivers than at present; and they were somewhat removed from the great Hudson River, out in the Meadowlands of New Jersey. Nevertheless, they were still considered to be very much a part of New York Harbor. The corps also did some dredging in Newark Bay, already the focus of industrial development. Later, in the 1960s Port Newark and Elizabeth on Newark Bay would become vital container ports, the busiest shipping areas in New York Harbor.

The Corps of Engineers made other contributions to the development of New York Harbor. For many years, the corps has been responsible for removing the floating materials found in the waterways. Those materials can nick a propeller pretty badly, or even cause a sinking if a boat in the harbor should hit a floating piece of debris head-on. The Corps of Engineers also became involved in removal of derelict piers and shipwrecks. The legislation that involved the removal of shipwrecks that interfered with navigation was clear-cut, and the corps was fairly successful in dealing with shipwrecks. It has been less effective in getting rid of abandoned piers and old vessels. In Newtown Creek and Gowanus there are several abandoned pier buildings, and in the Kill Van Kull there are a number of derelict, rotting vessels to be seen. In fact, at a number of places around the harbor there are still to be seen old ferries, rotting at their docks. There is one at Rikers Island and another on the Hudson at Haverstraw, to mention two that come to mind.

THE CORPS OF ENGINEERS AT PRESENT

The Corps of Engineers is responsible for dredging the channels in the harbor under the current program to make the channels deeper and thus accommodate the new containerships. Originally, as mentioned in the chapter on the Port Authority, it was proposed to dredge to a 45-foot depth, with a later project to dredge to a 50-foot depth. Then, it was reproposed to do it all at once to a 50-foot depth. Congress approved the latter proposal. In a meeting with the program manager for New York Harbor, the author was told that the Corps of Engineers is proceeding to dredge the Kill Van Kull up to the Newark Bay turnoff,

Newark Bay, and the Kill Van Kull a short way past the Goethals Bridge to 50 feet. It is only "studying" the other areas for the 50-foot depth. The Corps of Engineers has said that as a matter of priority it had already decided it would not be feasible to dredge the Brooklyn Channels to 50 feet.[28]

The Corps of Engineers, along with the Port Authority, has been criticized for being unmindful of the environment when carrying out its projects. Dredging, in particular, has come under fire.[29] For its part, the Corps of Engineers has taken the step, along with other harbor agencies, of developing the Dredged Material Management Plan for the port of New York and New Jersey. For example, the rock taken from the Bergen Point area in Kill Van Kull is supposed to be used for a fish reef off Shark River, New Jersey.[30]

As a federal agency, the U.S. Army Corps of Engineers has a broader charter than just serving the harbor of New York. It may seem somewhat incongruous that an army agency would be involved in the waterways of the United States. One might think it would more likely be the U.S. Navy. However, throughout the history of the United States, it was the Army Corps of Engineers that had the expertise to put the chain across the Hudson, to lobby for the cessation of dumping in New York Harbor, and dredge the channels in the rivers. The Corps of Engineers has contributed a great deal to the evolution of New York Harbor. It has been criticized as well, to be sure, mostly on environmental issues having to do with dredging and what to do with the dredged spoil. The corps has been under much pressure in other ways as well: The head of the Corps of Engineers was dismissed over a budget quarrel in 2002.[31] There have been calls for a reorganization of the corps.[32] A *New York Times* editorial says that every president has found the corps to be difficult and cites environmental issues having to do with the engineering policies of the corps. The editorial also refers to legislation that would overhaul the corps, sponsored by several members of Congress.

In spite of this proposed legislation the Corps of Engineers will probably get through this storm and continue with their dredging, maintaining the waterways—changed perhaps in some ways, but still applying their expertise in carrying out their engineering projects.

Railroads

RAILROADS ACTIVE IN HARBOR
FROM ABOUT 1850 TO 1950

Railroads are vital to the operation of the harbor as a shipping port, although they are less crucial now than they were some years ago. The term *intermodal* is becoming more common nowadays, and applied to shipping it means the use of various means of transportation to get a product from one place to another. One of the advantages of New York as a port is that it has good transportation links to move the cargoes from the ships to the hinterland, and, in reverse, the products from inland points to New York so they can be loaded on ships and exported. "Pretty good" would be a better phrase for it in the sense that New York is mostly a series of islands and special means have to be taken to get products from the mainland of New Jersey to other parts of the port of New York.

When the Erie Canal was opened in 1825 it was a great plus for New York Harbor. The canal opened up access to the Great Lakes area and middle America, much as the railroads in the 1800s provided a way of getting cargoes from New York to other parts of the country and western territories. Railroad lines like the Pennsylvania, the Erie, New York Central, and the Jersey Central competed with one another to get the port of New York freight, and expanded by leaps and bounds in the New York–New Jersey area. The railroad tycoons battled with one another to get into the lucrative New York market.[33] Railroads were the primary means of long-distance transportation from about 1850 to 1950.

It is difficult now to believe there was a time when it was not possible to get by rail from one place to another in the United States. The railroad lines coming from the west ended in New Jersey up until the early 20th century. It was only in 1910 that the Pennsylvania Railroad built a tunnel under the Hudson River to get access to Manhattan, terminating at Pennsylvania Station. The New York Central had access to Manhattan via the bridge at the Harlem River at Spuyten Duyvil, ending at Grand Central Station (coming from upstate New York); but it wasn't until 1917 that the Pennsylvania and New Haven Railroads got together to construct the Hell Gate Bridge. Until that time there was no direct rail connection between New York and New England.

As was emphasized earlier, New York is a metropolis consisting mainly of islands. The Bronx is the only one of the five boroughs that is topographically connected with the mainland. The others are islands, or parts of islands. This feature gave New York its extensive waterfront. It also made it rather inaccessible other than by boat until the bridges and tunnels were built, and even then the tunnels and bridges served as bottlenecks to vehicle travel. The railroads found that to be the case as they built their railroad terminals in New Jersey. They were faced with difficulty in getting their cargoes to the boroughs of New York City, so they did what they had to do. They used car floats, long wooden barges, to carry the railroad cars to various points in New York Harbor. These were towed, usually alongside, by tugboats owned by the railroads. The railroads developed "navies" consisting of many lighters and tugs.[34] The Erie Railroad had 236 marine craft, and that was not the largest maritime fleet.[35]

The lighters were constructed like barges, usually with buildings on deck for keeping the cargo out of the weather while it was transported. They served the purpose of carrying the cargo to or from the ships that were anchored out in the harbor. The lighters had no propulsion of their own; they had to be towed by tugs. Many of the lighters had cranes on board to handle the cargo they carried,

Fall River steamboat pier. The Fall River line operated in the 1800s, running to New England ports (Library of Congress).

a large mast and boom that dominated the vessel and gave it the nickname "stick-lighter." The railroads, when they were active on the waterfront, had many of these lighters and one would see them going to and fro in the harbor, usually towed by railroad tugs. There are still a small number of lighters servicing ships that are moored at the various anchorages, but the railroad tugs are rare these days; they are towed now by the few remaining other towing companies.

The railroads also went into the business of operating steamboats. The Fall River Line, which operated between New York and New England, was owned by the Pennsylvania Railroad. It was common until fairly recently for the railroads to operate marine vessels that would complete the travels of their rail passengers, to get them from one place to another — entirely. It was a way of extending their reach. A person traveling from St. Louis to Boston would come to New York by rail and then complete the trip by steamboat from New York, out Long Island Sound to Boston. (This is one of the reasons why it was so important to get Hell Gate cleared of rocks — so the boats could go through without accident).

The railroads built large facilities called classification yards in New Jersey. In these yards, consisting of miles of tracks lined up one beside the other, the railroad cars would be separated according to their ultimate destination. They would then be loaded onto car floats and be towed by railroad tugs to whatever part of New York Harbor they were destined for. The New York Central had a terminal in the Bronx; its car floats would be taken up the East River. Other car floats would be taken by the railroad tugs to Brooklyn. In Manhattan on the West Side there were several "pier stations" into which the car floats were taken and moored alongside piers. These piers had warehouses on them into which the cargoes were unloaded. Sometimes they would be loaded directly onto waiting trucks. Most if not all of the cargo for the pier stations was of the less-than-a-carload, or breakbulk, variety.[36] The yard operated by the Central Railroad of New Jersey, for example, was built on a peninsula abutting the Hudson River in Jersey City. It was huge, more than 1,000 acres. The yard had many railroad tracks in parallel running from the west toward the water. The switching engines used these tracks to shunt the railroad cars onto one track or another depending upon destination. At the end, on the waterfront, was the enormous terminal of the Central Railroad of New Jersey, referred to earlier in this book. It was a very dominating feature overlooking the river. For the immigrants landing at nearby Ellis Island, this terminal was the first place they would set foot on the mainland United States. Many of them landed at this terminal to board trains to their final destination in the United States.

The railroads were the predominant form of transportation during the first half of the 20th century. By the end of the 1950s, the situation had changed. Among other things, the road system had been built. Bridges and tunnels had been constructed over the East River and the Hudson River. A whole infrastructure for road transportation into and out of New York City had been developed. Robert Moses, the great power figure in New York, had built the parkways on Long Island. He built the Bronx-Whitestone Bridge. The East River Drive along the waterfront in Manhattan was a reality. The Triborough Bridge system had been constructed. New Jersey saw the advent of the Garden State Parkway and the New Jersey Turnpike. All of these roads, tunnels, bridges, and many more, came into existence. They changed the face of New York Harbor.

DECREASE IN RAILROAD OPERATIONS

The railroads gradually decreased their operations. Their marine assets became costly to operate, especially as their business diminished. The ferry operations fell into disuse. Many fine, big, powerful ferries operated by the railroads were laid up, moored to docks or piers only to decay. Docks and train yards became derelict and rotted. Just as the railroads had replaced the Morris Canal, the eastern end of which was adjacent to the Jersey Central yard, the railroads were replaced by the airplane, the truck and the automobile. That trend has been the way of life in New York Harbor, a continual process of change. A system would flourish and then be replaced.

The railroads are still important to New York Harbor, maybe more impor-

Lehigh Valley railroad tug *Capmoore* coming into a slip with covered barges alongside (South Street Seaport).

tant than ever when one considers the desire to transport more containers by rail at Port Newark or the call for more car floats from the Brooklyn container operations. Nevertheless, railroad operations are much less extensive now than they were in the first half of the 20th century. At one time there were four rail terminals in Brooklyn. They were combined into the Cross Harbor Railroad, which is the only remaining shoreline railroad in Brooklyn. This railroad still maintains car float operations between Brooklyn and New Jersey. So, a few railroad tugs and car floats can be seen in the Upper Bay, but not such as would have been seen long ago. The railroads, which had once been so prominent in New York Harbor, on the water as well as on the land, cut back their operations. The extensive yards which the Jersey Central had in Jersey City have become Liberty State Park, a recreational area.

Rail Tunnel Proposal

Part of the problem with the use of Brooklyn as a shipping center is that Brooklyn has no direct rail link with the hinterland of the continent. Other than the small amount of cargo that is carried in railroad cars on car floats to and from New Jersey, the Brooklyn terminals are dependent upon truck transportation to carry the goods to other states. To remedy this problem, a study by the New York City Economic Development Corporation recommends a freight train tunnel connecting Bay Ridge, Brooklyn, to either Jersey City or Staten Island. This proposal would link the Brooklyn rail-freight network to the rest of the system. Reactions to this proposal have been mixed. Critical comments include that it is hard to predict what the requirements for freight transportation would be 10 years from now. Ten years is the anticipated completion time for the project. This criticism seems groundless, given that the predictions are for increases in shipping in the coming years. The Port Authority has invested billions based on expectations of future growth.

Most of this growth predicted by the Port Authority is for the New Jersey parts of the harbor. However, if the problems with the Brooklyn shipping operations are rectified, namely the current need for trucks to traverse the New York City streets, the whole harbor could benefit from the increased shipping business. Most argue an "either-or" type of decision: put the investment money into either New York or New Jersey.[37, 38] The thinking should be that we can build up both the New York and the New Jersey shipping operations.

Some New Jersey people feel that the Brooklyn Terminals represent only a small portion of the total shipping processed by the harbor, so it would not be worth the expense of building the tunnel, which is estimated at $1.4 to $2.5 billion. That view may be biased in that the Brooklyn share of the shipping business could increase proportionately. That would likely please New Yorkers.

SLIGHT INCREASE IN RAIL TRANSPORT OF CONTAINERS

In spite of the reduction in operation of the railroads in New York and New Jersey, the container terminals at Port Newark and Elizabeth are served by a number of railroads at present, including the Canadian Pacific, CSX and Norfolk Southern. The Port Authority is enhancing the facilities for these railroads. Although most of the cargoes coming into the port are handled by truck, the Port Authority is fully aware of the importance of rail travel to the transportation of cargoes onto the continent of North America. In fact, its aim is to increase rail capacity in hopes of easing the strain on road traffic and decreasing pollution. The Port Authority developed an on-dock system called ExpressRail that allows international shippers a way to reach consumers in the midwest, New England and Canada. The 35-acre ExpressRail terminal opened in 1991. The Port Authority is currently planning to expand the terminal to 70 acres. Also, in the current plan is a provision to construct overpasses on the truck streets around the container terminals so the trains can move freely without tying up the track traffic.

In spite of all these plans, the railroads are not likely in New York Harbor to return to the glory days of the past. Some operations still exist, such as the Greenville Yards in New Jersey. More car float activity has been proposed between the Brooklyn waterfront and the Greenville Yards in order to alleviate the truck congestion on New York City streets.[39] This proposal should receive serious consideration. It would help materially in realizing the shipping potential of the port.

Sandy Hook Pilots

A VENERABLE PROFESSION

The Sandy Hook Pilots over the years have played a key role in the development of New York Harbor. On the wall of their Staten Island headquarters is a letter, carefully framed, from Governor George Clinton, dated 1784, commissioning the Sandy Hook Pilots to carry out the responsibility of guiding ships into New York.[40] They have a long history behind them. The seal of their organization has a date of 1694. Since that date they have been shepherding ships across the Sandy Hook bar into what was to become the harbor of New York.

COMPETITION AMONG PILOTS IN THE 1700S AND 1800S

The Sandy Hook Pilots went through some difficult times. In the terrifying blizzard of 1888, 12 pilot boats went down in the windswept waves. The Sandy Hook Pilots had been operating for a long time, but until that time they were not organized. The pilot boats roamed far and wide, sometimes going quite a way out to sea, vying ferociously to be the first to reach a ship as it approached the New York Bight. It was a race against time. Speed of the pilot boat was most important. When the pilot boat approached a ship, the procedure was to burn a barrel loaded with tar up forward on the deck of the boat. The ship would see this flare up and know there was a pilot on hand who could guide them over the shoals of Sandy Hook and the Lower Bay.

Picture a pilot boat of that era racing to meet a ship coming into New York. The boat is rising up on each wave, fighting for its life against a sea that is providing its livelihood. The boat has sails up, but they are tightly reefed because the wind is howling with a tremendous roar. Each gust of the wind sends the boat lurching down the backs of the waves and heeling rail-down in the water. Unmercifully tossed about by the waves, the boat is first on the crest of a wave, a second later in the depths of a valley of water. It seems like the boat must go down, it is so thrown about by the sea. Finally, the pilot sees the ship, a gray image in the fog fighting its way against the foamy waves. A light is lit up forward on the pilot boat. The ship sees it. Now the pilot boat has only to get the pilot aboard the ship, no mean feat in this stormy sea.

The pilots of those days, at a time when they sailed in schooners, had to confront difficult conditions at sea, especially in winter. Feats of great seamanship were everyday events. The pilot boats roamed far away from New York Harbor to compete for a ship to guide into the port, as far away as Nantucket to the east (there are reports of pilots going even farther, to Sable Island, Nova Scotia) and off Delaware Bay to the south. When they spotted the ship, they would put a light up forward as a signal and then launch a "yawl boat," a rowboat the pilot would use to get aboard the ship. They battled fiercely with the waves, bringing the yawl boat under the lee of the ship. Only then could the pilot begin the precarious process of grasping the ladder to get on board the ship. It was a dangerous occupation and many were lost offshore.[41]

ORGANIZATION OF THE PILOTS

In the disastrous blizzard of 1888 many pilots were lost. The remaining pilots carried on. Then the state commissioner of New York and of New Jersey said the pilots needed to form a single group to maintain a boat at the harbor entrance for purpose of meeting the ships as they came in. The aim of the states was to eliminate the competition, and the pilots agreed. In 1884, the modern-day Sandy Hook Pilots Association was formed. Actually, there are two associations: the New York Sandy Hook Pilots Association and the United New Jersey Sandy Hook Pilots Association. The reason there are two associations is that the pilots are governed by state law, hence separate laws for New York and New Jersey. They operate as one, however.

The idea of maintaining a boat at the entrance to the harbor for the pilots to stay on while they were waiting for the ships was written into the law, and it exists to this day. The Pilots Association has a fleet of smaller boats to bring them out to the large boat, which is always on station near Ambrose Light, and to take the pilots from the large boat to the ships.

The notion of eliminating the competition between different pilot boats made sense because it freed the pilots from any obligation to the ship owners. For example, the pilot does not have to be concerned about financial pressure to get the ship into or out of port because of scheduling. The safety of the ship is uppermost in the mind of the pilot. Needless to say, not having to go a long distance offshore to find a ship to guide into port is a great boon to the pilots. Most of the vessels nowadays arrange in advance to pick up a pilot at the entrance to the harbor. Under current security rules, they have to notify the Coast Guard in advance of their intention to enter the harbor of New York. (Tugs coming into New York Harbor do not need a pilot — they usually know the waters well enough. Most of these tugs stay offshore in their approach to the harbor, but occasionally they come close to Sandy Hook using the False Hook Channel. Tugs approaching from the northeast use the Long Island Sound entrance and go through Hell Gate.)

100

DESIGN OF PILOT BOATS

Design of pilot boats was important. In the days of sail, many of them were schooners. The schooner *America*, the first winner of the America's Cup, had a design based on a pilot boat. The pilot boats did not have to carry cargo, and their primary requirement was speed. Also, they had to be very seaworthy because they had to be out in all kinds of weather. In the old days, the pilot boats, like all the vessels of that time, were built of wood, and they were equipped with sails. Now pilot boats are built of aluminum or steel and they are propelled by powerful diesel engines. Some of them, such as the *New York* or *New Jersey*, which the pilots alternately maintain on station near Ambrose Light, are large and relatively comfortable to be aboard because they have sleeping accommodations and lounges for the pilots in which to wait for their ships.

OPERATIONS AND EQUIPMENT OF THE PILOTS

As the pilot guides the ship into New York Harbor, his relationship with the captain of the ship is an interesting one. The captain, of course, is responsible for the ship at all times. However, he relies on the pilot, who knows the waters of New York Harbor better than he does. In fact, ship captains over the centuries have welcomed the pilot who could take them safely into the harbor. Wearing the traditional jacket and tie, the pilot comes on board and takes over the guiding of the ship. The captain is ever watchful but stands in the background, conferring occasionally with the pilot on matters such as characteristics of the ship. Such information is very important, particularly draft of the ship. Some of these ships are so large that they scrape the bottom of even the deepest channels. Captain W.W. Sherwood, the president of the New York Sandy Hook Pilots Association, says that they will build ships to whatever depth the channels are. The pilots will clear a ship that is two and a half feet less than the channel depth. This situation gives only minimal clearance, and they must wait for high tide with a ship with that much draft.

Pilot boats are very important to pilots. These boats are their means of getting to the ships they guide into the harbor. Two kinds of boats are involved in the pilot operations. The pilots have two fairly large boats, and a number of launches. The two larger boats alternate on station at the harbor entrance for six months each. The pilot boat *New York*, built in 1972, is 185 feet long. Its speed is 13 knots. Captain Sherwood has said it is a fine boat and that he would go anywhere in the *New York*. The other large boat is the *New Jersey*, 149 feet long and built in 1986. When the *New York* or *New Jersey* finish their six-months tour of duty on station at Ambrose Light, they are brought into port and completely refurbished. They need it, especially the *New York*, which stays on station at Ambrose during the challenging winter months.

These boats are "floating bunkhouses" where the pilots wait for the ships that they will service. The boats are always under way when on station, either drifting or steaming slowly in a triangular area marked out on the chart near Ambrose Light. The pilots go out to the larger boats on 24-foot launches. Also, the larger boats always have a launch alongside to bring the pilots to the ships. The pilots association recently acquired two new launches. They are built of aluminum, and they are very fast, an important requirement because the new container ships go as fast as nine knots even when they are at dead slow. The old wooden launches would only make eight knots at top speed. With the new launches, the pilot boats can match up with the new container ships in speed and get the pilot on board.

RIGOROUS TRAINING

The Sandy Hook Pilots are an expert, well-trained group. Individually, they have many years of experience. To obtain his license a pilot has to know almost literally every inch of the harbor, the channels, the depths, the currents. They know all the navigational aids, their location, characteristics, and they have to keep up to date on changes, and when specific navigational aids are not working. In past days, pilot trainees were recommended from within the association. This meant most pilots were sons and even grandsons of former pilots. It was a matter of family tradition in many cases. That situation has changed in present times. Now, they are more open in their recruiting of new pilots, selecting on the basis of aptitude, primarily. Additionally, there now are a few women pilots.

An article in the *Star-Ledger* (Newark, N.J.) talks about the training of Sandy Hook pilots (among other facts about the Sandy Hook pilots).[42] One of the requirements now is a college education. The fledgling pilots enter the Pilots Association as apprentices for a period of six years. Then they serve as deputy pilots for about another six years. By this time they have learned the harbor well (10 times over) and they become full-fledged pilots.

CHANGE COMES TO THE SANDY HOOK PILOTS

The harbor is changing for these pilots, just as it is for other harbor boatmen and ship operators. In 1962, the pilots handled over 26,000 ships. In 2002, the number of ships guided into or out of New York Harbor was down to about 11,000. Similarly, the association's membership is shrinking: they included 147 pilots in 1962. Now they are down to 84. Part of this decline is because the ships have become so much larger; it just doesn't take as many ships to carry the same amount of cargo. The *Regina Maersk* is so large it reportedly holds at least 4,500 containers. However, most of the ships are smaller, and there are just not as many of them coming into New York Harbor.

Someone sailing in the area of Sandy Hook will hear the chatter on the VHF radio of ships calling to arrange a rendezvous with a pilot, or calling the *New*

York or *New Jersey* to arrange for a pilot to be picked up. It happens every day and through all hours of the night. The harbor is changing, and the Sandy Hook Pilots are affected by the changes, but in some ways they are the common thread over the centuries.

Tugboats and Towing

A Changing Picture on the Waters of the Harbor

It has been said that there were 1,000 tugboats in the New York Harbor when they were at their peak. In 1960, it was reported that there were some 430 tugs in the harbor, and in 2000 there were only 90 tugs, according to the web feature "The Last of the Family Tugs."[43] The tugboat business in New York Harbor really shrunk from the way was in the early part of the last century.

Towing in the harbor is a good example of how every business has to deal with the changes that occur around it. Such changes are economic in nature — those are the obvious ones. Others are more subtle, like changes in the attitudes of the many customers they serve, or changes in the conditions in which people live. Some of the tugboat companies survived, even prospered, like Moran and McAllister, which took advantage of the growth of deep-sea towing. They had the breadth of vision to expand out of the New York Harbor market. They also capitalized on the berthing of ships, a commerce that grew as more and more ships came into New York Harbor. Other towing companies, such as Red Star, saw themselves mainly as towing between the creeks of New York Harbor. The Tracy towing company at one point had many towboats and barges. The company was too specialized, however. They serviced the many power plants in and around New York Harbor by towing coal barges to supply their furnaces. When coal went out of the picture, they failed to adapt to the change.

Consolidation of Tugboat Firms

There has been a consolidation of tugboat firms going on for some years now. The Turecamo Towing Company was recently taken over by Moran. The Moran Towing Company, probably the largest and best-known company, is active in many ports in the United States. Moran started in New York Harbor many generations ago. The McAllister Towing Company is another big firm, family-owned but very large, with corporate offices in the Whitehall Building in Manhattan at 17 Battery Place. These firms do a great deal of ship work, that is, docking of ships, but they also engage in offshore towing, oil rigs and the like, towing anything that will float on barges or on the water itself. McAllister did a lot of work in Saudi Arabia in connection with oil production, but that project was only a relatively small portion of its work activity.[44]

Some firms are more diversified in their operations, such as Weeks and Don-Jon Marine. They do much dredging work, but they have tugboats to support their operations. Other firms are smaller than Moran, Reinauer Maritime Group for one. A few of them are family concerns, like Thomas Towing, described as one of the last small family-owned companies. The author talked with Captain Thomas Brown, founder of Thomas Towing, in his home on Staten Island. He is semi-retired now, but still helps with running the towing business from his home. They have two tugs now with a third one on order. Captain Brown says that he hopes can pay for it.[45]

CHANGES IN THE TOWING INDUSTRY

Captain Brown talked about how it was in the 1940s, when he was on the tugs as a young man, and why there are fewer boats on the rivers nowadays. He talked about how many boats a company like Tracy Towing had. The Tracy Company had many tugs and coal barges and specialized in towing coal to the power stations in New York and Long Island Sound. When the power plants converted to oil, Tracy lost their business and liquidated the company. The Tracy towing line is an example of a company which had narrow assumptions about what its business should consist of. To a certain extent, most of the companies in the tug-boat industry in New York leaned toward this kind of thinking. The economics and culture changed around them and they failed to adapt to it. The towing companies which were primarily engaged in towing barges and scows around the harbor were especially vulnerable to the changes that occurred. When the bridges and tunnels were built and the highway network in New York City and environs was completed, that sounded the death knell for many of the tugboat companies.

Captain Brown went on to talk about the sand and gravel from Long Island which was towed on scows to New York and up the Hudson. Captain Brown said sand and gravel are not towed from Long Island at present. Although items such as sand and traprock would seem to lend themselves to bulk transportation and be particularly suited to scows, the trucking industry seems to have taken over. It is a matter of economics, and that is what makes businesses run.

SHIPS ASSISTED BY POWERFUL TUGS

One of the uses of tugs in New York Harbor, as in any harbor, is in escorting and assisting in the berthing of ships. The two big companies are Moran and McAllister, but other towing companies occasionally are called upon to help the ships into and out of port. Ships are getting larger all the time and they frequently need assistance staying in the channels and negotiating their way into their berths (aided by the Sandy Hook Pilots, who work hand in hand with the tug captains). Weather conditions, especially the wind, have a great effect on these ships. The tidal current is also an influence that the ships have to contend with. (It should

A McAllister tug steams north on the Hudson River. The Lackawanna Ferry slips are seen on the right.

be noted that technology developments are encroaching on the need for tugs to help dock large ships. This is discussed below.)

At one stage in the history of the port, tugboats assisted in the docking of transatlantic passenger ships. That source of business is long gone. Now the ship traffic would more likely consist of ships laden with containers, bound for Port Newark or Port Elizabeth. As the tugs increase in power, it takes fewer of them to berth a ship. Also, as mentioned, the container ships are getting larger, so there are fewer of them coming into port. The few cruise ships that are coming into New York Harbor are not only getting larger but they are equipped with bow thrusters. A bow thruster is a propulsion mechanism in a tunnel through the bow of a ship that vastly increases the maneuverability of the ship. Some of the newer ships even have rotatable propellers at the stern, which gives them great maneuverability. Needless to say, these ships have less need for assistance from tugs to get into a dock.

Clearly, the towing companies that provide assistance to ships have to deal with change also. The big ones are diversified enough that they may be expected to deal with the changes that are going on in the harbor.

TODAY'S TUGS IN NEW YORK HARBOR

The tugs in the present day have powerful engines, some of them up to 6,000 or 7,000 horsepower. By comparison, the *Takana*, a tug from the 1940s (mentioned previously) had only a 250 horsepower diesel. Danny Gallagher, captain of the

Tug pushing an oil barge up the East River, approaching the Manhattan Bridge. This tug, with its squared bow, is not typical of New York Harbor tugs.

Takana, said she didn't have enough power "to pull a whore out of bed." Captain Gallagher worked for Red Star Towing and Transportation Company, a family owned line that was ultimately sold to Ira S. Bushey. (Bushey had its shipyard on the Gowanus Canal.) Additionally, it owned a company that transported petroleum on barges and tankers. Red Star had its headquarters at 17 Battery Place where the Moran dispatchers had a balcony above Pier 1 at the Battery. The boatmen at Pier 1 could hear when the dispatcher came out on the balcony with his big megaphone to yell orders to the Moran tugboat below.

Present-day tugboats are loaded with all kinds of electronic equipment: depth meters, knot meters (speedometers), GPS positioning equipment, and VHF radio. Some tugs even have chart plotters on board, connected to the GPS, which show a chart on the screen with a blip to show the tug's location. The harbor tugs of today also have windlasses located near the stern. These windlasses are utilized to haul in the hawsers when then they are let go on the barge. (The hawsers stretch astern of the tug when the tug is towing a vessel.) Windlasses began to be installed only in the 1940s—before then, the deckhands had to pull the hawsers in by hand, a grueling task.

Although the tugs of today are much different from earlier tugboats in terms of equipment, the tugboats in New York Harbor have not changed drastically from the tugs of the early 20th century in superficial appearance. They are more powerful than they were in days gone by and they have more electronic equipment. Also, they are pilothouse controlled, which means the engine controls are in the pilot house and the captain or mate controls the engine, not an engineer down below. The old tugs had a system of jingles and gongs by which the person in the pilot house who was controlling the boat, signaled the engine room "ahead slow," "slow astern," "full speed ahead," and so on. The captain of the tug, who had very respectful relationship with the engineer, had to ask him politely to give any special power to the engine, such as when the boat had a tide to buck. The engineer, who zealously guarded the engine he tended, might be coaxed into providing a little more power. Now, the captain (or mate) has direct control over the use of the engine.

The tugboats of New York Harbor still have a basic squat hull, rounded off at the stern, with a long deckhouse and a pilot house on the second deck. Aft of the pilot house is a smokestack, crucial in the days of steam; it is less important for the diesel tugs but still needed to release the exhaust from the engine. Other harbors have some tugs of more modern design. Some are tractor tugs, very contemporary looking, with angled glass in the pilot house windows. These tugs can go sideways as well as forward and back. They can turn within their own length because their propellers are directional. Some tugs have Kurt nozzles, a design which as been around for a while. This design has a "tunnel" around each screw to direct the water flow. Also, modern tugs have "Z-Drives" in which the propellers are turnable.[46]

Some few new tugs destined for New York Harbor are coming off the ways with "Z-Drives" and Kurt nozzles, but that is not typical. Each harbor has different requirements, and the tug companies choose the design that suits their needs. To handle the big ships and the heavy towing jobs they need powerful tugs, and for the New York Harbor tugs, high propulsion power is a feature they have been emphasizing.

The Coast Guard has been raising requirements as well. Now it requires all tugs which tow petroleum barges to have twin screws. The Coast Guard wants to minimize the chances of oil spills resulting from accidents. Since New York Harbor is the most active port in terms of petroleum products, this requirement has far-reaching effects on the towing companies.[47]

Sometimes one will see around New York Harbor tugs with high pilot houses. In fact some of them have towers built over the conventional pilot house in which there is a smaller pilot house from which the captain or mate can control the boat when he needs, for visibility's sake, to get high up. Visibility from the pilot house has been a problem on tugboats in towing a vessel alongside. The vessel being towed alongside, a barge, scow, or a ship, could block the view

Tug tending a ship on the East River. Downtown Manhattan is in the background.
Tugs tending ships do only ship work, generally. They do not ordinarily tow barges
and scows. Undated photograph (Museum of the City of New York).

from the pilot house, particularly if was light (unloaded) and high out of the water.

Will the Tugboats Continue to Be in the Harbor?

It can be said that the towing industry is healthy. It is much smaller than it used to be. The towing business has matured quite a bit. To survive, the companies have to apply sophisticated business techniques. It is a big business now. When there were many small companies in the harbor, the competition was keen and they had their ups and downs with the economy. At times, the companies had to tie up their boats, at least some of them. The companies that operate at the present time in New York Harbor seem to be doing well. They are adding boats to their fleets, and that is a good sign.

There are some compensating factors that point to increased business for the tugs. For example, on occasion ships at the docks do not have enough water under their bottoms to be fully loaded. These ships will have to go to the anchorage to be topped off by lighters. The lighters have to be towed out to the anchorage by tugs. Also, cement and other materials are still transported on barges and scows. Captain Brown talked about his company's towing sand from South Amboy, New Jersey. The pattern of transportation changes. The towing companies have changed with it over the years. However, many of them have gone out of business or have been acquired by larger firms.

One will still see tugs in the harbor, but not as many.

Return of the Ferries

Ferries, Then and Now

In the past, almost every scene of New York Harbor had at least one ferry-boat in it. The ferries were very much a part of the port. Before bridges were built and tunnels were dug beneath the East and Hudson Rivers the ferries were in their heyday. New York is divided by many waterways, and the ferries provided the only means of transport between the boroughs. Their heyday gradually ended around the middle of the last century, in the 1950s. The ferries met their match with the increase of automobile travel over the bridges and through the tunnels which had been built from New Jersey into Manhattan and between Brooklyn and Queens and Manhattan. For many years there were no ferries in New York Harbor, and that accounts in part for why there was very little vessel traffic in the East River and the Hudson River after 1967. It was in that year that the last ferry line in New York Harbor closed down, except for the Staten Island ferry which has gone on and on. In 1987, Arthur Imperatore started up the New York Waterway line, and that was the beginning of the rebirth of ferries in New York.

The Early Ferries

When America was first settled by Europeans, ferries were just rafts pulled along ropes stretched across the rivers, although the rivers of New York Harbor were too wide, and there was too much traffic, to do it that way. Among the first ferries in New York Harbor were the "periaugers," small boats which were propelled by sail and oars. After that came the horse team boats such as the ones operated by the Hoboken-to-Barclay-Street Ferry. The power was provided by a team of horses that walked in a circle. The power was transmitted to paddle wheels.[48]

Robert Fulton tried out his first steamboat in 1807, and the ferries became steam operated, with paddle wheels to propel them. In addition to Robert Fulton, another person associated with ferry development in New York Harbor was Colonel John Stevens. He incorporated the Hoboken Steamboat Ferry Company in 1821 after operating the horse-propelled ferries for a number of years. He is the person who developed, among other things, the rack to guide the ferryboat into the slip, and the bridge that formed the link between the boat and the dock, which was raised and lowered with the tide. Ferries also crossed in other parts of the harbor. There were ferries from Brooklyn to Staten Island, ferries from

Fulton Ferry as it was in the 1700s. Manhattan is across the East River (Library of Congress).

Brooklyn to Manhattan and ferries from the Bronx to Queens. There were no bridges and tunnels at that time. The Brooklyn Bridge, completed in 1883, was the first bridge in New York Harbor. Shortly after the Brooklyn Bridge was built, the ferry that had taken people from Brooklyn to Manhattan, not surprisingly went out of business.

The first steam ferryboats were built not only to carry passengers but to transport vehicles as well. These boats had gangways on board for the cars and trucks, and places for the passengers to sit. When the first steam ferries were built, they were limited to one deck, but eventually they included a second deck for the passengers to sit in or stroll around to watch the scenes on the water. The terminals were constructed so that some of them led the passengers directly onto the top deck of the ferryboat when it was in the dock, and the terminals themselves were elaborately built and visually attractive. The ferries of New York Harbor were all double-ended boats; that is, they could go back and forth across the river without having to turn around. They were designed with two pilot houses, two propellers (the first screw propeller came in 1802, although it would not become commonplace until 100 years later), and two rudders. One of the duties of the deckhands was to drop the pin to fix the rudder in what was going to be the forward end of the vessel.

Steam engines were vastly improved over the years. Boilers for making steam were made safer — they occasionally blew up in the early stages. The ultimate design in engines was the powerful Uniflow engine, and that was important because more powerful ferries make faster trips.

Railroad Ferries

It was natural for the railroads to extend their business of transportation into ferrying cars and passengers across the rivers of New York Harbor. As the railroads became predominant in the harbor, they added to their already large fleets of tugs, car floats and lighters by operating ferries, primarily across the Hudson River from New Jersey to Manhattan. They built terminals on the New Jersey side of the river and in Manhattan as well, to receive the passengers or to drop them off at the end of their trip. Some of these terminals were quite elegant, with classical woodwork. They had plush seats and benches to make the passengers comfortable while they were waiting. People commuted from New Jersey to downtown and midtown Manhattan by the thousands on the ferries, encouraged by the reasonable fares.

Before the Throgs Neck Bridge and the Bronx-Whitestone Bridge were built there was a ferry from College Point in Queens to the Bronx. The ferry was the only way to get across the East River at that point. When the bridges were built, the ferry fell into disuse and eventually was discontinued. The Triborough Bridge added another route for automobiles to go to or from Queens, the Bronx, and

Manhattan. The Verrazano Bridge was built across the Narrows which provided access to Staten Island or New Jersey from Brooklyn. The last ferryboat, the Erie Lackawanna ferryboat *Elmira*, made the final trip in 1967 to close out an era. When ferry service was no longer needed, public choices were decisive. Ferry service in New York Harbor fell by the waterside.

Reemergence of the Ferries

Arthur E. Imperatore Senior and his son Arthur E. Imperatore Junior initiated the revival of the ferry service into New York City.[49] It was an amazing example of entrepreneurship, and certainly forward-looking on their part. It seems so obvious after the fact: The five boroughs of New York City, and parts of New Jersey, are divided by water. The ferry was an obvious means of transportation for New York Harbor, especially with the now heavy vehicular traffic, in Brooklyn and Manhattan, particularly. However, it took the Imperatores to take the step, and they had the resources to do it.

It was in 1986 that they founded their ferry company, known as New York Waterway. Operating out of what they called Port Imperial in Weehawken, they implemented service to West 38th Street in Manhattan. Now they have many more lines operating across the Hudson and around the harbor. They have a route originating at East 96th Street and going to Pier 11 which is located downtown on the East River. It made sense to have ferries in New York Harbor to connect the boroughs which were separated by waterways. As Manhattan and the outer boroughs became more and more clogged with vehicles, the ferries relieved some of this congestion. The PATH subway, from New Jersey to downtown New York, had taken many commuters to their jobs in the financial center of Manhattan. When the World Trade Center was destroyed in 2001, the PATH system was partly closed down because it lost its station at the World Trade Center. A great many people took the ferry as an alternative, and some liked the convenience of taking the ferry. Ferry service, which had been growing every year, had 35,000 riders before the 2001 attacks. After that, the ferry ridership grew to 70,000. The World Trade Center disaster had the by-product of increasing the ferry traffic over the waters of New York Harbor.

There are more ferryboat companies now in New York Harbor. Some of the routes are across the East River. Some of them go as far as Highlands, New Jersey, on the Lower Bay. There is also a ferry leaving from Atlantic Highlands on the Lower Bay in New Jersey, and New York Waterway inaugurated a route from Belford, New Jersey. Of course these routes cost more than those transporting across the rivers because they have to go a longer distance, across the Lower Bay, through the Narrows and through the Upper Bay to Manhattan. This means of transportation is taken mostly by the more affluent workers in the financial district of Manhattan who live in central New Jersey.

Competition in Ferrying People

There is competition now for New York Waterway — six companies, in fact. Their routes connect all the boroughs, but Manhattan is the center of attraction. People now commute to their jobs on the ferries. The ferry companies encourage people to take the ferry for recreational purposes: to see the harbor or to cruise around Manhattan. Officials of New York Waterway hoped that even though the PATH trains started up again after 2001 that New Jersey commuters would stick with the ferry. Apparently, it is questionable whether ferry riders will continue using the ferry. A 2004 article in the *Star-Ledger* comments that since the PATH station at the World Trade Center was restored, ferry use has dropped off.[50] The article says that this factor, among others, has resulted in New York Waterway having financial difficulties. Meanwhile, the management of New York Waterway continues to be optimistic.

The present-day ferries do not carry cars and trucks. Even the Staten Island ferry, most of whose boats are designed to carry vehicles, no longer does. There is enough traffic in New York City now — what is needed is to relieve the traffic situation, and the ferries do that admirably. Alan Ohmsted and members of his staff are enthused about a new water taxi that started in operation in 2002. (Alan

Modern ferry coming up the Hudson River off New Jersey waterfront. This ferry is one of the front-loading types plying New York's waterways.

Water taxi departing from a pier on the lower East River. The Brooklyn and Manhattan Bridges are in the background.

Ohmsted is head of the Ferry Office in the New York City Department of Transportation.)[51] Consisting of much smaller boats (capacity 49 passengers) this service takes people from one part of Manhattan to another. When the ferry service to the two sports stadiums in New York City, Yankee Stadium and Shea Stadium, was inaugurated, some fans were happy to ride the water, and outgoing Mayor Giuliani as well as his successor, Mayor Bloomberg was quite proud of that accomplishment. Carter Craft, director of the Metropolitan Waterfront Alliance, provided this author with information that a regional ferry network had been established, so the ferries have a good start at making a comeback, in spite of some difficulties they have encountered.[52]

Present-Day Design of Ferryboats

The ferryboats in general are much smaller than they were previously, and thus they are lighter and faster. At first, the operators obtained crewboats from the oil fields. They soon found out that these boats did not work well. The side-loading boats took too long to load and unload the passengers, making the

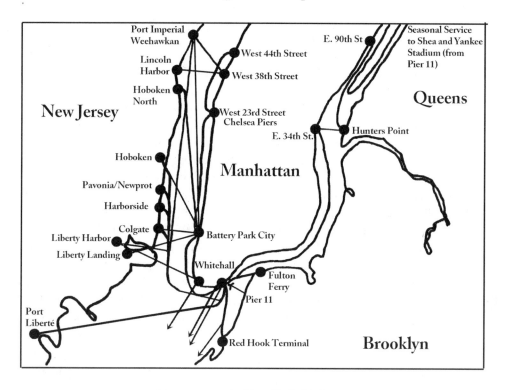

Ferry routes in New York Harbor.

turnaround time too long. Also, crewboats were expensive to operate for short hauls.

The ferry operators also experimented with catamarans, feeling the catamarans were easier to drive through the water. Catamarans are boats with two hulls, linked together by a common deck and deckhouse, so above the water they seem like conventional vessels. The first catamarans were not strong enough in the way their hulls were linked together. The boat builders found a way to make the connections stronger, and now most of the new ferries are of the catamaran type, and they are front loaders. The ferryboat managers find it is much faster to have people walk to the bow of the vessel in the unloading process, and it is easy enough to bring the boat bow-in to the dock. Diesel engines are getting lighter, too, and more powerful all the time. (The price of fuel is a potential problem). It all adds up to the catamarans being less expensive to operate than other ferries. The people at the Department of Transportation say that another advantage of the catamarans is that they are of shallower draft.

Some of the monohulls still are in use, however. (Monohulls are conventional boats with a single hull). These boats are used on the shorter runs. The distance from Highlands to downtown Manhattan is 28 miles. Catamaran boats are used on that run. They go quite fast and make the run in close to 30 minutes.

ADVANTAGES OF THE FERRY

How is it to ride the ferry? The commuters who ride the ferry every day know the answer to that question. A typical ferry ride might begin at the ferry terminal in Weehawken, on the New Jersey side of the Hudson. The ferry terminal at Weehawken is located on a flat plain about a half-mile wide, situated at the base of the Palisades, an immense outcropping of rock that overlooks the Hudson. The terminal, oddly enough, consists of an old ferryboat, moored at the dock. It seems unusual but strangely appropriate. Some commuters buy their tickets at the counter on the ferryboat terminal, but most have commuter tickets.

The ferry comes in that will carry the commuters across the river to their jobs in Manhattan. The ferry loads up quickly, and before the commuters know it the ferry is backing out of the slip. The ferry in this case is of a monohull design, built originally as a front-loading ferry with diesel engines. As the ferry proceeds across the river, some of the riders are in the cabin, avidly reading their papers. Others are on the top deck of the ferry, looking at the sights around the water. They have a marvelous view of Manhattan. The buildings in Manhattan are etched in silver, gleaming against the yellow-gray of the sky. Surely, many of the commuters are thinking about how taking the ferry is much better than

Leaving Whitehall Terminal in dowtown Manhattan, this Staten Island ferry is passing Governor's Island and heading for St. George on Staten Island.

116

traveling through the tunnel on a bus. Less than 10 minutes go by. By this time the ferry is approaching the terminal at West 38th Street in Manhattan. The commuters' trip across the Hudson is over.

The ferries are back. They are different from the ferries of the past. The ferry operators are optimistic that they are here to stay, as are the people at the New York City Department of Transportation. Much depends upon the reopening of the PATH station at the site of the World Trade Center. (It was reopened in November 2003.) Will the riders stay with the ferry? Cost will be a big factor and you can be sure that each person involved will be comparing the fees charged by the ferries with the charges for the PATH line. As ridership increases, the costs per passenger should decrease, though at the same time, inflation drives costs up. All in all, it is likely that the modern ferries will continue to be part of the vista of New York Harbor, at least for the near future.

3

Contemporary Issues

Dredging

Need for Dredging

Dredging, as far as New York Harbor is concerned, is a never-ending task. Dredging has to do with the deepening of the water. It applies mostly to the channels which criss-cross the waters of New York Harbor. Also, the area around the docks and piers has to be dredged from time to time. Silt is the reason dredging is necessary. Every river, bay or creek of the harbor has in it sediment, solid particles which settle to the bottom and cause the harbor to become clogged. This process is encouraged by the ebb and flow of the water due to tides and currents.

The Hudson, which has its origin in upstate New York, flows downstream toward New York City. It carries with it all the silt gathered up in its travels. The river deposits much of the silt when it gets to New York Harbor, where it encounters the full force of the ebb and flow of the tide. The East River has tidal currents flowing through it each day, so it is relatively deep, except where there is not much flow of the tide, like around the piers where the current is likely to be less strong. Where the current from the tide flows strongly, the bottom is apt to be relatively deep. Examples are the Hudson in the middle of the river, or the point at Sandy Hook where the water is deep right in close to shore.

Where the water is polluted by chemicals, the disposal of the dredged spoil is particularly sensitive for the government and environmental groups. What is dredged up is called "spoil." In New York Harbor, as in other areas as well, industrial plants have dumped into the waters PCBs, mercury, dioxins and other pollutants. These pollutants have become mixed up with the silt or sand at the bottom of the waterway.

Harbors Clogged with Silt

On the other side of the world, there are two harbors, Ephesus and Ostia, that silted up during the course of history. Ephesus, which is in Turkey, was once a glorious port, not nearly as spread out as New York Harbor, but once very active.[1] Ephesus is an archaeologist's delight because of the classical ruins that are continually discovered there. A river flowed into the bay of Ephesus, and that was its ultimate downfall as a harbor. The residents cut down the trees in the countryside, the earth was carried by the rains into the river and downstream, and over the years the harbor became clogged with the sediment that was deposited on the bottom of the bay.

Like Ephesus, Ostia, which was the main harbor for Rome when Rome flourished as the "capital of the world," silted up so that much of it could not be used.[2] Like Ephesus, Ostia was a tiny port compared with New York. Ostia is popular with tourists because of the ruins that exist there. The silt kept the local residents from taking the stones from the ruins. It also protected the ruins so the archaeologists found buildings almost perfectly preserved.

Every harbor is subject to silting up at least to some extent. That is the reason for maintenance dredging of the channels and the area around the docks, and other parts where the silt is likely to build up.

TYPES OF DREDGES

There are two basic approaches to dredging: these are best exemplified by the hydraulic dredge and the digger dredge.[3] The hydraulic dredge is based on the fact that solid particles are suspended in the water. The dredge pumps those particles mixed with water through pipes and hoses. Often it pumps the mixture onto a scow or barge. Frequently, it pumps the silted water right up on the beach where it is deposited (in beach replenishment) or to a disposal site. In this technique, there must be a powerful pumping mechanism because the ratio of silt to water is very slight. The pumps have to pump a lot of water. However, there are powerful pumps nowadays, but that was not always the case. The dredgers who took on the Lower Bay in the 1800s found that they could not meet the output required in their contract. The contractors thought they could power their pumps with steam engines, which were new at the time, but the pumps were not powerful enough to dredge up enough material from the bottom.

A common type of dredge is the cutter suction dredge. It employs a cutter at the end of the element which goes down in the water to bring the muck up into the dredge. This kind of dredge is universal, combining the cutting action with the hydraulic technique of bringing the silt up to the surface.

Another common type of dredge is the digger dredge, and it is used frequently in New York Harbor.[4] This kind of dredge has a bucket that goes into the water and digs into the muck below. It raises and dumps it, usually in a scow alongside. There are many types of buckets. Some buckets are quite large. Others are of the clamshell type, buckets that open on hinges.

Frequently, dredges employ both techniques to get the muck up from the bottom of the waterway and dispose of it. They pump it through pipes that go over the water to the beach or disposal area. Some dredges are of the trailing suction hopper dredge type. Such dredges trail a large pipe in the water that sucks up the silt from the bottom. These dredges are often self-propelled — they are literally ships built for dredging. They have the advantage that they can transport dredged material to the disposal site.

As a part of the large project that is under way at present to dredge New York Harbor, the dredgers who are operating in the Kill Van Kull near Bergen Point have to deal with rock on the bottom of the waterway, among other things. That situation will be met by blasting. The managers overseeing the project estimate that 10.5 tons of rock have to be excavated. They reportedly plan to deposit it to form an artificial reef off the Shark River in New Jersey.[5]

AN ISSUE FOR NEW YORK HARBOR

Officials and organizations are concerned that dredging in New York Harbor will bring up chemicals from the bottom along with the uncontaminated material. There is a trade-off of variables in this case. There are economic considerations to think about, and they have predominated up to now. The Port Authority and the Corps of Engineers have a plan to make New York Harbor deep enough to accommodate the new ships that are being built. Congress has approved the money. The Corps of Engineers has already awarded contracts for the dredging and part of the work has been completed. Officials and community organizations are monitoring what is being done, being sure that all goes according to the law and what is best for the people around the port.

HARS, the former mud dump site off Sandy Hook, is the subject of much controversy. Clean Ocean Action and other anti-pollution organizations are still raising questions about the spoil dumped there by the dredging companies.[6] Questions about HARS will probably end up in the courts. The spoil will still be there while the courts try to work out legal remedies. Nevertheless, some improvements have been made. The water is becoming somewhat cleaner, and the general public is enjoying the water of the harbor more.

Dredging in the harbor has to continue. There will be compromises as all parties attempt to reach the optimum balance between the elements of society that have different stakes in the outcome.

The Environment of the Harbor

POLLUTION IN NEW YORK HARBOR

The Environmental Protection Agency (EPA), as well as a host of other organizations associated with preserving the environment, has been interested in New York Harbor for many years. With the passage of the Clean Water Act in 1972, a number of actions were taken to make the harbor cleaner. The harbor was pretty dirty during the 19th century and the first half of the 20th century. In contrast, when the first Dutch settlers arrived in the 1600s the harbor was virginal. It was in a completely natural state. There were fish and oysters for the taking. There are stories of many sharks being taken in the East River. There were dolphins in the Upper Bay. The shores were as nature intended, with sloping sand bottoms and wetlands extending around the islands.[7]

As the growth of commerce occurred in the harbor, there was a need to construct bulkheads where the land met the water. Docks and piers were built and the water around them was deepened. The sand was used to fill in behind the piers to make an artificial line of demarcation: land, dock, then relatively deep water along side the dock. Finger piers were built jutting out into the rivers, so much so that in 1855 the city fathers became concerned about the docks protruding out into the river, and they passed a law regulating the length of the piers. Still, these finger piers became a characteristic of the harbor. Soon after, in the 1800s, the industrial revolution came along to make its mark on history. Many factories were built, and they were constructed along the waterways where the transportation was relatively good in those days.

Unfortunately, one of the by-products of industry was pollution. With no controls or concern for pollution in those times, the factories and plants generated foul chemicals, and it was all too easy to discharge it into the nearest waterway.

Meanwhile, the population around the port of New York grew by leaps and bounds. Most of the sewage generated by the millions of people ended up in the rivers and creeks of the harbor. Some of these creeks, like the Gowanus Canal and Newtown Creek, were literally open sewers. Preservation of the environment was not a major concern during the first 350 years of New York Harbor's history. The growth of commerce was. This was before a time when people tried to work out a balance between economic development and concern about the environment. In earlier times the cultural attitude was to accept the pollution as normal. Also, the citizens did not understand the health hazards involved with pollution. Persons working on the boats in the harbor, especially in the Gowanus Canal or Newtown Creek, smelled the odors that were there. They associated the smells with boats and took it for granted.

Environmental Protection Agency

Things got better in terms of the pollution in the harbor during the last half of the 20th century. People became more conscious of the environment that they lived in. A number of federal, state and local laws were passed. Private organizations were formed, interested in the improvement of the harbor and surrounding waters. The 2001 status report of the New York–New Jersey Harbor Estuary Program lists 15 such organizations.[8] These are in addition to the many city, state and federal organizations that look after the environment. There is a question as to whether all of them are necessary, but in a democratic society it is good to have many people looking after such issues.

After the Clean Water Act was passed, a number of improvements were made in the sewage plants around the city of New York, as well as other locations in the harbor. The plants now process the sewage to get rid of the contaminants. A problem that these plants have is that some of them can be overwhelmed by storm water runoff, as occurs during an especially heavy rain, resulting in occasional discharge of untreated sewage into the waterway. This is probably the cause of the detritus seen on the surface of the Lower Bay. The EPA is trying to solve this problem, as noted in a 2002 meeting.[9]

The New York–New Jersey Harbor Estuary Program (which is part of the EPA, Region 2) intends to restore the wetlands in the harbor, such as Jamaica Bay and the Kill Van Kull between Staten Island and New Jersey. Great strides have been made in improving the habitat for wildlife. There is much pristine, untouched land abutting the waterway along the Kill Van Kull and Arthur Kill. Unlike the East River sections, and Manhattan and New Jersey along the Hudson River, entire portions of the Kill Van Kull and Arthur Kill are still unoccupied by refineries and tank farms, unlike so much of the rest of the area. Wildlife abounds here, and organizations such as the Estuary Program and others are giving these areas careful attention. These government operations, at times, have been accused of doing too much planning and not providing enough action. One organization, Clean Ocean Action, expressing its frustration over offshore dumping, says it has reached the limit of its tolerance, claiming that sufficient studies have been made and that what we need now is action.[10]

SOURCES OF POLLUTION

The U.S. Army Corps of Engineers has carried out a number of construction projects having to do with the waters around the country, as described in a previous chapter. In the course these many construction projects, the Corps of Engineers has been accused of tampering with the environment. Like the Port Authority, the Corps of Engineers is determined to achieve its goals— such as the dredging of New York Harbor. But where to put the dredged spoil? That is a matter of continual discussion. It has been estimated that about 65 million cubic yards of dredged material will have to be disposed of over the next 10 years from New York Harbor dredging.[11] Much of this dredged fill is contaminated with PCBs, mercury, lead and other metals put out by the plants and factories that lined the waterfront in the past.

Many chemicals also get into the waterways through rainfall runoff, as do "floatables," materials that are washed into the rivers and creeks, such as packaging materials, cigarette butts, and even emergency medical materials. These are the floatable materials that cause beach closings around the harbor. EPA is concerned about issues like these and it reports significant improvement in this area. Another issue is the presence of fecal coliform bacteria in harbor waters. Again, beaches are closed when the bacterial count gets too high. Fortunately, there has been improvement in this area as well.

Optimistic Look for the Future

While New York Harbor is not entirely clean as yet, many concerned organizations and officials are optimistic. Improvements have definitely been made in the environmental condition of the harbor. The waterfront has changed. Neighborhood associations are getting more involved in planning for use of the waterfront. They want access, and parks and esplanades. All of these changes in the cultural outlook — how people spend their time, the growth of recreational pursuits — are potentially beneficial to the environment. In addition, economic factors enter into the situation. A great deal of shipping has left New York City. The focus has shifted to New Jersey and the state, similarly, is very aware of environmental effects. At the same time, the Port Authority, while concerned with economic issues, has also recognized the objective of preserving the environment.

Some questions about the environment remain to be answered. How do we best remove the contaminants on the river bottoms? Where do we put the contaminated material when we remove it from the rivers? Still to be dealt with is the question of storm water runoff and the pollution that results when sewage plants get flooded with too much water to process. "Floatables" are still a problem, although much less so than formerly. Despite these ongoing problems, aquatic life is coming back. There is still a way to go, but the forces at work in the region are favorable to improving the surroundings. The future of the harbor looks good in respect to the environment.

Tides and Fast-Moving Currents

The Ebb and Flow of the Tides

New York is a beautifully protected harbor. Twice each day the water from the Atlantic Ocean floods into the bays and rivers and creeks that make up the harbor, and twice a day it ebbs out of these bodies of water. Actually, the cycle takes about 25 hours, so the change occurs approximately an hour later each day. The mariners who sail in the harbor know the effect of the tides on the depth of the water and the tidal currents that come with the flow and ebb of the waters. They know that to get in Flushing Creek they have to have high water, or to get out of Eastchester with a tow they must do it quickly before the water ebbs enough that they run aground.

The tidal range for New York Harbor is about five feet. That is not a really significant change for all practical purposes, and it is one of the assets of the port of New York. In many ports it is much higher. In the Bay of Fundy, up Nova Scotia way, it is over 40 feet! That is the result of the water flowing up the bay and being squeezed into narrow rivers. On the other hand, in certain parts of the world, the Mediterranean area for instance, there is practically no change at all in the tidal level of the waters. The effect of the tidal change depends upon, among other things, the topography of the bottom of the body of water.

The wind also makes a big difference in the tidal effect. When the wind is blowing toward the harbor from the ocean it "pushes" more water into the harbor and makes the tide higher. Conversely, when the wind is blowing away from the harbor the tide is lower than average. The wind direction in relation to the current flow also has an effect, and it can be a nasty one. When the wind blows against the flow of the current it can create an uncomfortable chop on the water, maybe even breaking waves. Through the Narrows, for instance, there are stories of a rapidly flowing ebb tide and a strong wind from the southeast causing large breaking waves that could turn the hair gray on the most seasoned small-boat sailor.

A Historical Incident

The tides made a big difference in one situation. When British ships were in New York Harbor in 1781, they could not leave the harbor because there was not sufficient depth of water over the bar of Sandy Hook. The ships heaved at anchor off Staten Island, and the crews sweated, waiting for the tide to get high enough that they could cross the bar. Finally, the tide became high enough that the ships were able to sail out of the harbor. They sailed down to the Chesapeake, but they were too late to come to the aid of their brethren in Virginia. So, the course of history was different from what it might have been.[12] At that time, ships had to wait for high tide to get into or out of the harbor. That is why the channels that were dredged eventually were so important to the utilization of the harbor.

Causes of the Tides

What causes the tides? Most people know that it has something to do with the moon and the sun. It is a matter of gravitational pull, and that is a matter of the *mass* and the *distance* of the body.[13, 14] The moon has a two-to-one effect on the tides of the Earth compared to the Sun. The reason is that the Moon is much closer than the Sun even though the Sun has much greater mass. From the point of view of the Earth as an astronomical body, the gravitational pull of the Sun and the Moon create a bulge on the ocean at high tide. This bulge creates a flow of water into the harbors which causes the tidal currents. Similarly, the water flows out of the harbor when the tide on the ocean is lower.

Tides vary in height from one time to another. When the Sun and Moon are in a direct line, which happens from time to time, we have what is called a spring tide, higher and lower than normal. In contrast, when the Sun and Moon are at 90 degrees to each other in respect to the Earth we have neap tide, less extreme in range. These differences are not great in the New York area, maybe one foot, but they could be significant to a marina owner if a high spring tide floods over his dock. Fortunately, most docks are high enough that it does not matter.

The Tides in New York Harbor

New York Harbor is fortunate in one respect in having two entrances; it can be entered through Long Island Sound as well as the Ambrose Channel. This means the harbor has water flowing into it from both sides, from the Long Island Sound as well as into the Lower and Upper Bay. The East River is a tidal strait connecting the Lower and Upper Bays to Long Island Sound. The inflow of water from the two entrances meets at Hell Gate, which means much of the water from broad Long Island Sound converges on the narrow Hell Gate stretch and the water from the wide Upper Bay flows through the relatively narrow East River to Hell Gate. This is why the tidal currents are so strong in these parts of the harbor.

Another aspect of tidal currents is that they do not always run strongly. When the tide is fully high or fully low (called "slack water") the current is nil, standing still, as placid as a sleeping pussycat. The current runs strongest about halfway between high and low tides. The experts have figured this all out and there are tables showing time of low and high tides, current speed, and level of the tide for each date. Harbor mariners consult these tables all the time.

Meanings of the Tide

The stages of the tide have a different meaning for different people. When the tide is out, some areas of the harbor, mostly in the bays and backwater creeks, are well drained out and the bottom is exposed. The smell often associated with low tide is due to organic matter exposed by the shallowness of the water, especially in the creeks. The mud is evident. One can go clamming or gather mussels when the tide is low but not at high tide. When it is low tide, it is comparatively unsightly. Shoal areas are readily apparent. Mussels are seen on the dock piers and on the rocks. The docks seem to stand taller, almost out of the water in some places. When the tide is "in"—high tide—the water looks better, up to where should be, it seems.

New York Harbor includes several beaches—Jacob Riis Park and Gateway National Park at Sandy Hook, to name two. The beach at Coney Island is quite famous; it is not on the ocean directly, but on Lower New York Bay. Most people prefer high tide on such a beach, although if the contour of the depth of the water is a gradual incline it does not make a great deal of difference. It is true that the beach is considerably wider at low tide.

Fishermen say it is better to fish on an incoming tide; the fish are feeding then. However, it is questionable whether research bears that out to be true. In the harbor itself, around Manhattan, the average person is less aware of the stage of the tide because the seawalls and the piers tend to minimize the effect; the river bottom is never exposed. Mariners prefer high tide because they can go places with their boats where otherwise they could not go. The channels have more depth to them at high tide; the boats do not scrape the bottom. When the tide is high the harbor is full and fertile. It seems as though the harbor is closer to its natural form.

The commerce of the harbor follows the ebb and flow of the tides. On the ebb tide the marine traffic in the East River and the Hudson River tends to come down both rivers toward the Battery (the lower tip of Manhattan). That is especially important for the tugs with tows. Their objective is to reach the Battery right at the ebb. Then, they catch the beginning of the flood tide when it pours up the East River (or the other way around if they are going in the opposite direction).

Similarly, boats and ships in the harbor that want to go through Hell Gate try to time it so they reach Hell Gate just when the tide is at the change from flood to ebb. That way, they ride the flood current up the East River toward Hell Gate. Then they ride the ebb current out the sound. Ships leaving port usually depart with the ebb tide. That way they have the tidal current to carry them through the Narrows and out through the Lower Bay. Similarly, ships coming into the harbor pick up their pilot at Ambrose Light and ride the flood current through Ambrose Channel into their berth in the port.

Mariners Have Respect for the Tides and Currents

The traffic in the harbor is less sensitive to the tides in the present day. That is because the modern boats and ships have more powerful engines. At one time, particularly in the age of sail, the boats could not go against the tide as they can nowadays. Still, mariners know that it is better to get a boost from the tidal current, so they will plan their voyage through the harbor to take advantage of the current if they can.

The people who steer the vessels of the harbor, the pilots, the ferry captains, the mates on the towboats, have years of experience in dealing with the various situations that develop. They know that when they get in a certain part of the Upper Bay, the outflow from the East River on the ebb tide will cause a cross current. They consider it a routine part of the job. The ferryboat captains have to deal continually with the tidal currents. Approaching their slip when the current is running strongly, they have to gauge the effect on the boat of the current and counteract it accordingly. When one considers that they have the wind to deal with as well, in some conditions they have their hands full. All these mariners also have great respect for the tidal condition and they keep it, at the very least, in the back of their minds at all times. It is part of sailing in the harbor.

Recreational Use of the Harbor

THE BOATING PUBLIC DISCOVERS THE HARBOR

The local inhabitants and the tourists are making increased use of the recreational aspects of the harbor. This is not to say that the local inhabitants of days gone by did not do so. Judging by photographs of the 1800s the harbor was filled with pleasure yachts of all types at that time. In those days the vessels were sailboats for the most part, and people enjoyed themselves sailing on the bays and rivers of the harbor. Around the turn of the 20th century, the city constructed a number of recreational piers on which people relaxed and had the satisfaction of being by the water. A number of swimming pools on barges were provided for the public. Through the first half of the 20th century, gleaming white-painted excursion boats with gilt trim took people on trips up the Hudson or to Long Island where they held picnics and had other forms of recreation. (The infamous *General Slocum* fire in which so many people died was one of these excursions, as described later in this book.)

However, later in the 20th century, people less often looked to the harbor to satisfy their recreational needs. Their attention was distracted by other, more pressing situations, like the Depression and World War II. In the middle of the 20th century people were too busy to be concerned with the use of the harbor for recreation. Since that time, a vast cultural change has occurred. The citizens of yesteryear were satisfied to leave the waterfront and waterways to the shipping people, the tugboats, the ferries. The harbor vessels were crewed by people who made their living on the water. Now, many more people want access to the waterfront for a wide variety of reasons.

MORE MARINAS IN THE HARBOR

The growth of marinas in New York Harbor is one of the expressions of this cultural change, a consequence of the growth of pleasure boating in general. Economic times have been good overall. With shipping decreasing in the New York City parts of the harbor, it was natural for pleasure boating in New York Harbor to take its place.

The 79th Street Boat Basin, off Manhattan's West Side, has caused some concern. When that yacht basin was established by New York City some years ago, it was designed to be a marina that boat owners could utilize when they were passing through New York Harbor, a haven where owners of boats of all types could tie up and spend the evening seeing the sights of Manhattan. During recent

Motor yacht in Lower Bay, with the Verrazano Bridge and the Narrows in the background. There are boats fishing in the bay.

years, it has developed into a haven for "liveaboards," people who enjoy low rent, living in a highly desirable area of Manhattan. The city has tried to get the boat owners to move, but without much success. Meanwhile, the liveaboards just go on keeping their boats at 79th Street Boat Basin. It is said that there is a long list of people waiting to get in.[15]

MORRIS CANAL

Another of these marinas is in a place called the Morris Canal.[16] In a tour of the harbor on a police boat, this author visited the Morris Canal, on the New Jersey shoreline next to Jersey City. Actually, this area is at the *end* of the Morris Canal, which used to run across the state of New Jersey to Phillipsburg. The Morris Canal, opened in 1831, was constructed at a time when water transportation was particularly important, before the railroads came to the fore. When the railroads came, the canals were doomed. A large part of the canal has been filled in by now, especially in the urban areas, although portions of the canal are still intact farther out in New Jersey.

At an earlier time, Morris Canal bustled with commercial activity, and there were many working vessels tied up there, among them tugs, barges and lighters. At the present time there is a large marina on the canal which was built a few years ago. Many contemporary pleasure boats are docked there, mostly power boats, a few sailboats. On the north side of the canal, a new condominium is going up, right on the water's edge.

FISHING IN THE HARBOR

Because the waters of New York Harbor are becoming cleaner, there is an increase in the recreational fishing taking place in the port. Fishermen go for sea bass on occasion in the Upper Bay. Even the East River is becoming clean enough that there is some interest in fishing in those waters, although not yet a great deal. There is still a problem with fishing in the harbor. The problem is mercury. The government continually puts out warnings against steady eating of seafood caught or collected in the harbor because it is still contaminated by the metals that are found in the water.[17] The level of contamination has decreased considerably but apparently it is still of concern.

As one sails through the Narrows, into the Lower Bay, one can usually see a host of fishing boats anchored or drifting slowly, fishing for fluke or bluefish on a sunny day. The boats come out of places nearby, like Sheepshead Bay or Atlantic Highlands, their fishermen eager people who have paid for a day's outing, hoping they will catch fish to take home for supper. Sheepshead Bay, in Brooklyn, is an old port with a history to it. It is, in effect, like many ports around New York City, a harbor within a harbor. There is a fishing fleet in Sheepshead Bay; they are called "headboats," boats that take people out to the fishing areas for so much a head for a half day or a whole day. There are also several yacht clubs on Sheepshead Bay. It is a small harbor, so that the anchorages seem to be in the "backyards" of these yacht clubs. The yacht clubs are small and not affluent; their clubhouses look like houses.

RECREATIONAL ACTIVITIES ON THE HUDSON

A tugboatman coming down the Hudson River, approaching the battery, would no longer be surprised to see a large speedboat roaring down the river. It takes tourists and people of the metropolitan area out for a ride at so much a head. Nor would he be surprised to see a boat towing a parasailor high in the sky. These are some of the recreational activities the harbor is providing now. (The tugboatman would no doubt be derisive of such antics.) The Downtown Boathouse in Manhattan on Pier 26, just north of Chambers Street, lends kayaks to persons who dare to contend with the tidal currents of the Hudson River. Perhaps they go out only at slack time when the current is not running strongly.

There are also dinner cruise boats that go out of the Lower West Side of Manhattan. These are the boats that served so admirably in ferrying passengers during the World Trade Center disaster. There are cruises to the Statue of Liberty and Ellis Island leaving from the Battery. Also, the Circle Line makes trips around Manhattan. Most of the people who take advantage of these benefits are tourists visiting New York City, but local residents also realize that these cruises have a great deal to offer. The waters of the harbor are becoming more inviting to the general public all the time.

Farther up the west side of Manhattan are the Chelsea Piers.[18] They are now a vast sports complex, with a restaurant and several smaller eating places. The Chelsea Piers complex maintains a golf driving range on one of the open piers. It seems odd as one goes down the river to see a golf driving range on a pier that in the past was a shipping terminal, but there it is, in all its fenced-in majesty, incongruous perhaps, but serving a purpose. There is a marina between two of the piers, and on the second floor of one of the terminals is an ice rink. That is the direction the waterfront is going in: entrepreneur-operated, but oriented toward use by the general public for recreational pursuits as the shipping and industrial users move out.

CITY ISLAND

At the other end of the harbor lies City Island, situated where the East River meets Long Island Sound, out past the Throgs Neck Bridge and Stepping Stones Light. City Island has a long history as a boating center. The Minneford Shipyard is here, where the 12-meter boats for the United States entries into the America's Cup races were built. Now, Minneford is just a marina, though a large one. In fact, marinas and yacht clubs encircle City Island and occupy most of the shoreline space. The main avenue, which goes down the center of the island, has many motels and restaurants as well. The island is connected to the mainland of the Bronx by a bridge, so it is very much a part of New York.

OPSAIL AND NAVY VISITS

The OpSail events, which are planned every few years, bring back the age of sail to everyone who has a gleam in his eye for the sea.[19] Many countries are represented by sailing ships in these events. The United States has the bark *Eagle*, a Coast Guard training vessel with tall masts and shining white sails. OpSail 2000 was a big event when the ships came to New York Harbor during that year. They entered the harbor one by one, many of them under sail. The ships berthed at docks around the city, schooners, square riggers, all decked out in their shipshape best. Men, women and children from the metropolitan area visited these ships. As part of the celebration, the ships paraded up the Hudson River.

Also, the U.S. Navy visits the port of New York each year. The ships anchor in the Hudson River or berth at the docks in the harbor. The sailors spend a merry time in Manhattan or other parts of the port. Visitors are allowed to inspect the ships. Everyone involved has a good time.

Many ports are visited in each of these events, but the highlight of the cruise of these ships has to be their visit to New York Harbor. (The Coast Guard is involved in coordination of these visits. Even though they are fun events, the Coast Guard is serious about them, especially now that security of the port is such an issue.)

Concern About Increase in Recreational Boats

There are some people who worry about the increase use of the harbor for recreation.[20] Some vessels do go rather fast, like *The Beast*, a speedboat that takes people, tourists mostly, for breathtaking rides on the Hudson River. As one website points out, there are no speed limits.[21] Other boats are sailboats or motor cruisers that use the harbor, mostly on a "passing through" basis. True, there are occasional accidents, some quite serious. However, the harbor is very large and there are not that many recreational vessels.

Increasing Interest in Being On or By the Water

The boating community is developing increasing interest in New York Harbor. The port is becoming more friendly to the average boatman. It is becoming perceived as a port to visit or pass through on the way to Long Island Sound, the mecca for area recreational boaters.

The harbor, with all its esplanades, walkways and parks along the waterfront, is becoming more aesthetically pleasing. The New Jersey shoreline of the Hudson River sports many marinas and restaurants overlooking the water. Newport, a large condominium development in Jersey City, has oriented itself toward the harbor. With marinas, restaurants, and esplanades designed with a view toward the waterfront, businesses have capitalized on a growing interest of people to live at the harbor's edge.

This developing trend is part of the transition that the harbor is going through. It is caused by a number of factors, not the least of which is the drying up of shipping in the New York City parts of the harbor.

The Rise of Community Organizations

Influence of Local Organizations

More and more community organizations have come into existence in the last few years. They have a great effect on what happens in New York Harbor. The emphasis of the community organizations has been on the environment for the most part, but they have also pushed for other issues such as access to the water, non-marine use of the waterfront, public parks and other such projects. Many industries which were on the waterfront in New York Harbor have moved away or closed down. These industries were along the waterfront because they were marine-related or desired to be close to the water because waterborne transportation was so important in past years. In modern times, community organizations have a say in how the land that these industries once occupied is to be reused. The current thinking is to revitalize the waterfront, to make it young again with fresh new businesses that people can enjoy and which will serve the overall economic objectives. Little by little, these organizations have made great strides. They have not met their objectives entirely but they are making progress.

GOWANUS CANAL COMMUNITY DEVELOPMENT CORPORATION

A typical community organization is the Gowanus Canal Community Development Corporation.[22] Founded in 1978, it is a not-for-profit organization. It was put together by a number of citizens who were concerned about the deterioration of Gowanus Canal. Applying to the New York City part of the harbor, there are 59 community organizations "officially recognized" by the New York City Council. Many council members are key members of these community organizations. Several are charter members. Waterfront localities in New Jersey have community organizations as well. In fact other, non-waterfront, communities have them also. Many readers of this book are likely to be members of such organizations. Local governing bodies pay attention to these organizations. It is the democratic way. These organizations usually have a small group of public-spirited citizens at their core. Other members may not have the time to commit to the organization but share in the objectives of the group.

COMMUNITY GROUPS IN OPERATION

Another organization is the Metropolitan Waterfront Alliance.[23] The Metropolitan Waterfront Alliance is a New York City group. The author talked with Carter Craft, the director of the group.[24] He says the alliance is actually part of a group called the Municipal Arts Council but they coordinate the activities of many parallel groups, such as the Gowanus Canal Community Development Corporation and the Newtown Creek Alliance. It serves as an "umbrella" over these organizations, helping them with fund-raising, public relations efforts and so forth.

Why are community groups more effective these days? Fostered by the natural attraction for the water, as industry moved out of waterfront areas, community groups moved in to fill the gap. Aided by the real estate boom of recent years, many community projects along the water were accomplished. For example, the "Gold Coast," the New Jersey cities of Jersey City, Hoboken, Weehawken and others, have built along the waterfront restaurants, condominiums and the ubiquitous marinas, all for people who work by the water or live there. Often, the developers have conflicting motives, or they have good intentions but come up with what the community organizations think are the wrong answers. For example, the Fund For A Better Waterfront, a Hoboken, New Jersey–based group, thinks that a group of homes on the waterfront should have been built facing the water. Instead, the builder put the backyards on the water side. Granted, the builder built a pedestrian path bordering the water, but the community organization thinks that interferes with the privacy of backyards. Still, the public officials who approved the project thought they were deciding in the public interest.

Community organizations are very much interested in environmental conditions affecting the water around them. In this respect, the Clean Water Act was a big help because the federal government became involved in improving the waterways.

COMMUNITY ORGANIZATIONS EXERT THEIR INFLUENCE

How do the community organizations exert their influence? They continually voice their opinion on relevant issues. They speak with a concerted voice expressing their aspirations and their hopes. They do this by contacting their representatives in the legislature directly or by publicizing their objectives through the media. The media is an especially powerful force. The organizations write letters to the editors of newspapers. In some instances they write articles for the newspapers themselves. An example is the New York City web site *Gotham Gazette*. The *Gotham Gazette* frequently has articles written by key members of the community organizations.

Members and officers of these organizations often testify before legislative bodies and in court cases. The organizations may bring suit in legal hearings if it feels strongly about its position on an issue or if it feels it has a justifiable case.

Frequently, these organizations have members who are involved in government organizations, and are thus able to carry the message of the community organizations directly to the governing bodies.

THE COMPUTER AND COMMUNITY ORGANIZATIONS

Almost everyone has a computer nowadays. Asked whether the Internet had any effect on the rise of community organizations, Mr. Craft replied in the affirmative. He said he had received much positive feedback about the website of his organization — viewers thought that the website made them aware of the possibilities that the community organization could bring about. It did that by presenting for all to see the goals of the organization, who was involved, and other interesting facts about the body of water that it represented. Usually, the organization of the unit is spelled out, and key people are listed to contact. There is a host of information available for the casual viewer. The website is not the most important tool of the community organizations, but certainly a helpful one.

COMMUNITY ORGANIZATIONS AFFECT THE HARBOR

Community organizations do not always get their way. Newtown Creek is still polluted. The Gowanus Canal is still a long way from being the "Venice of

New York," but they have come a long way from the way they were. The trade-off with the governing bodies is usually the availability of money, and trade-off with the press is that they have other topics to devote attention to. Legislators are always trying to optimize the outcome, weighing the voters' options against the broader legislative possibilities. Community organizations have by definition a relatively parochial point of view. In fact, Carter Craft thinks they are most effective in pushing their local issues. When they become involved in issues pertaining to the harbor in general, they have less impact. The reason is probably that members have a deeper stake in the neighborhood issues and are likely to press harder for such issues.

Waterfront organizations have their problems as well, as all groups do, to be sure. They have their politics as members struggle for power within the organization. While not everyone has the same view and there are differences of thinking in the group, the members seem to work it out to the satisfaction of most. There is consensus on the goals, for the most part.

In short, community organizations have a great effect on New York Harbor. These organizations will even have more effect in the future. As shipping concerns and other industry move out community organizations will continue to assert their influence in how the waterfront is developed.

4

Major Events in the Harbor's History

The Dredging of Ambrose Channel

Dredging Ambrose Channel

At the present time, the main ship channel into New York Harbor is Ambrose Channel. Before the early 1900s, the way into the harbor was through the Gedney Channel and the Main Ship Channel. (These channels are now called Sandy Hook Channel and Chapel Hill Channel, respectively.) The Lower Bay has been silted up from the effluent of the Hudson River, and there were, and still are, many areas showing particularly shallow water. Channels had been dredged on the west side of the Lower Bay, providing a rather circuitous route across the shoals into the harbor. The east side had been neglected to a great extent, although there was a channel there called the East Channel, but it was only 16 feet deep. Several officials recognized that deepening the channel on the east side of the bay would provide a more direct route into the harbor since this channel ran in a straight line, that is, directly into the harbor from what was to be Ambrose Light.[1]

While the advantages of dredging the east side of the bay were being talked about, the consensus of the time favored the pre-existing channels on the west side of the Lower Bay, the Gedney Channel and the Main Ship Channel. Congress voted an appropriation of $200,000 in 1884 (a sizable amount at that date) to dredge Gedney channel to a depth of 28 feet. Dredging technology was in its infancy at that time. After a few aborted attempts it was possible only to dredge it to 26 feet. By 1893, after a few improvements in dredging techniques and another appropriation from Congress, it was possible to dredge the two channels to 30 feet.

Need for Deeper Channels

Meanwhile, the age of steam had come into being and bigger ships were being built. Bigger ships meant then, as it does now, deeper draft; hence the push to dredge deeper channels so the new ships could get into New York Harbor. Among others, the Cunard line petitioned the Corps of Engineers to deepen the approach to New York Harbor.[2] Among those who lobbied for congressional support for dredging the East Channel was John Wolfe Ambrose. Ambrose was a well-to-do engineer who had been involved in improvements to the Upper Bay. He was, among other things, a board member and part owner, of a ferry company based in Brooklyn. His efforts to influence Congress paid off. In 1899, Congress appropriated the money, and it was to be used for dredging the East Channel. Ambrose is largely credited with leading the way in getting the East Channel deepened.

Congress had worded the legislation so as to put the burden on the dredging contractors to perform on time and within specifications. Snags developed. Years went by with little progress made. A contractor died. A contractor tried and failed — he had the idea of using pressure to stir up the bottom. He hoped the tide would clear the suspended sand from the intended channel. It did not work; there were more delays. Finally, the Corps of Engineers built its own dredges and put them to work. The East Channel's depth now ran between 35 and 38 feet.

Completion of that stage of the dredging of Ambrose Channel occurred just in time for the *Lusitania*'s visit to New York. In September 1907, the *Lusitania* arrived and proudly sailed into the harbor by way of the East Channel, soon to be renamed the Ambrose Channel. It had just been built, a large, new passenger vessel. It was a significant event. The *Lusitania*'s coming to New York meant that the harbor now could accommodate the gigantic ships that were to be coming off the ways.

By 1908 five dredges were working on the channel. The project continued until 1914, at which time the channel had been dredged to a depth of 40 feet with a width of 2,000 feet. By 1944, the channel had been dredged to 45 feet.

How Large Will Ships Be?

It is interesting to note that the same drive to accommodate the larger ships that caused John Ambrose to make his plea for having the East Channel deepened is at work right now to deepen the channels in New York Harbor still further for the new containerships. Will a maximum size be reached for ships? When the giant containership *Regina Maersk* made its first visit to New York Harbor in 1998, the workmen had to remove the mast so the ship could fit under the Bayonne Bridge.[3] Perhaps the bridges will put a limit on how big ships will be in the future, or at least on the height of the ships above the waterline. Maybe the depth of the harbor and how deep the dredges can dig will establish a limit eventually. The Port Authority has pointed out that no new advances have been made in the technology of dredging for quite a while. The dredges are able to dig to the currently proposed depth, which is 50 feet for New York Harbor (other ports have dredged to a depth of 55 feet). However, they will reach the limit of their capability unless a new technique for dredging is developed (which probably will happen eventually).

The Clearing of Hell Gate

A Treacherous Body of Water

An action that had a great effect of the growth of New York Harbor was the clearing of the rocks from Hell Gate. This accomplishment owes a lot to John Newton. Newton was a colonel in the U.S. Army Corps of Engineers. He was a determined man who had a spirit of inventiveness and the courage to carry through on his convictions. He led the program that cleared the way through Hell Gate, a hellishly narrow passageway that ships choosing to use that entrance had to go through to get to New York Harbor.[4]

The alternate route to Ambrose Channel for entering New York Harbor is via Long Island Sound. Boats and ships that come that way pass Nantucket or Block Island. Then they come through Long Island Sound, a body of water that is about 12 miles wide toward the eastern end of Long Island but narrows toward its western end. Eventually the vessels end up in Hell Gate, ready to go down the East River into the harbor proper.

Hell Gate is the name of the body of water at the upper (east) end of the East River. In a way, it connects the East River with Long Island Sound. The river narrows at Hell Gate, and that is the reason for the treacherous tidal current. In the 1850s, when all kinds of ships and boats were coming and going to and from New York Harbor, the passage at Hell Gate was riddled with rocks. Currents as high as 10 knots were encountered by some vessels that were audacious enough to try to go through when the current was running fully. Many vessels tried, some with disastrous results. The current is much weaker now, although still plenty strong, 4–4.5 knots. (A knot equals one nautical mile per hour — slightly more than the land measure of miles per hour.) The current is slower because the rocks have been removed and the water has more of a chance to flow through Hell Gate unimpeded.

An Episode in Hell Gate

Many vessels met their doom in Hell Gate before the rocks were cleared. One story is tragic, yet comic in some ways. The story refers back to the time at which there were many rocks in Hell Gate. A tug was towing a lighter, a barge which was used to carry cargo out to the ships at anchor. Like many lighters, this one had a derrick mast and boom on board to load and unload the cargo. The tug had run behind on its schedule, so it had missed the optimum time of slack water. It found itself going through Hell Gate with a strong current behind it. As often happens in that situation, the barge, propelled by the strong current, had a mind of its own; it did not stay passively behind the tug. This barge took off, hit a rock and proceeded to sink. As the barge went to the bottom, the barge captain scampered up the mast. He had with him a suitcase holding all his belongings. So here we have a barge captain clinging to the top of the mast, which was just barely sticking out of the water, holding tight to his suitcase! Fortunately, the tug was able to retrieve him in short order.

INITIAL MOVES TO CLEAR HELL GATE

Since the early 1800s, there had been talk of clearing the obstacles in Hell Gate. Sailing ships "going east" in the coastwise trade came and went that way. Can you imagine sailing through Hell Gate in those days, subject to the vagaries of the wind, trying to negotiate through all those rocks? No wonder that in the 1850s one vessel in 50 did not make it through; they often crashed into a rock or ran aground. Many of them sank outright. A history of the Corps of Engineers reports that in an average year at the time, 1,000 ships ran aground in Hell Gate.[5] Even ships propelled by steam had their share of difficulty navigating through Hell Gate.

Hell Gate was more critical as an access route to New York Harbor in those days because the main entrance to the harbor, the Sandy Hook Bar, had only 24 feet of water at low tide. In 1855, Great Britain began building larger ships with the new steam engines. These ships would have difficulty crossing the bar at the entrance to New York. Some New York Harbor people thought the answer to this situation was to increase the use of the Long Island Sound entrance, coming through Hell Gate. Hell Gate was deep enough; if only it did not have those devilish rocks. This line of thinking, as well as the normally high use of the Hell Gate entrance at the time, spawned a push to clear the rocks from Hell Gate, an enormous task, to be sure, but one that had to be done.

CLEARING THE ROCKS FROM HELL GATE

In view of the enormousness of the task, there was an alternate plan which received some consideration. The alternate plan was to build a canal across the community of Astoria, a part of Queens adjacent to the river at Hell Gate, thus bypassing the violent waters of Hell Gate. That plan, which was talked about and supported by a few people, never got off the ground. Eventually, it was dropped when Congress finally acted on the clearing of Hell Gate.

In 1850, a "public-spirited citizen" named Merriam lobbied for the clearing of the river at Hell Gate, and in 1852 Congress approved an appropriation of $20,000, a significant sum at that time. As a result the engineers on the project tried to clear a major hazard from the treacherous waters. They worked on an obstacle to navigation called "Pot Rock." They placed charges on top of the rock and blasted continuously, but the blasting did not work. The project was abandoned for the time being, but not forgotten. This project was going to take a long time.

In 1867, Lt. Col. John Newton of the Army Corps of Engineers was put in charge. He proposed to clear the reef at Hallet's Point. Hallet's Point is a portion of Astoria that protrudes out into the East River. It still does to this day; but at the end of Hallet's Point at that time began a reef that was three acres in area, ranging from 0 to 26 feet of depth. This reef extended out into the river another 300 feet from Hallet's Point. You can imagine the hazard that reef presented to a ship trying to pass by the area. The ship had to veer toward the Manhattan shore to avoid striking it.

From the "Pot Rock" experience, the engineers had long since learned to drill holes into which to put the charges. In only that way would the charges have the desired effect of blowing apart the rock. To take advantage of this line of thinking, Newton designed a drilling barge in which the drills were driven by steam. The barge was positioned over the rock that was to be removed by explosives. The barge drilled the holes, the charges were placed, and the rock was blown into pieces. Then workers used grappling hooks to remove the shattered rock. It

Hell Gate in the 1770s. Many of the rocks referered to under the etching were cleared in the latter half of the 19th century (Library of Congress).

sounds simple; the only problem was that the passing ships and boats kept running into the barge. Reportedly it was hit as often as three times in one day. It sounds incredible that so many vessels could run into the work barge in that manner, but there was a lot of traffic passing through Hell Gate in those days and the boats were difficult to control because of the strong current and frequent adverse wind conditions. In addition, in some cases fog led to the collisions. Nevertheless, in spite of problems and delays, progress was proceeding on the Hell Gate clearing. The progress was gradual, but over the long run, the workers were coming closer to their goal.

In view of the shortcomings encountered in using the drilling barge, Newton came up with another plan to get rid of Hallet's Point Reef. He decided to tunnel under it to plant his explosives. A 310-foot coffer dam was constructed, and then the crew dug down to a depth of 33 feet. They dug tunnels out of the rock horizontally, leaving only relatively thin walls between each tunnel and a relatively thin ceiling above the tunnels. The idea was to use explosives to blast the entire reef at one time. It was to be the biggest manmade explosion in history. The newspapers and many officials had misgivings about the expected effects of the explosion. They waited with bated breath. The year was 1882. Finally the day arrived. Mr. Newton, who did not want lawsuits from perceived damage from the blast, had his engineers spread around the city to observe any untoward effects. Everybody was waiting expectantly. The plunger was pushed and the water erupted. Many pictures were taken of the tremendous explosion, and nothing unforeseen occurred. The blasting was a complete success. Subsequent underwater surveys showed that the entire reef had been shattered. A total of 90,588 tons of rock were removed. The reef was cleared. Now ships and boats could pass close to Hallet's Point.

FLOOD ROCK

Meanwhile, work had begun on clearing another major obstacle from the river. It was called Flood Rock, a large rock formation in the East River just south of Hallet's Point. Flood Rock was clearly a hazard to navigation and had to be removed. John Newton's plan was to tunnel under the rock and use explosives to blast it into pieces, a similar plan to what he had envisioned to remove the Hallet's Point Reef. The crew started digging the tunnels, but encountered repeated work stoppages for one reason or another. Several times they ran out of funds. Eventually, they were in position to place the explosives. The tunnels were flooded to contain the force of the explosion, as they had been for the Hallet's Point explosion. This time, there was more confidence that the tremendous explosion would cause no harm to the surrounding community. Fortunately, it went off as planned. It was a complete success, and John Newton, who was now a brigadier general, was widely acclaimed.

Other rocks were cleared from Hell Gate. The project was completed in 1890. Now it is possible to navigate through the passage with relative ease. Many boats with powerful engines go through even against the current. Still, most ships bide their time until about high tide when the current is not running. That way, they have the ebb to take them down the East River or out the Sound. There is a noticeable increase in traffic at the time of high tide (slack water) in Hell Gate. Much of this increase consists of recreational cruisers or sailboats. It is not like the 1800s when there was a host of commercial vessels using the Hell Gate entrance to the harbor.

A Useful Alternative Entrance to the Harbor

There is no doubt that the clearing of obstacles in the Hell Gate passageway, including the clearing of Flood Rock, was a great contribution to the navigability of New York Harbor though fewer ships, proportionately, use the sound and Hell Gate entrance to the harbor today. Ambrose Channel, in the Lower Bay, is the entrance of choice nowadays, especially for the ships approaching New York from the south. For one thing, these ships stay in the ocean; they do not have to navigate with land hazards all around them. (This fact was brought home to the *Queen Elizabeth II* when it left the channel and tore its bottom on the rocks near Martha's Vineyard. It was headed for New York Harbor via Long Island Sound, Hell Gate and the East River).

On the other hand, from a strategic point of view, it is beneficial to have an alternate entrance to the harbor. During World War II, a great many convoys left New York Harbor by this "back door." To this day, tugs towing barges containing oil and other commodities to New England ports use this route. A great deal of commerce passes through Hell Gate in relative safety.

The General Slocum *Steamboat Excursion Disaster*

New York Shocked by Steamboat Tragedy

In 1904, disaster occurred that greatly shook the communities of New York Harbor. The United States and even other nations reacted to it. A fire in a vessel on the water is a fearsome event whenever it takes place, but it had a devastating effect on this excursion boat full of passengers expecting to have a festive day. The misfortune that overtook the steamboat *General Slocum* on the 15th of June, 1904, underscored the unsafe nature of passenger-carrying vessels of the time. Some said it was an accident waiting to happen; some said it was the fault of the operators of the steamboat; some said it was the shabbiness of the boat inspection made shortly before the disaster. All agreed the incident could have been handled better, avoiding the loss of so many lives.

The *General Slocum* was a paddlewheel steamer that sailed around New York

Harbor, taking people on excursion trips. Its captain was William Van Schaick who had been sailing for many years. He had much misfortune with the *General Slocum*, but nothing as bad as what was to come on that fateful day. There had been a few groundings and a collision. On a June day in 1904, he went on board with his crew and brought the boat to the East River pier where they were to pick up their passengers for the day.[6, 7] The outing was for the parishioners of the St. Mark's Evangelical Lutheran Church, a group of German immigrants who were clustered in the east side of Manhattan. They lived in an area of the Lower East Side called Kleindeutschland (Little Germany), after the country they had come from. The annual event was scheduled on a Monday. It was slated to be a steamboat excursion to Locust Point, Long Island, where they were scheduled to enjoy a fun-filled day on the picnic grounds. The participants never arrived there.

Most of the passengers arrived at Pier 3 on the East River at the appointed time, around 8:30 in the morning. The passengers, mostly women and children, were in good spirits. The men, for the most part, had gone to work. The passengers boarded the boat, deckhand John Coakley clicking off each person on his counter. Reports are that he did not count too carefully, however. His count of the passengers, what would have been an important piece of information, could not be relied upon, as it later came out.

The band was already on board. They played "Ein Feste Burg Ist Unser Beste Gott." The Reverend George F. Haas and his wife and daughter had stationed themselves on board the *General Slocum* among the members of their parish. The happy throng was looking forward to a delightful day.

The boat backed out into the river with a great churning of its paddlewheels. The band played melodically and rather loudly, and laughter and gay sounds wafted across the water. The boat headed up the river. Reverend Haas took up his position in the after lounge. Others strolled about the deck admiring the tall buildings of Manhattan; they were not used to seeing the buildings from the vantage point of the water. Some persons bought hot dogs from the counter. Some of the men took advantage of the opportunity to have a beer at the bar that had been set up by a member of the party.

THE BOAT BURNS FIERCELY

Crew member John Coakley (one of the many villains in this unfortunate episode) went to the storeroom to investigate a report of smoke, raised by a boy passenger. On entering the compartment, he found that a barrel of straw had caught fire and was burning brightly. He tried to place a tarpaulin over the fire, but it continued to burn. Instead, he grabbed two bags of charcoal that were nearby and tried to smother the fire with them. That did not work either; the charcoal merely added fuel to the fire. He decided to get assistance. Meanwhile the fire had accelerated considerably, aided by the draft created by the open door behind him.

By this time the boat had passed Blackwell's Island (now called Roosevelt Island), had passed Astoria, and was entering Hell Gate. Hell Gate had been cleared by this date of rocks and reefs, but mariners still respected it as a challenging body of water to go through.

Coakley had apprised the first mate of the fire, but no one had yet told the captain that the boat had caught fire. By this time the boat was almost clear of Hell Gate. Some of the passengers had already jumped overboard. The shore was so close by in this narrow body of water that jumping looked liked a safer choice to some, but the current was flowing strongly and carried swimmers to their deaths.

First there was smoke, which terrified the passengers. Then there were flames which terrified them even more. It all happened very quickly and the crew lost many minutes with which to fight the fire while it was still manageable.

Finally the captain was told that there was a fire on the boat. By this time the *General Slocum* had passed out of Hell Gate and proceeded up the river past Port Morris in the Bronx. It was headed for the narrow gap between North Brother Island and South Brother Island. Because of the fire on board, the captain opted to turn the boat toward Port Morris. The docks there seemed like an opportune place to land the boat and get the passengers to safety. The fire was burning more fiercely now. Panic had seized the passengers and they were crushing one another in their efforts to move toward the stern of the vessel, away from the flames. Carried by the swift current, the boat was moving at 13 knots, and the breeze was fanning the flames, carrying them throughout the boat in a destructive onslaught. Constructed of wood, as boats were at that time, and freshly painted, the vessel was a tinderbox. It burned quickly, the flames starting up forward and consuming the lounges and open areas. Deck by deck the fire rose, passengers trying to save themselves from the ravenous flames. Many passengers threw themselves overboard to escape the flames, only to find a watery death by drowning. Others were pushed overboard by the pressing crowd. At one point a railing burst, spilling yet others over the side. Those who could swim were the lucky ones. Even they had a tough time because of the cumbersome clothing.

CREW TRIES TO DEAL WITH THE FIRE

The crew tried to react to the fire. Upon discovering the fire, they unrolled a fire hose in the hope of taming the flames. The hose had many kinks in it when they turned on the water pressure. The hose proved useless when it sprung leaks at each of the kinks. Life preservers also proved of little avail for the most part. They were held to the ceiling by wire screening and many passengers tried to get them down but could not. Those passengers who were able to obtain a life preserver found that they were made of defective cork which crumbled out of the canvas containers. Many of the passengers who went into the water discovered that the life preservers became water-soaked and weighed them down. Many persons drowned because of that.

143

All of this calamity happened within minutes. As far as the passengers knew, the entire episode took place within 20 minutes. As the ship angled toward Port Morris, people on the shore waved it off. The persons on shore pointed out the fuel docks they were headed for — a burning ship would cause the docks to catch fire with possible explosions. The captain instead headed for North Brother Island with intentions to beach the boat there. It was only a matter of minutes, but with a fire raging on board it meant many lives were in the balance. Edward Van Wart, who was at the wheel, tried to beach the boat sideways to the shore, but he could not get the boat around before the vessel slammed into the rocks on North Brother Island. The vessel was now beached, but most of the frantic passengers were at the stern which was sticking out in the water. There was a desperate attempt by the people to escape the flames that were licking at their backs. The clothing of many of them was afire. Mothers were calling for their children. Children were looking for their parents. All was in chaos.

NEARBY BOATS COME TO THE AID OF THE STRICKEN VESSEL

The boats in the area tried to help the stricken passengers of the *General Slocum*. Boats of all types came to the rescue, tugboats, ferries, a fireboat, a launch, even rowboats. A tug cut loose a tow and came up to the burning excursion boat. Another tug cut loose a schooner that it was towing. The boats maneuvered around the flaming steamboat and their crews busied themselves recovering the flailing victims from the water. Some desperate people jumped from the *General Slocum* to the deck of a nearby boat. Some passengers missed, falling on the rocks alongside. One woman lost all her teeth by landing face first on the rocks when she jumped. A tug stood offshore, fearful of running aground itself, but lowered a lifeboat which went among the people struggling in the water to pick up anyone within reach. Scattered among the people struggling in the water were many bodies of persons who had already succumbed to drowning. The rescuers left the bodies and concentrated on recovering the survivors. Eventually, the dead bodies were brought into shore, many found some distance away, carried by the strong current.

Aboard the ill-fated *General Slocum*, there was a crush of people trying to escape the heat of the fire. By this time the fire was raging and the boat was being completely consumed. The people who had yet to leave the boat were doomed. Their clothing was on fire. Families were trying to stay together, motivated by the relationships they had built up over the years, looking to each other for the security they needed at the moment. Many of those who managed to stay together perished in the raging fire. The decks collapsed, burying the passengers under a mass of wreckage.

AFTER THE TRAGEDY

A morgue was set up in a hospital on the shore of North Brother Island. Immediately after the disaster, 498 bodies were placed in this morgue. Then the bodies had to be identified. Relatives wandered among the bodies with grim faces, weighted down by the unpleasant task they faced. Estimates of the death toll increased steadily. The exact number of the dead will never be known, but the official estimate is 1,021, the second most savage accident occurring to a vessel on U.S. waters. (The worst accident occurred in 1865 when the paddle-wheel steamer *Sultana*, loaded with 2,000 Civil War veterans and 376 regular passengers, experienced a boiler explosion and the boat went ablaze. More than 1,450 people died in that disaster.)[8]

After the survivors had been taken ashore by the rescuers and the bodies had been recovered, to keep the conflagration from spreading to the hospital the *General Slocum* was pushed out into the river. The floating hulk was carried by the current down the river to a place called Sunken Meadow, there to sink to the bottom with its starboard paddlebox sticking out of the water. By then, the boat had burned to the waterline. All that remained above decks were the paddleboxes containing the paddlewheels, the smokestacks, the walking beam, and remnants of the hogbacks, the heavy structural members that excursion boats were designed with to keep the hull from sagging at the bow and stern. The hull was eventually raised and towed to the New Jersey part of the port to be outfitted as the barge *Maryland*. It served for a few years as a barge but was later lost in a storm off the coast of New Jersey.

REACTIONS TO THE DISASTER

The president of France wrote to U.S. president Theodore Roosevelt offering condolences for the tragedy. The mayors of many cities corresponded with the mayor of New York. New York Harbor was incensed at the burning of the *General Slocum*. Newspaper accounts of the disaster infuriated the populace, particularly as the deficiencies of the captain and crew were described. Also, there were deficiencies in the safety equipment on board the *General Slocum*. An inspection of the boat by the U.S. Steamboat Inspection Service had recently been conducted. Why had not this inspection revealed the deficiencies in equipment and training of the crew?

A coroner's hearing was conducted. The hearing revealed the shortcomings of the inspectors who had conducted a survey of the boat just weeks before the incident occurred. Witnesses testified as to the defective life preservers, the rotted hose, the inaccessible lifeboats. The owner of the *General Slocum*, the Knickerbocker Company, weakly testified in its defense. The captain, William Van Schaick, received his share of the blame. The ultimate outcome was that the captain was indicted for manslaughter as a result of the disaster. He was the only one who was held for trial. No action was taken against the corporation that owned the boat, much to the surprise of many people. Even more surprisingly, no action was taken against the two inspectors, who seemed very culpable in the affair. (Eventually, they were fired.)

Captain Van Schaick was placed on trial. In the wave of strong public revulsion caused by the tragedy, he was found guilty of negligence (the charge of manslaughter was reduced) and sentenced to 10 years in prison. He was sent to the infamous Sing Sing prison where he spent three and a half years. His wife succeeded in obtaining a pardon for him from President Taft and he spent the remainder of his years on his farm in upstate New York.

SAFETY IMPROVEMENTS OF PASSENGER VESSELS

One result of the burning of the *General Slocum* was a recommendation that all of the steamboats in New York Harbor should be inspected immediately. This recommendation became very controversial. The newspapers of New York and the nearby municipalities took up the drumbeat for reinspection. The owners of the boats protested vehemently. The controversy went back and forth for a while. Eventually, many boats were inspected, and the inspections were carried out in a stringent manner. These inspections undoubtedly drew attention to the need for better safety and the boating public was protected accordingly.[9, 10]

More inspections were held in New York Harbor in the years immediately following the *General Slocum* disaster. The U.S. Customs Department and the Harbor Police stopped excursion boats in the harbor for boarding and inspection. Most important, they drew attention to the problem of maritime safety.[11, 12]

Another result of the excursion steamboat disaster was a review held at the federal level in Washington, D.C. The secretary of commerce and labor, George B. Cortelyou, became involved, and his commission filed a report to the president. In that report they confirmed the conclusions that had been reached at the New York level: that the U.S. Steamboat Inspection Service had been derelict in its function, that the equipment on the *General Slocum* had been faulty, that some of the crew of the steamboat had exercised poor judgment, and that the owners were culpable. The commission recommended a number of changes in legislation. Congress responded by strengthening somewhat the laws regulating vessels carrying passengers. The circumstances were unfortunate in one respect: The laws were already on the books; they had merely to be enforced. The U.S. Steamboat Inspection Service inspectors, in spite of the fact that they were at fault in the incident concerning the *Slocum*, really did not have much power. The U.S. Steamboat Inspection Service was overhauled to a degree, and the inspectors who were involved with the *General Slocum* were terminated. However, it was not until much later, in 1942, that the U.S. Steamboat Inspection Service was disbanded and the inspection of vessels turned over to the U.S. Coast Guard.

New York was severely affected emotionally by the *General Slocum* disaster. Much of a whole neighborhood was wiped out by the tragedy. What had been an area of immigrants, Kleindeutschland, was never the same after the accident. People moved away. An area of the Upper East Side known as Yorktown became the new neighborhood for German immigrants. The neighborhood probably would have changed in any event — neighborhoods change just as New York Harbor has changed.[13] St. Mark's Church is still there; it is a synagogue now. A monument stands in Tompkins Square, in what was Kleindeutschland. On it is inscribed, in silent testimony to the young people who succumbed in the tragedy: "They Were the Earth's Purest Children, Young and Fair."

The Black Tom Explosion

It is early Sunday morning. In the areas around New York Harbor almost everyone is sleeping. Suddenly, a tremendous roaring, thundering explosion pierces the air, rocks the beds, and sends a shutter through the buildings. Windows are shattered. The Brooklyn Bridge is taken by the scruff of the neck and rudely shaken.

The explosion occurred on July 30, 1916, on the docks and on the water near Jersey City. The explosion blew people out of their beds in nearby New Jersey and Manhattan.[14] It broke most of the windows in downtown and midtown Manhattan. The pressure from the cataclysm was felt in Spring Lake and Long Branch at the Jersey Shore, as far away, in fact, as Maryland. It was a great concussive force that shook people awake from far and wide.

The locus of the explosion was a loading pier where ammunition of all kinds was stored in warehouses or on barges and lighters to be taken out to the waiting ships anchored nearby. The ammunition was destined for Russia, Great Britain and France. At this time, during World War I, the United States was trying doggedly to stay out of the fray but still siding with the Allies in many ways. While the United States was formally neutral at that time, great factories from all over the northeastern United States and the Midwest were producing explosives to ship to friendly nations overseas. The explosion at Black Tom Island was, as it turned out, a result of that involvement.

ALL IS QUIET AT BLACK TOM — FOR A WHILE

On the night of the explosion at Black Tom Island, the docks had grown quiet. The longshoremen, having finished their work for the day, had gone home, fortunately for them. The only people around the piers as the clock approached midnight were the security guards. It was cool as the night progressed and there were many insects in the air. The guards wanted a fire to ward off the mosquitoes. Someone brought up some smudge pots and lit them. (It was later established that the smudge pots, as many people had thought, had nothing to do with the explosions. The motives involved in the case were much more sinister.) The guards saw a fire in one of the freight cars. The guards hastened to put out the fire because they knew the freight car held ammunition that was could blow sky-high at the slightest spark. They were too late.

The first of a series of explosions went off at 2:08 A.M. Soon, the area was a scene of utter chaos. The guards scampered to safety over the bridge separating the island from the mainland. Bombs, shells, and other forms of ammunition went off with extraordinary force. Liberty Island, nearby, was peppered with shrapnel from the blast. On nearby Ellis Island, immigrants who were housed there came out of the buildings screaming, unaware of what was going on — they knew only that all hell was breaking loose and they wanted to get away. Two boats from the New York City Police Harbor Squad went to Ellis Island in response to a call from officials there. The immigrants were getting panicky. Boats eventually took the people to New York City where they were relatively safe. A building on Ellis Island caught fire from the embers that were flying all around. Liberty Island was completely evacuated during the night.

The skies lit up over the harbor, and shells burst in the air. A hail of sparks and debris rained down over the docks which by then had been almost completely destroyed. Tugboats responded to the catastrophic situation. They methodically towed some of the ships from the docks where they were exposed to the fire. Many barges caught fire, however, or were obliterated by the explosion of munitions on board.

There was panic among the people in Manhattan, Hoboken, Jersey City and other areas of New York and New Jersey. People heard the explosions and did not know what was going on. Many wandered in the streets in their bed clothing looking for answers. Shattered glass was strewn around in many streets and people had to step gingerly to avoid the broken shards. There was a rumor that the Standard Oil plant in Bayonne had blown up. There were other rumors as well. It was only later that morning when people had an inkling of what had happened. One thing was sure: It had been something to do with the harbor — something big to create explosions of such force.

Miraculously, very few people were killed in the incident. Perhaps the perpetrators deliberately planned it for a Saturday night when they knew the workers would not be there. The *New York Times* ran major articles on the explosion on Black Tom Island on Sunday and Monday, July 30 and July 31. One among the many articles in those cataclysmic days included the headline "The Harbor Raked By Shrapnel for Hour." The article described the damage to the plant of the National Storage Company, the company that was assembling munitions to send overseas. The *Times* printed a picture of the wrecked plant and the many barges docked nearby that were loaded down with explosives.[15]

What Caused the Explosion?

Almost immediately, officials tried to determine the cause of the disaster. At first, the guards were suspected, especially since they had made fires to ward off the mosquitoes. Fires — with all those explosives around! Heaven forbid. Investigators soon narrowed the cause down to two freight cars which were burning and set off the explosions. There were other issues. Officials decried the violations of regulations that had been found. For example, a barge loaded with ammunition was supposed to leave for Gravesend Bay that afternoon; instead, it remained tied up the dock at Black Tom Island, despite the fact that it was loaded with explosives. Other infractions were involved, not the basic cause of the disaster but adding to it substantially. The presidents of the National Storage Company and the Lehigh Valley Railroad were arrested, then released on bail awaiting grand jury action.

What had caused these tremendous explosions? It was not until years later that evidence of a sinister plot, a picture of sabotage by the Germans, began to emerge. As investigators worked to gather evidence, the "Mixed Claims Commission" was established in August 1922 by the United States and Germany. Germany was represented by a commissioner at first. The German commissioner resigned later in an attempt to have the commission abolished. Meanwhile, Hitler rose to power and the commission continued with its consideration of the evidence year after year, under much controversy. Finally, in 1939, the commission ruled that Germany was guilty, and later that year awards of approximately $50 million were made to the claimants in the Black Tom disaster. (Plus those claimants of several other explosions at munitions plants—the German saboteurs were busy that year.) Germany protested, but the claims were upheld. World War II was under way by that time and the Nazi regime, desirous of establishing its credit in the world markets, made good its payment to the claimants.

German Agents

The story of the German agents who caused the Black Tom explosions is virtually beyond belief, a story of clever and not-so-clever manipulations by a varied group of individuals, a story of incredible naiveté and complacence by the American people. The tale is told by Jules Witcover, who researched the files of the Mixed Claims Commission when they were released and published a book about the disaster and its aftermath.[16] He described how the German saboteurs came and went quite easily between New York City and the New Jersey cities of Hoboken, Jersey City and Bayonne. Frequently cited as the top of the hierarchy of the German spy ring in the United States was Captain Franz Von Papen. He was a military attaché in the German Embassy. He was supported by Captain Karl Boy-Ed, naval attaché. There were many others involved, but the most believable theory about who actually set off the explosions at Black Tom that night concerns three men: Kurt Jahnke and Lothar Witzke, aided by their lackey Michael Kristoff. Although the testimony overwhelmingly pointed to the Germans as responsible for the explosions at Black Tom, the commission never ruled on exactly how it was done.

Witzke and Jahnke probably approached the piers in a small boat (as several witnesses testified) and planted explosive devices in a boxcar and on a barge named the *Johnson 17*. Their accomplice, Kristoff, a waterfront worker who lived in a rooming house in Hoboken, came from the land side and helped them set the fires which led to the two big explosions and many smaller ones.

At the time, New York Harbor was deeply affected by the Black Tom explosion. Over the long run, it is difficult to say how seriously hurt was the population. Not many people connected with the harbor today know about Black Tom. However, many boats took part in the rescue effort, just as they did in the terrorist attack on the World Trade Center many years later. In fact, there are many parallels in the two incidents. Both showed a lack of preparedness on the part of the people and the authorities. There were many more casualties in the World Trade Center disaster — the injuries and deaths were relatively light in the Black Tom Explosions, mostly because it happened early on a Sunday morning when the longshoremen and railroad workers were away from their jobs.

New York Harbor was a bustling port at the time of the Black Tom disaster. It was busier still in World War II, as will be described. Wars provide a need for increased shipping between nations. The Black Tom explosion is one of the issues that led the United States into the war with Germany, not the most compelling issue, but certainly a contributor. By the time the commission settled the matter, in 1939, the United States was close to becoming involved in World War II.

World War II and New York Harbor

NEW YORK HARBOR ALREADY HELPING THE ALLIES

The United States became involved in World War II even before Congress declared war in 1941. The nation supported England in its war with the Axis powers by providing destroyers to add to the British fleet in the famous lend-lease arrangement. Already, U.S. transport ships were forming convoys in New York Harbor to lend assistance to the Allies. U.S. destroyers were shepherding these convoys part way across the Atlantic — the arrangement was for U.S. ships to guard the convoys halfway. Then the British ships would take over.

The port of New York became busy toward the latter part of the 1930s because the Great Depression was lessening and the economy was starting to heat up. However, when the war came along, the harbor really became clogged with vessels with all the added activity caused by the war effort.

It seemed natural for the U.S. government to use New York Harbor as its number one port. It was arguably one of the best ports in the world, and it was already quite busy. The New York State Museum website mentions that there were 600 individual ship anchorages for ships awaiting berthing or awaiting convoy assignment. On one record-setting day in March 1943, there were a total of

543 merchant ships at anchor in the port of New York. At another point it mentions that there were over 575 tugboats in the New York Harbor.[17]

There were shipyards all over the port of New York — 39 of them.[18] Also, the New York Naval Shipyard — the Brooklyn Navy Yard — was making a strong contribution to the war effort. It was the navy's biggest shipyard, and probably the biggest shipyard in the world, employing 71, 000 workers at the time of World War II. (The New York Naval Shipyard is described in another section). The shipyards built ships and boats for the U.S. Navy. The Brooklyn Navy Yard produced aircraft carriers such as the *Bon Homme Richard*, the *Bennington* and the *Franklin Delano Roosevelt*, as well as the battleships U.S.S. *Missouri* and *North Carolina*.[19] (These were built in addition to the ships mentioned previously in the section on the East River. To sum it up simply, Brooklyn Navy Yard built a lot of ships.)

The Todd Shipyard at Erie Basin built LCPs (landing craft personnel) for the war effort.[20] A division of the Sperry Gyroscope Company was located in Brooklyn at the base of Manhattan Bridge, and the Brooklyn Army Terminal, a large building of several floors, served as the New York port of embarkation for the armed services. The terminal was the embarkation point for more than 1 million troops who were sent overseas, and was the coordinating point for half the war-destined cargo of the East Coast.

The U.S. Maritime Commission was contracting with the shipyards to build many ships. There was emphasis on productivity, overtime hours, putting in long working days, and the shipyard workers, many of them women, labored intensively. Women were taking the place of men in the shipyards in many cases. ("Rosie the Riveter" was widely publicized.) The ships were being launched at an astonishing rate. U.S. ship losses were high in the early stages of the war, but the industrial engine of the United States was building ships faster than the Axis powers could sink them.

Other signs of the war came to the area around New York Harbor. At Coney Island in Brooklyn there were guns defending the harbor. Where Kingsborough Community College is at this time, at the end of Manhattan Beach in Brooklyn, there was a training school for the Coast Guard and Merchant Marine. Also, numerous anti-aircraft gun emplacements were established around the harbor. The state merchant marine training school at Fort Schuyler and the federal Merchant Marine Academy at Kings Point, Long Island, were busy training officers for the merchant marine, a very important arm of the service during World War II.

SECURITY OF THE HARBOR

Security of the harbor was an important issue, both security from attack and security from foreign agents. There were posters all around the harbor saying "Loose lips sink ships," and the government did not want another Black Tom explosion that had rocked the harbor in World War I. Also in the way of security, every vessel flew three code flags to show its identity according to how they were registered with the Coast Guard. The U.S. Army had fortifications at key points in the harbor. The harbor was well protected as far as attack from ships. Fort Hancock on Sandy Hook protected that entrance to the port. The big guns of the fort are still available for inspection by the public. There were many other forts, such as Fort Wadsworth and Fort Hamilton at the Narrows, and Fort Drum on Governor's Island. Fort Schuyler on the East River in the Bronx and Fort Tilden in Little Neck Bay protected the harbor from invasion via the Long Island Sound route. All had gun emplacements, and personnel there were prepared to shoot enemy ships out of the water. Some of the forts are not in existence any longer. Fort Hamilton was demolished as part of the construction of the Verrazano Bridge. It was located where the Brooklyn tower for the bridge now stands. Fort Tilden, at the eastern end of the harbor, has been closed down.

No enemy ships tried to enter New York Harbor during the war. Probably, the separation provided by the Atlantic Ocean presented too much of a logistical problem for the Axis powers, except for submarines, that is. Although German submarines were a menace right off the coast of New York Harbor, no enemy vessels tried to penetrate the port.

The U.S. Navy had several installations scattered around New York Harbor. Floyd Bennett Naval Air Station was one, a large installation of navy planes situated near Canarsie, a part of the borough of Brooklyn. The navy had its headquarters for the Eastern Sea Frontier located in Manhattan and it established with the U.S. Army the Army and Navy Joint Control Center at 90 Church Street in Manhattan. From this control center, defenses against the German submarines were coordinated.

German Submarines Outside New York Harbor

In 1942, although New York Harbor was already becoming busy with shipping activity as a result of the war, the average person in the New York area was relatively uninvolved in it. The German submarine command changed that attitude by bringing the war right off the shore of the United States. It launched Operation Drumbeat, *Paukenschlag* in German, in which submarines were dispatched to the U.S. coast. There they wrought havoc through the early part of the year, sinking tankers and cargo ships right off the coast, until the United States finally mounted a defense. The United States was caught completely off guard. The U.S. Navy did not respond until later that year.

Michael Gannon wrote a book about the German submarines' operation off the coast of the U.S. called *Operation Drumbeat: The Dramatic True Story of Germany's First U-Boat Attacks Along the American Coast in World War II*.[21] He researched in German archives to unearth a wealth of information about the activities of those submarines. He relates a story about *U-boat 123*, after sinking several ships in the Atlantic, approaching the shore of Long Island and prowling about at the entrance to New York Harbor. *U-boat 123* had already sunk the *Cyclops* and the *Norness* on its way to New York. Now, it was off the shore of Long Island, looking for the Ambrose Lightship at the entrance to New York Harbor. After it found its way to the entrance to New York Harbor, it headed east again and sank another ship 27 miles off Long Island. That ship was the *Coimbra*, a British ship of 6.768 GRT (gross registered tonnage), which went down in a yellow haze of flames and smoke.

Those were difficult times for Americans. People heard about ships sinking near New York Harbor almost every day. There were reports of oil, wreckage and bodies floating up on the beaches, yet the United States was slow to respond. There was not even a blackout of New York City. A brownout was ordered eventually, but the commercial interests along the shore resisted a complete blackout, which the seafarers recommended. Eventually the navy became geared up to the situation. Destroyers and other vessels like anti-submarine trawlers were put into action. Additional planes were put on patrol. There were many kills of the German submarines once the defenses were implemented. Eventually, after a six-month offensive, the German submarine command recalled its submarines from the east coast of the United States. The submarines did much damage, however, especially to the tankers who were carrying much-needed oil to power the engines of war for the Allied forces.

A submarine net had been put up early in the war stretching from Norton's Point to Hoffman Island. This net, strategically located in the Lower Bay, just before the entrance to the Narrows, effectively blocked submarines from entering the harbor. Mines were also planted outside the harbor, and the defensive vessels employed a system called ASDIC, an early electronic underwater detection device.

THE S.S. *NORMANDIE* INCIDENT

One incident that affected New York Harbor was a fire that took place aboard the *Normandie*.[22] The year was 1942 and the war was in full progress. The ocean liner *Normandie*, a proud ship, had carried passengers back and forth across the Atlantic since being launched in 1932. It had been taken over by the Coast Guard from France and was being readied to serve as a troop transport. While the *Normandie* was undergoing renovation at Pier 92 on the West Side of Manhattan, a strange event occurred. The ship was undergoing conversion to transport duty, destined to carry thousands of soldiers to the war fields overseas. That destiny never came to pass. The *Normandie* mysteriously caught fire and burned. It was learned later that most probably a worker had been careless with an acetylene torch and had caused the fire, which quickly spread throughout the freshly painted ship. The New York City Fire Department was called. Firefighters battled intensely

Normandie (right) in Pier 88 in New York Harbor before it was damaged by fire. The ship on the left is *Roma;* center is *Queen Mary* (South Street Seaport).

with the flames, pouring millions of gallons of water into the ship. Laden with the water that had entered its hull, the ship lost stability, turned on its side and settled to the bottom at the dock where it was moored.

What a tragedy. This magnificent ship had become a desolate hulk lying on its side at a pier in New York. Newspapers, New York and nationwide alike, chastised the fire department and the navy for allowing the ship to capsize at the dock. The ship was a total loss, at a time when the U.S. government needed every asset it could get its hands on to further the war effort. A plan was implemented to raise the vessel. Navy divers sealed the underwater portions of the vessel. (In 1942 the U.S. Navy established a diving school at the site). Now the ship was ready to be pumped out. Slowly, the vessel rose and was righted. It was towed to the shipyard at Kearny, New Jersey, only to be sold as scrap.

There was a great deal of concern that the ship had been sabotaged by German agents. There were a few reports to that extent. The Federal Bureau of Investigation (FBI) conducted an investigation but could find no evidence of foreign nationals having been involved in the incident. The FBI concluded that the calamity was a result of the carelessness of the workers renovating the ship.

It was an accident remembered to this day, an unfortunate fate for a great ship.

A BUSY HARBOR

World War II had a great effect on New York Harbor. All parts of the harbor were kept busy contributing to the war effort in one way or another. Shipyards built ships and boats. Tugs towed barges laden with war materials. Kill Van Kull was the main operation on the East Coast for the petrochemical industry, as it is today. Torpedo boats were tested in the East River. Convoys formed in the many anchorages about the harbor, and troops were sent overseas. New York Harbor was filled with boats and ships during World War II; it is not that way now.

The World Trade Center Attacks of 2001

A DEVASTATING EVENT

September 11, 2001, shook New York Harbor to the depths of its rivers and bays. When the airplanes were deliberately guided into the Twin Towers it brought devastation to the area and it snuffed out the lives of thousands of people who had occasion to be there — the wrong time at the wrong place. But those people had a right to be there, of course. Some of these people worked at the World Trade Center. Others were the firefighters who went into the buildings to help the persons inside. Included were the Port Authority police officers who wanted to give aid to the thousands of people still inside the towers.

When the towers collapsed, thousands of people on the streets, many of them dazed by the awesome events that happened right before their eyes, struggled to escape. They went down William Street. They went up Broadway. Most of them went eventually in the direction of the waterfront. They knew their way out was to get off the island of Manhattan and that Manhattan is an island was brought home clearly by the tragedy. The bridges and tunnels were closed because of the emergency. The Staten Island ferryboats were not running. There was no vehicular traffic on the East River bridges. The bridges were crowded with pedestrians crossing over to Brooklyn. Nobody at the time knew what was going to come next.

The harbor people responded beautifully. They had the boats to take people off the island. A group of pilots from the Sandy Hook Pilots Association were meeting at the Coast Guard Headquarters in Staten Island.[23] When they heard about the attacks on the World Trade Center, they offered their pilot boat to the Coast Guard. The Coast Guard loaded its Vessel Traffic Service personnel on board and immediately went to the Battery to coordinate emergency measures. There was a lot to coordinate. Boats were going all over the waters around the Battery. There were thousands of people wandering around, some simply standing in the water with nowhere to go, trying to escape the dreadful catastrophe that was going on around them.

HARBOR VESSELS PLAY A KEY ROLE

Coast Guard personnel added a note of stability to the chaos of the moment on that fateful morning. They communicated with the boats and the boats communicated with them. There was an air of urgency in the voices of the radio operators, an air of excitement, but there was also a steady rationale to their orders, this boat goes here, this boat goes there.

Coast Guard communication could be heard on Channel 13 (VHF):[24]

> "Please go down to the Battery. Go down to Pier 11 on the East River.
> Be careful of the people in the water, get people off the island of Manhattan."
> "John J. Harvey. Get rid of your passengers as fast as you can. We don't have any hydrants. We need your water."

The *John J. Harvey* is a restored fireboat.[25] Saved from the scrapyard by marine enthusiasts, it became a floating museum. Previously it had spent many years in New York Harbor in commission as a fireboat. It was at the *Normandie* fire during World War II and fought many fires along the piers during an active career. It is housed now at Pier 63, at the foot of West 23rd Street. Its keepers fired it up and traveled to the Battery, where it pumped water for the firefighters at the World Trade Center site, along with two other fireboats. None of the hydrants on shore worked — they had been damaged in the catastrophe. So these fireboats, including the *John J. Harvey*, supplied water to the firefighters for about a week.

Four tugboats from the Reinauer Transportation Company were on their way from their base at Staten Island. As they approached the Battery they radioed the Coast Guard and were told to pick up people at the seawall at the Lower Battery, near the Whitehall Ferry Terminal. They loaded 100 to 150 people on each boat. Most of these persons were covered with soot, and some of them were crying, shaken by the experience they had been through. The boat crews asked the people where they wanted to go. They took them there. Other tugboat companies sent boats. By one estimate, there were 35 tugboats available to take people off the docks and carry them to New Jersey, Brooklyn and Queens. Peopled wanted to go home, to see about their families, to feel the warmth and security of their homes after the dreadful ordeal.

The ferries responded in force.[26] New York Waterway, the biggest ferry organization, pressed 22 of its 24 boats into service. In a similar manner, Circle Line, which takes tourists around Manhattan on its cruise boats, moved its boats into action. Also, the dinner cruise boats were part of the operation. Spirit Cruises, an excursion line, shuttled evacuees from Chelsea Piers to Lincoln Harbor Yacht Marina in Weehawken, New Jersey. In four and a half hours, 8,000 persons were moved. The cruise boat *Spirit of New York* was given permission to dock at the North Cove Marina, where it served as a floating rest stop for the workers. Among other contributions to the emergency effort, the boat distributed food donated by area restaurants.

As a result of the 9/11 tragedy, the city of New York put a former ferry in service between the Brooklyn Army Terminal and the Whitehall Terminal on the Lower East Side. It is one of the old-fashioned ferries; passengers have no access to the outside. It's just a means of transportation in an emergency, but people use it to get back and forth. It is still operating at the time of this writing.

The periodical *Professional Mariner* described what occurred after the calamity took place. In the New York Passenger Terminal, cruise ships were diverted to ports such as Philadelphia, Baltimore and Boston. At first, the boats took people anywhere in the harbor. Later, they placed signs on the boats showing where the boats were going to go. The Seamen's Church Institute provided space for the rescue workers to rest, and provided hot meals, clothing and other supplies. Tugs supplied fireboats with emergency fuel, and fire trucks as well. A suggestion was made: bring a fuel barge to Battery. The need for permits was dispensed with under the circumstances. Finally, the John Deere Company supplied six-wheeled utility vehicles to the rescue effort.[27]

In addition to taking passengers off Manhattan Island, many of the boats carried doctors and other emergency personnel to the disaster site. A staging area was set up in Liberty Park in Jersey City, just across the Hudson from the World Trade Center. A triage center, an emergency medical treatment station, was set up there, and many boats shuttled back and forth across the Hudson. A number of firefighters were transported there for rest or emergency medical treatment.

Supplies were brought to the World Trade Center site in large quantities as the workers tried to sift through the wreckage to find possible survivors. These supplies were brought in mostly by boat. Food supplies were in great demand. The workers had to be fed and boats were asked to ferry victuals of many kinds along with the other needed equipment, such as gloves for emergency workers. Companies and organizations donated so much that authorities were all but overwhelmed. They had to ask, reluctantly, for some organizations to hold off.

Three days after the attacks on the World Trade Center, a person standing on the New Jersey shore opposite downtown Manhattan would have seen the navy hospital ship U.S.S. *Comfort* outlined against the buildings of the financial district.[28] It was moored there to render assistance to the emergency workers. The ship, which was docked near Ground Zero, as the site was called, functioned as a rest center. It provided meals, emergency medical care and even had chaplains aboard who said Mass, blessed the firefighters ("They asked for it"), and provided a listening ear for those emergency workers who needed supportive attention. A hospital corpsman described his experience treating two policemen. One, he said, suffered from dehydration and the other had a knee injury. They were crying from the stress of their experiences. They had suffered the loss of two other policemen from their unit. At last they broke down completely.

AFTER THE ATTACKS

In another incident, a man cried when he recognized that the Twin Towers were gone, no longer standing tall and proud where they once had been. He was a dock builder who was used to lining up the pilings with tall buildings to be sure the pilings were perpendicular. In his dock-building work on the New Jersey side of the Hudson, he unconsciously tried to line up his piling with the World Trade Center off in the distance. Then he felt a twinge of sadness when he realized the twin towers were no longer there. [29]

The harbor experienced a decrease in shipping operations after September 11. The harbor was closed entirely for several days after the incident. Then commercial ships were allowed to enter after being carefully inspected. It was a long time before recreational vessels were allowed into the harbor. The cruise ships that had seen a flourishing of their operations in the several years prior to 9/11, were hit hard by the disaster. People just stopped going on cruises. Added to that situation, the Coast Guard prohibited cruise ships from coming into the harbor, a prohibition that for a long time has been lifted. The New York City pier that served as one of their landing places in Manhattan on the West Side was turned into a supply depot for the World Trade Center emergency but has since returned to its original use.

The North Cove Marina figured prominently in the World Trade Center disaster. Being near the lower tip of Manhattan, it is close to the World Trade Center site. It was an important departure point for many evacuees who boarded boats at the marina. Also, it provided a docking space for boats that assisted directly in the emergency operations by bringing supplies or by serving as rest stops for the volunteer workers and emergency crews.

As pointed out a number of times, New York Harbor consists of islands for the most part. That fact has importance for the development of the harbor and the directions the changes take. It had particular importance in the reaction of the harbor people to the World Trade Center calamity. There were many thousands of people who had to get off Manhattan Island, and the way many of them had to do it was by boat. It has been estimated that 1 million people were evacuated from Manhattan by boat, all of the boats volunteering their services. The boatmen did what they felt was the natural thing to do, to help out. The evacuees appreciated being transported at their time of need.

There is no telling how much the World Trade Center disaster will affect New York Harbor. It is clear that it will have a deep and lasting impact on the port, as it will on the whole country and the world. The Coast Guard has been severely affected, if only because it is concerned with the security of the harbor. The transportation patterns in and around the City of New York have been affected, and that in turn affects the harbor. The ferries benefited when the PATH train line that went to the World Trade Center was out of operation. (The station now has

The twin towers of the World Trade Center stand tall and proud before they were destroyed on September 11, 2001. A memorial is being planned for the site.

A small Coast Guard vessel patrols the East River as part of the port security which was increased after the September 11th attacks.

been restored and is operating.) The ferries took up the slack. The managers of ferry operations have increased the number of boats in operation. They also increased the number of ferry terminals and construction is underway to improve and expand the ones that already exist. Some people believe that the ferries are on the verge of an unprecedented expansion. Already, one sees the dominant presence of the ferries in the harbor, especially after the 9/11 attacks.

AGAIN, RESIDENTS WANT ACCESS TO THE WATER

Some organizations are reacting to the disaster in terms of what occurred during the emergency. Battery Park City residents took note of the difficulties some evacuees had in getting to the boats.[30] Fences and railings on the esplanades had to be cut in order to gain access to the water, and the seawall was damaged by the boats taking off the evacuees. The thinking is that they want to *use* the water, not just to be near it, and to see it. Presently, there are federal restrictions to building out from the seawall at the Battery. Some of the residents want marinas and docks so they can get access to the water. The Port Authority of New York and New Jersey and New York Waterway obtained federal approval to build a ferry terminal near North Cove Marina, in the area of the former World Trade Center. Local residents see that approval as a precedent. They have hopes of other construction in the area which would give them more ability to use the waterfront.

Reaction to the Tragedy

New York Harbor was severely shaken by this tragedy. The people of the U.S. thought it could never happen here, so the attacks caused the people to stop and think. A barrage of protective mechanisms were put into effect to defend the United States against the recurrence of such an onslaught. The harbor was considered to be especially vulnerable. A great many of those protective mechanisms affected the harbor. A ship could sail into the harbor loaded with explosives; a container could be shipped holding a nuclear bomb. A CNN television program on terrorist activity explored, among other things, this very possibility.[31] U.S. authorities are inspecting the containers in overseas ports as well. These inspections of containers, before they arrive here, are possible because the containers are sealed upon being looked at. The problem, it seems, is that they cannot look at every container. They have to do it on a sampling basis. Some people think that is not enough.

As far as the harbor is concerned, a good deal of the responsibility to protect the populace from terrorist attacks was placed in the hands of the U. S. Coast Guard. (See section on U.S. Coast Guard.) One good that came out of the attacks on the World Trade Center was that the disaster brought out the innate qualities of beneficence and charity of the local people. The response of the boats in the harbor is an example. They were magnificent in the way they transported thousands of persons off Manhattan. The boats helped out in the emergency in many other ways.

The tight security that now grips New York Harbor will probably go on for a while. Eventually, it may be relaxed. One thing is sure: The harbor will never be the same.

5

Conclusions: A History and Future of Constant Change

Change Comes to New York Harbor

REACTION TO CHANGE IN THE HARBOR

Change has always been a characteristic of New York Harbor. Shipping activity has decreased in the New York City parts of the harbor. Other changes have taken place, as described previously in this book. All of this change happened without fanfare and acclaim. It just happened, without anyone paying special notice. Maybe the populace should have been incensed that it was happening. Maybe the press should have been aware it was going on. It was, to a certain extent. It was aware that there were changes taking place in the harbor. But there was no overall reaction. No screaming with rage over the inevitable trend of events. No wringing of hands. Perhaps it was the inevitability of it all that made everyone in New York City accept it. Probably, it was the gradual nature of the change that made everyone adjust to it as it happened. People in responsible positions who are knowledgeable about the harbor seem to accept the status quo in respect to the decrease in shipping activity and other changes It is as if they are saying, "This is the way it always was. This is how the harbor is."

SOCIOLOGICAL CHANGES

Since the 1950s, the changes in New York Harbor have coincided with several sociological changes that the culture surrounding the port has experienced. One change is growing community involvement in matters affecting the collective welfare. Another social development has been the decrease in commercial shipping activity in the New York City parts of the harbor. Thirdly, there has been economic growth overall. In short, the United Sates has become a relatively wealthy country. Another change in U.S. culture is the growing concern about the environment. These changes in the way of mass thinking of the population have had a decided effect on developments in New York Harbor.

COMMUNITY INVOLVEMENT

A whole new collective consciousness has developed, broadly defined as a consciousness of the environment. But it becomes more specific than that. It consists of concern about the things that are going on around us, the proposals for development, the political issues. "How is it going to affect me?" has become the basic interest. Prompted by the expansion in media communication, the public has become more aware of what is transpiring. A case in point is the proposal for Westway, the highway and parks development for the Upper West Side of Manhattan, initially proposed in 1974. Community groups opposed Westway because they feared such development would negatively affect their neighborhoods. (Among other issues, community groups were concerned that the waterfront land would ultimately be developed commercially.) Westway became a national issue because part of the funding would have been provided by Congress. The newspapers got involved; each successive governor of New York State was involved; environmental groups got involved. Westway remained mired in controversy until 1985, when the project fell apart after the Federal Funding that would have paid for most of the work was withdrawn. There are other examples, more positive, perhaps—the community groups that made some improvements in the Gowanus Canal, for example. Community groups have served as watchdogs over such organizations as the Corps of Engineers and the Port Authority in relation to the disposal of dredged spoil, especially contaminated material.

IMPORTANCE OF THE ECONOMIC CLIMATE

U.S. economic health has been strong overall from the beginning. There have been recessions, to be sure, and the depression of the 1930s really set the country back. However, the trend has been favorable, and when times are good there is money available for new planning and construction. With the recent recession of the economy, there is not so much money available for waterfront projects. In spite of this presumably temporary setback, impetus has continued to develop the waterfront of New York Harbor so that the general public can use it. This impetus applies to the New Jersey parts of the harbor as well as to New York City. The thinking now is that there should be at least a balance of interests involved. The granting in 2000 of Brooklyn waterfront property to the city to become a park by the Port Authority of New York and New Jersey illustrates this point.[1] Grants have been available for community groups from various governmental bodies to pursue worthwhile ventures, and cleaning up the environment has certainly been considered worthwhile.[2]

The growing concern about the environment in the past few decades has

resulted in a spate of legislation. Two pieces of legislation that had special implications for New York Harbor are the Clean Water Act of 1980 and the Oil Pollution Act of 1988. These two pieces of legislation resulted in a significant
improvement in the condition of the waters of the harbor.

REVITALIZATION OF THE WATERFRONT

Many communities in New Jersey that border on New York Harbor, such as
Hoboken and Jersey City, have done a great deal to revitalize the waterfront. Jersey City has reclaimed the land formerly occupied by the Jersey Central Railroad,
a large switching yard that was key to much cargo activity in the harbor. The area,
consisting of 156 acres, is now Liberty State Park.[3] The Science Museum is part
of that facility. The waterfront areas are available to the general public for walking, jogging, and fishing and contain a boat-launching ramp. Hoboken has
revamped its waterfront area as well. The former ferry terminal has been restored
and the town officials have provided access to the water for the public at large.
Access to the waterfront has become important in current thinking about the land
bordering the water.

PLANNING FOR THE WATERFRONT

Where land meets the water — the waterfront — is as much a part of New York
Harbor as the waterways themselves. The heliports on the east and west sides of Manhattan, the marinas around the harbor, the parks on the waterfront, and the tramway
to Roosevelt Island are included in the vista that makes up the harbor. Some of the
changes that have taken place on the waterfront are a result of the spurt in community interest, many of them made possible by the burgeoning economy that expanded
until 2001. In fact, economic issues have had an especially large effect on developments around the waterfront. In lean years, the rate of progress is relatively slow.
In good times, things happen fast. The real estate sector has continued to be strong
in spite of the recession that is now being experienced. The development of the New
Jersey side of the Hudson River is an example. Municipalities such as Jersey City,
Hoboken and Weehawken have experienced great change during the past few years.
At the same time, the decline of industry on the New York City waterfront has caused
areas such as Newtown Creek in Queens, a scene of decaying docks and empty,
weed-covered lots, to become increasingly derelict. This result has been so widespread on the waterfront that in 1999 New York City made a review of all the waterfront properties in the city and came up with recommendations for development.[4]
Industry is still reluctant to invest in waterfront property in those few areas zoned
for shipping development. The New York City Department of Planning has zoned
most of the city waterfront for recreational or community use.

A great deal has changed in New York Harbor. Perhaps the greatest change
has been in the attitudes of the local inhabitants toward use of the waterfront.

Reasons for Change in the Harbor

A Continuing Process

New York Harbor, like everything in this world, has gone through a process of change, and it will change in the future. It has changed drastically from the 1940s and 1950s, when it was still arguably the greatest shipping center on Earth. Until that time the port was a bustling cauldron of activity. The rivers and bays were filled with boats and ships going hither and yon. It has been a main purpose of this narrative to explore why the changes took place.

Airplanes took over from the great transatlantic ships that once carried passengers in grand style to and from ports in Europe. Gradually, the ships left the West Side piers that berthed them, the *United States*, *Île de France*, *Queen Mary;* and, going farther back, the *Lusitania* and *Mauritania*. On the New Jersey side of the river, North German Lloyd, Dollar Line, and Holland America Line once berthed their ships, but not anymore. The *Queen Elizabeth II* still makes an occasional trip across the Atlantic, but almost everyone traveling to or from Europe flies nowadays. The great steamships that were welcomed with a fireboat streaming plumes of water and tugboats swarming around to render docking assistance are no more. The pictures of large oceangoing vessels berthed at the Chelsea Piers are relics of the past.

Containerization as a shipping and cargo-handling technique came into its own in the 1960s and brought with it the great shift in activity from the New York City parts of the harbor to the New Jersey terminals, mostly Port Newark and Elizabeth. Now the large container ships go into the Kill Van Kull, under the Bayonne Bridge, and turn to starboard into Newark Bay. Some of them continue through the Kill Van Kull to the Howland Hook Terminal on Staten Island. There are far fewer ships than previously going into the East River and Hudson River.

Technological Change

Technological advances are upon us. Shoreside changes have been made. There are a number of improvements in handling cargo, such as the large cranes that load and unload the containers on and off the ships. These cranes have been specially designed to deal with containers. Being very tall, they are easily seen lined up along the docks at containerports. Such cranes identify the port as a depot handling containers as opposed to breakbulk cargo-handling (an old-fashioned process of handling cargo piece by piece). In addition, the large forklift trucks that lift the containers in the terminals ("yard jockeys" as Howland Hook Terminal director Brad Winfree calls them) make easy the handling of containers that would have been impossible years ago.

Societies do not always accept the changes that new inventions thrust upon them. In fact, as history shows, they resist change for the most part. There are many examples. Going back a ways, the British maritime interests failed to implement as a regulation the drinking of lime juice by the sailors for about 100 years, even though they were sure it would prevent scurvy. John Ericsson surely lamented the slow adoption of the screw propeller to power the ships of his time. Shipowners were content to stay with paddle wheels—they were more comfortable that way. Nowadays, nuclear power plants are receiving similar resistance in the United States. Nuclear power is much more popular in Europe, whereas the United States is abandoning several of the plants. Timing is important. The population has to be ready to accept the new technology. This point was brought out by Frank T. Kryza in *The Power of Light*, his 2003 book about solar energy.[5]

The population seems to be more accepting of technological change that affects New York Harbor. Cruise ships are being built with bow thrusters and turnable propulsion systems at the stern (which affects docking tugboats). The Port Authority is pressing for the development of new dredging techniques, although no radically new techniques had come up by 2002.[6] Maybe that says something in itself.

In the present day, some of the ships that go into the Kill Van Kull for New Jersey or Howland Hook destinations are unloaded in 24 hours. It used to take a week or more for the many stevedores to go on board to unload the cargo piece by piece. Unloading ships and getting the cargo out to where it will ultimately be used is more efficient than it used to be, but it is far from a perfect system, even now. As discussed in the chapter on the Port Authority, many problems of infrastructure having to do with shore transportation remain to be solved.

Innovations Bring Social Change

The building of tunnels and bridges across the East River and the Hudson River changed the face of New York Harbor. This development eliminated the need for the ferries that criss-crossed the rivers around the harbor. The only ferry that is designed to carry cars, although it does not nowadays, is the Staten Island ferry, which has run for many years from Whitehall in downtown Manhattan to St. George on Staten Island. It is used mostly by Staten Island commuters, but to a certain extent by tourists and sightseers as well.

Construction of roads, which occurred in great part during the Eisenhower administration in the 1950s, had a great deal to do with the demise of tugboats in New York Harbor. Much of the cargo that had been carried on barges and scows (sand, gravel, traprock, coal) was picked up by the trucking industry, which grew by leaps and bounds after the road network was built.

The development of pipelines to carry the oil that had previously been transported on oil barges lessened the need for tugboats in the harbor. New York Harbor is still the major port for petroleum products, but much of it is transported on tanker ships. The tugs still take the oil barges from the terminals on Staten

Island up the Hudson River, and they still go out Long Island Sound to Connecticut ports occasionally.

RAILROADS FADE IN INFLUENCE

The railroads had a strong presence in New York Harbor in years gone by. The New Jersey banks of the Hudson River were sprinkled with railroad activity. Via the yards at Jersey City, the Erie Lackawanna, the New York Central and the Pennsylvania Railroad were just a few of the many railroads that played a central role in the shipping here. The railroads used tugs, lighters and covered barges. They had many tugs, most of them with strong propulsion systems. The tugs towed the railroad floats back and forth to terminals in Brooklyn and the Bronx. The railroads also operated a number of ferries that took commuters and vehicles back and forth across the East River and the Hudson River. As the harbor changed, the railroads could not compete with the trucking industry, which was aided by the improved road system. The railroad ferries succumbed to the building of the bridges and tunnels and the increase of automobile and bus traffic via these routes.

LARGER SHIPS

Another change for the harbor is that the ships entering it are getting larger. These larger ships not only require the dredging of the channels to new depths, but the bridges are becoming more and more of a problem as the ships get higher above the waterline. When the *Regina Maersk*, a new containership, came into New York Harbor, it was close to the bottom of the channel.[7] It is 1,043 feet long, a veritable behemoth of a ship that is capable of carrying 4,500 to 5,000 containers. It barely fit under the bridges when it came into the harbor. It was purposely only partly loaded to decrease its draft because the channel was not deep enough. The superstructure of the vessel was higher out of the water. The height of the bridges continues as a potential problem. When the tanker *Brooklyn* was constructed in the Brooklyn Navy Yard, some of the superstructure was left off to get it under the Brooklyn Bridge.

The increase in size of the ships means fewer ships have been coming into the harbor, which means in turn fewer tugs overall are required to help them in docking. Firms such as Moran and McAllister have felt the difference, although they have enough diversified activity in other harbors to keep them busy. The Sandy Hook Pilots are also affected by the fewer number of vessels coming into the port. The number of pilots has decreased considerably over the years.

U. S. NAVY IN NEW YORK HARBOR

The U.S. Navy's pulling out of New York Harbor had some effect on the overall level of activity here, especially their leaving the Brooklyn Navy Yard, which happened in 1966. The Brooklyn Navy Yard used to be located off the East River, just north of the Brooklyn Bridge. There is an indentation in the shoreline there called Wallabout Bay, and the Brooklyn Navy Yard was located on that indentation. Many noted vessels were built there, among them the *Maine* of Spanish-American War fame and the battleship *Missouri*. Many navy vessels came in there for maintenance work, as well. It was especially busy during World War II. A great number of persons were employed there during that period.

The closing of the Stapleton base on Staten Island, which was used only for a relatively short while, had a lesser effect on the harbor overall. The Staten Island neighbors were against the shoreline facilities being used for a naval base, and New York City mayor David Dinkins and his administration were wary of the nuclear weapons possibly carried aboard the navy vessels which would come into the port. Since the navy had a policy of not declaring whether nuclear weapons were aboard any of its vessels, the siting of the base in New York Harbor was very much in dispute. The navy left without fanfare. It still maintains a base at Earle, New Jersey, on the Lower Bay, used for stocking navy ships with ammunition.

CORPS OF ENGINEERS

The U.S. Army Corps of Engineers has a great deal of impact on what goes on in the harbor and will likely continue to do so for the foreseeable future. Federal legislation gives the corps control over the dredging in the harbor, and that dredging is crucial to the role of the port in the international shipping picture. The corps is under fire at present, mostly because many officials think it has a narrow-minded perception of their mission: to build dams or accomplish dredging with no thought toward preserving the environment.

RELATIVELY QUIET HARBOR

The decrease in support activity for the shipping interests, shipyards and shipbuilding, has resulted in the harbor's becoming a relatively quiet place at present. In the history of New York Harbor, there were shipyards galore to support the shipping industry. In the latter half of the 1800s and the early 1900s, the Lower East Side of Manhattan was the site of sailmakers, ship chandlers, and provisioners that supported the ships that came into port. In recent history, the Todd Shipyard in Hoboken serviced many large ships. It closed down in 1967. The tourist-oriented South Street Seaport is the only remaining vestige of these enterprises. It has a sincere interest in preserving the heritage of New York Harbor.

Finally, New York Harbor does not exist alone as a port in the United States. There are other ports as well, and some of them are progressing very well as shipping centers. The port of Los Angeles/Long Beach in California has more shipping activity than New York Harbor. Also, in Washington, the port of Seattle/ Tacoma is very active. On the East Coast, Charleston Harbor in South Carolina and Baltimore, Maryland, have been very busy. In Nova Scotia, the port of Halifax gives New York a great deal of competition. Competition from other ports plays a part in the changing fate of New York Harbor. Other ports have been very aggressive during the past few years in pushing for development of their harbors. They have been competing for federal dollars, and they have been getting attention. The federal government has been supporting the growth of other ports in the country as well as the port of New York.

In the overall scheme of things, New York Harbor is no longer the biggest port in the United States in volume of shipping. Nevertheless, the harbor needs to plan for continued growth, in the container operations especially, and most of that burden will fall upon the Port Authority of New York and New Jersey.

The Future of New York Harbor

GROWTH OF THE PORT

New York Harbor is still one of the great ports of the world, and it will continue to be a very important harbor for the economy of the United States. The overall predictions are for continued growth in the shipping business for New York Harbor, but they will be in the New Jersey portions of the harbor for the most part. One reason why New York Harbor will be busy (on a concentrated basis, that is — the pattern has changed), is that the region around it constitutes one of the greatest market areas of the world. The Northeast has a vast population. Much of it is clustered in Connecticut, New York and New Jersey. When Long Island is included in the mix it makes a consolidated market area that uses large numbers of appliances, food and a whole host of other commodities in everyday living. A great deal of these items are imported through New York Harbor.

The optimistic predictions of growth for New York Harbor come down to one concept: globalization.[8] Globalization means the world is getting smaller. It means that new technology in communications and transportation has caused an integration of the economies of the world. What happens in the economy of one nation affects other economies. Nations are trading with each other at an increasing rate as trade restrictions are being lowered. There are divided opinions as to whether globalization is advantageous to the United States, as the demonstrations against the World Trade Organization in Seattle in 2001, and later demonstrations, showed. Yet there is a certain inevitability about globalization. As long as technological advances continue to be made and the cultures of the world continue to embrace the capitalist system, international trade will continue to grow. The ports of the United States will continue to develop, including the port of New York.

NEED TO INCREASE SHIPPING IN THE
NEW YORK CITY PARTS OF THE HARBOR

Most of the recent growth of shipping in New York Harbor has taken place in New Jersey, and will continue to do so. However, the growth of the Brooklyn shipping operations should be considered as well. It is said that a large percentage of the cargoes that are shipped via New York Harbor are used locally. Many of those items are consumed in New York City and Long Island. That is why it is very viable for New York City to cling to the expansion of the Brooklyn shipping installations. The Corps of Engineers has found recently that it is not feasible to deepen the channels to 50 feet in the Red Hook area.[9] So the city and the Port Authority will have to continue to service medium-sized ships in Brooklyn as they have done in the past. Captain Sherwood of the Sandy Hook Pilots says they should increase the amount of automobile imports going to Brooklyn. The ships that bring autos from overseas are of shallower draft and the channels in Brooklyn waters will accommodate them. [10]

Another step that can be taken to increase the amount of shipping passing through the Brooklyn part of the seaport is to increase the car float activity of the Cross Harbor Railroad. At the present time the Cross Harbor Railroad is transporting about one car float per day from Brooklyn to the Greenville Yards in Jersey City. There, the railroad cars are linked up with the railroad to the West and other regions. Most cargo coming into the Brooklyn part of the harbor, unfortunately, has to be carried away by truck transport. The problem is that the trucks that take the containers and breakbulk cargo have to negotiate the traffic of New York City streets, and contribute to pollution problems that go with such traffic. Part of the solution is to increase the amount of railroad transport. A railroad car holds as much cargo as 15 trucks, and there are 18 railroad cars on one car float, as pointed out by the *Gotham Gazette*.[11] The solution of the *Gotham Gazette*: Increase the number of car floats towed from the Brooklyn terminals to the Greenville Yards in Jersey City. Along the same line of thinking, New York City officials have been enthused about the idea of a tunnel linking the Brooklyn piers with either Staten Island or New Jersey. This idea is tempered somewhat by the current economic restrictions on spending. However, Congressman Jerrold Nadler has espoused the idea on a number of occasions.[12] In fact, he gets most of the credit for pushing the plan for the tunnel. The idea of a railroad freight tunnel beneath the waters of the bay would provide a way of shipping the cargoes that come into the port of New York to the mainland by rail instead of by truck, with all its associated advantages. The problem is that the tunnel would be expensive to build, about $2.6 billion. Also, some people contend that the resources available should be put into the New Jersey container operations where there is more potential for growth. The tunnel idea is gaining more support.[13]

Congressman Nadler has long been a champion of Brooklyn's waterfront.

He suggested that the Erie Basin and Red Hook operations be expanded considerably.[14] In an op-ed piece appearing in the *New York Times* in 1996, he (naturally) favored building up Brooklyn's shipping operations, pointing out the many benefits New York Harbor would accrue. One of the items he mentioned was deepening the Brooklyn port to 50 feet, which apparently did not happen.

TRANSPORTATION ACCESS BY NEW YORK CITY TO THE MAINLAND OF NEW JERSEY

To increase shipping activity in Brooklyn, there is a need to improve transportation access from Brooklyn to New Jersey. A train tunnel to New Jersey and putting car floats and tugs in operation to transport rail cars to and from New Jersey would help to achieve this objective. New York City is composed of islands, and New Jersey is part of the mainland United States. Even the Bronx is cut off to a certain extent by being sandwiched between the Hudson River and the East River. The Port Authority operations in Brooklyn need to be expanded, and it should be done soon. Time and money is being spent on diversionary projects. The Corps of Engineers has a project underway to improve the Gowanus Canal, which is a good objective in its own right, but priority must be given to rebuilding the shipping capacity of the New York City portions of the port. The development of the New Jersey operations is getting a great deal of attention, and that is all well and good. However, attention should be paid to building back the New York City part of the port shipping operations as well.

NEW JERSEY SHIPPING OPERATIONS

The New Jersey container operations are not without their problems. Truck traffic is a continual challenge for the Port Authority. It is confronting those problems head on. The Port Authority realizes that trucks are vital to transporting the containers to their final destination after they are unloaded from the ships. One solution they are trying is to spread the truck traffic over a 24-hour period instead of the present manner of operating which is mainly from 9 a.m. to 5 p.m.

Another problem is the consensus that the New Jersey Turnpike is saturated at peak times with truck traffic, or shortly will be.

These problems led the Port Authority to promote the increase of rail traffic from the container ports. The Port Authority is quite proud of the increases in railroad shipments from the New Jersey piers. Still, it is only a small percentage of the total.

The idea of a port inland distribution network is a further attempt to improve the infrastructure.[15] This plan involves setting up regional terminals, such as at Albany, New York, and Bridgeport, Connecticut. Containers would be barged on connecting waterways to such regional ports, thus relieving the congestion on the roads. It remains to be seen how this plan will work over the long run. If the regional terminals prove viable, there will be an increase in harbor traffic, probably not drastically, but more tows would be visible on the rivers.

NONCOMMERCIAL LOOK IN MOST OF THE HARBOR

Significant changes have taken place in the harbor with the decrease in harbor activity, particularly in the New York City parts of the harbor. Great strides have been made in cleaning up the pollution that characterized the harbor in days gone by. For centuries, the waterfront was thought of as a dirty, rat-infested place. The public attitude has changed. People no longer take for granted that the waterfront is dirty. The decline of shipping activity in the harbor has had a coincidental effect by allowing for the reshaping of the waterfront: As industry and shipping interests moved out, more public uses of the waterfront properties followed. At the present time, long stretches of the land bordering the rivers and bays, both in New York City and New Jersey, consist of seawalls, esplanades and parks. Going up the East River toward the north, one encounters finger piers on the Manhattan side below the Brooklyn Bridge. Farther up, one sees an apartment development and park at Corlears Hook. There is a power plant farther still, but then there is a seawall with an esplanade and park clear up to Mill Rock and the approach to Hell Gate. There is no place to land a boat, but the tidal currents flow very strongly there anyway. Almost the entire length of Manhattan on the East River side, except for a few piers on the Lower East Side, is noncommercial.

The same is true for large portions of the Brooklyn waterfront. In the Gravesend Bay area, the Belt Parkway goes along the shoreline. There is a seawall, esplanade, and public park area all the way to the Verrazano Bridge. Only beyond the bridge, toward Manhattan, does one see commercial installations such as the Brooklyn Army Terminal and the Red Hook and Erie Basin terminals.

New York Harbor is definitely not made up of wall-to-wall commercial shipping establishments. There is a large part of the harbor that is noncommercial, that is, not related to shipping, and the city and New Jersey communities seem to accept it that way. They seem to have accepted the loss of revenue from shipping activities. There is a school of thought that condominium development, restaurants, sports centers, even parks, have an upgrading effect that counters the loss in revenue for the city by the decrease in shipping-company and related taxpayers.

Communities seem determined to preserve the environment and give the public access to the waterfront. That is what the voters seem to want, and the administrations are influenced by such tendencies. It appears that the trend in non-shipping development of the harbor will continue. What commercial development there will be, will be very selective. Only very specific areas will be further developed commercially for shipping: in Brooklyn the Red Hook Terminal

Area, in Kill Van Kull the Howland Hook Terminal and the petroleum refineries, the Newark Bay area, Bayonne, Jersey City, Hoboken, Weehawken, and isolated piers on the West Side of Manhattan. These areas represent most of the commercial development related to shipping in New York Harbor. The remainder of the harbor is devoted to non-shipping installations for the most part.

Much emphasis is being placed on improving the condition of the harbor. The Environmental Protection Administration, specifically the New York–New Jersey Harbor Estuary Program is focusing on educational and restoration programs. Contaminants and storm water runoff are still a problem, but progress is being made in cleaning up the harbor. Agencies associated with the harbor are optimistic about the environmental improvements that are being made in the waters of the port. The expectation is that in the future improvements will continue to be made. The public consciousness has changed. The public will demand a clean harbor.

CHANGES IN THE FUTURE

Will we see more boats in the harbor in the future? There will be an increase in ferries zipping about, across the Hudson and East Rivers, out the East River to Flushing Bay or to Shea Stadium, from Manhattan out the Upper and Lower Bays to Atlantic Highlands. Fares may be brought lower as more and more people take to the water to get where they want to go and competition takes place between the ferry companies. The ferry companies and the city officials are determined to increase the use of ferries as a transportation mechanism around the harbor, which makes sense since the urban area consists primarily of islands.

These ferries will not be the traditional double-ended boats of years gone by. The days of steam and walking beams on the top deck are long past. Now, the boats are fast, many of them catamaran-hulled, with the helmsman seated in a cushioned, protective seat. These ferries do not carry vehicles, just passengers. The exception is the Staten Island ferries, which are designed along traditional lines, although they have modern diesel-based propulsion systems and all the latest electronic gear on board. Although they are designed to carry vehicles, since the World Trade Center attacks in 2001 security measures prevent them from transporting automobiles and trucks.

More technological changes will undoubtedly be upon us. In 1987, author Ernst Frankel predicted, among other things, that warehouses would be computerized, that there would be a continuous flow from ships to land transport.[16] That mode of shipping exists today with the advent of containers; they are lifted off the ships and onto waiting trucks for transport to their local destination. In some cases, the containers are lifted onto the docks to await the shore-based transportation (but not into warehouses). Frankel also predicted advances in ship docking. In approaching a pier, ships would be controlled by laser-powered distance devices, and line-handling will be done automatically. It is likely that ships will be able to dock themselves in the future, with the bow thrusters and rotatable propellers that are already coming into use (some cruise ships have them). That development does not bode well for the tug companies. However, there will be compensating factors. The Port Authority's proposed Inland Distribution Network might prove to be feasible. If that system works out positively, there will be more business for the towing companies. On the other hand, pilots will still be needed to guide the ships into the harbor, but the tugs will be involved in docking to a lesser extent.

The waterfront will change a great deal in the future. It has changed a lot in the past 50 years. The public is demanding greater access to the waterways, and it will come about if only because industry and shipping interests have pulled out. Community groups are gaining more voice than ever before, and through the political machinations they will continue to have influence. They will likely continue to press for the development of such waterways as the Gowanus Canal and Newtown Creek. By *development* they mean cleaning up the pollution in the waters, and shoreline construction of restaurants, marinas, shopping malls, parks and other similar facilities. Old, decrepit piers and warehouses will be replaced with new piers and new buildings. The property on the waterfront is still valuable. It should be used. It is strange that so much of it is unused at the present. The New York City Comprehensive Waterfront Development Plan recognizes the need to utilize the waterfront properties and has a number of development ideas. The planning places emphasis on non-shipping development, which is understandable given the long-range trends in decrease in shipping in the New York City parts of the harbor relative to New Jersey.

THE HARBOR IN THE WAR ON TERRORISM

After the World Trade Center attacks in 2001, the war on terrorism is fully upon New York Harbor. Security is tight in the harbor and will remain so in the foreseeable future. The role of the Coast Guard and the Armed Forces is very important in this regard. The probabilities are high that techniques for dealing with the terrorist tactics that affect the harbor will be developed. The U.S. economic system encourages new developments. For example, improved techniques for inspecting containers will be devised. They have to be. Also, arrangements for inspecting containers at the port of origin will be put in place more frequently than they are now. Some port officials think that is the way to go.[17]

THE GREATEST HARBOR

And so, the harbor changes as the culture surrounding it changes. New technology has its effect. So do the attitudes of the public. People take present conditions for granted. Many people think only occasionally of past years and times gone by. On the other hand, some people live with the nostalgia of the past. Regarding maritime affairs, there are a number of organizations that dwell on the past and keep alive the memory of the glories of bygone days. The National Maritime Historical Society (NMHS) is one. The NMHS has done a great deal to publicize marine history, and has aided in the restoration of many venerable ships. There are organizations which keep track of old tugboats. There is the Wooden Boat Association for old boat enthusiasts. Railroad buffs have organizations for them to join. The remembrance of recollections from the past gives perspective on views of the present state of things—and maybe of the future as well.

It is possible to be critical of the people who think the harbor was always the way it is now. Maybe they should have more historical perspective on how it got that way. This does not mean there is anything necessarily wrong with the way the harbor is at present; it reached its present state due to a lot of understandable reasons.

The persons who work in the harbor, the ferry crews, the mates on the tugboats, the officers on the ships visiting the harbor, the crews on the police boat, for the most part love their jobs. When a tow comes through the Narrows and the crew gets their first sight of the Manhattan skyline they must have a rush of adrenaline through their veins. As they approach the Battery, they can make out the individual buildings. They can see the Whitehall Building, old and traditional; they can see the World Financial Building, new and contemporary. All stand erect and proud, nestled one against the other, in all their magnificent glory. The crew does not say anything to one another; it would be taboo to mention the awe they feel, but inside they say to themselves this has got to be the greatest harbor in the whole world.

It *is* the greatest harbor.

Chapter Notes

Chapter 1

1. "Waterfront," *Gothamgazette.com*, 5 Dec. 2004, http//www.gothamgazette.com/waterfront/apr.01.shtml.

2. Port Authority of New York and New Jersey, *Portviews*, January 2002, Vol. 1, No. 2, p. 4.

3. Port Authority of New York and New Jersey, *Building a 21st Century Port*, October 2002, p. iv.

4. R. H. Westover, Chairman and CEO, SS United States Foundation, in a personal communication to the author, assured that the SS United States visited New York Harbor during the 1960s. He said, in fact, that New York was the home port of the ship. He commented that she still has "New York" painted on her stern. (His middle name is Hudson, appropriately enough, as pointed out by Peter Van Allen, an officer of the organization). November 2002.

5. Paul Lukas, "On Wings of Commerce," *Fortune*, 22 Mar. 2004, p. 109.

6. "For 2 ships: Goodbye, New York. Hello, Bayonne," *New York Times*, 4 Jan. 2004, Travel Sect., p. 3.

7. Kevin Bone, ed., *The New York Waterfront: Evolution and Building Culture of the Port and Harbor*, The Monacelli Press, New York, 1997, p. 39.

8. Museum of the City of New York, Research Department, Shipping, Piers and Docks file, Notes. No date.

9. Buttenwieser, Ann L., *Manhattan Waterbound*, New York University Press, New York, 1987, p. 214.

10. Joseph P. Fried, "A Nineteenth Century Pier, A 21st-Century Vision," *The New York Times*, 13 June 2004, Metro Sec., p. 48.

11. "Dropping the Hook New York Style," *Ocean Navigator*, No. 88, March/April 1998.

12. New York City Parks Department, *Improvement of Great Kills Harbor*, 1937.

13. David M. Herszenhorn, "New Jersey, Proud Owner, To Raise Flag On Ellis Island," *The New York Times*, 4 July 1998, Sec. B, p. 2.

14. Joseph J. Seebode and Thomas J. Shea, III, "Synergy in Port Development and Environmental Protection Within the New York/New Jersey Harbor Estuary," Paper presented at the Third Specialty Conference on Dredging and Dredged Material Disposal, May 5–8, 2002, Orlando, Florida.

15. Port Authority of New York and New Jersey, Press Release: "Port Authority Receives Approval to Begin $1.8 Billion Program to Deepen NY-NJ Port Channels to 50 Feet," 3 Dec. 2004, http://www.panynj.gov/pr/pressrelease.php3?id=244.

16. Revkin, Andrew C., "In Harbor, a Vanishing Era," *The New York Times*, 3 Jan. 1999, Metro Sec. p. 23f.

17. Meeting with Joseph Seebode, Corps of Engineers, July 23, 2002.

18. Meeting with Brad Winfree of the Howland Hook Terminal on December 14, 2004.

19. Kirk Johnson, "Dumping Ends at Great Kills, Symbol of Throw-Away Era," *The New York Times*, 18 Mar. 2001, p. 1f.

20. John Waldman, *Heartbeats in the Muck*, The Lyons Press, New York, 1999, p. 20.

21. Andrea Kannapell, "On the Waterfront; Developers' Glittering Dreams Are Alive Again Along the Hudson," *The New York Times*, 15 Feb. 1998.

22. Steve Chambers, "Gold Coast Hits Pay Dirt," *The Star-Ledger* (Newark, N.J.), 30 Aug. 2004, p. 11.

23. Susan Warner, "Lots of Work West of the Hudson," *The New York Times*, 26 Jan. 2003, Sec. 14, p. 1.

24. Barry Estabrook, "For 2 Ships, Goodbye New York. Hello Bayonne," *The New York Times*, 4 Jan. 2004, Travel Sec., p. 3.

25. Albion, Robert Greenhalgh, *The Rise of the New York Port*, Charles Scribner and Sons, New York, 1970, p. 13.

26. *Ibid.*, pp. 95–121.

27. "Governor's Island," *Columbia Encyclopedia,* 6th ed. Columbia University Press, New York, 2001.

28. John Coppola, "Fulton Ferry and the Brooklyn Navy Yard," 3 Dec. 2004, http://www.myc.org/Harbor%20Tour/History/Fulton_Ferry_Navy_Yard.htm.

29. New York Naval Shipyard, 3 Dec. 2004, http://www.fas.org/man/company/shipyard/new_york.htm.

30. Brooklyn Navy Yard Development Corporation, Brooklyn Navy Yard, 5 Dec. 2004, http://www.brooklynnavyyard.org/main.html.

31. Roosevelt Island Operating Corporation of New York State: History, 3 Dec. 2004, http://www.rioc.com/history.html.

32. "Roosevelt Island Report: A Cry for Independence ... and a Recommendation to Make Its Only Bridge an Immovable Object," *The New York Times,* 14 Jan. 2001, Sec. 14, Pg. 7.

33. New York City Department of Transportation, Macombs Dam Bridge Over Harlem River, 3 Dec. 2004, http://www.nyc.gov/html/dot/html/bridges/bridges/macombs.html.

34. Ann Buttenwieser, *Manhattan Water-Bound,* New York University Press, New York, 1987, p. 164.

35. Marion J. Klawonn, *Cradle of the Corps. A History of the New York District U.S. Army Corps of Engineers,* U.S. Army Corps of Engineers, 1977.

36. Harlem River and Spuyten Duyvil Improvement Association, *Report on Original and Present Condition of the Improvement,* 1893.

37. "Cash for the Channels. Millions Expended on New York's Harbor," *The Telegram,* 6 Mar. 1890.

38. *The New York Times,* February 1, 1893, p. 4, col. 2 (editorial).

39. Ellen M. Snyder-Grenier, *Brooklyn: An Illustrated History,* Temple University Press, Philadelphia, 1996, p. 152.

40. Gowanus Canal, "City Activates Gowanus Canal Flushing Tunnel," 6 Dec. 2004, http://www.ci.myc.ny.us/html/dep/html/news/gowanus.html.

41. Gowanus Canal Community Development Corporation, "Gowanus Canal Revitalization Program," 6 Dec. 2004, http://www.gowanus.org/gowproject.htm.

42. Jonathan Mahler, "Once Sprucer Gowanus Canal Aspires to Beauty Now," *The New York Times,* 8 June 2001.

43. Meeting by author with Mr. Joseph Seebode, Manager of Harbor Projects, U.S. Army Corps of Engineers, New York, July 23, 2002.

44. Andrew C. Revkin, "Flushing Out the Foul and the Frustration. A New Vista for a Dead-end Canal," *The New York Times,* 1 Feb. 1998. Sec. M, p. 1.

45. Newtown Creek Alliance, History of Newtown Creek, 3 Dec. 2004, http://www.newtowncreek.org/history.html.

46. Newtown Creek Alliance, "Sources of Pollution," 3 Dec. 2004, http://www.newtowncreek.org/pollution.htmln."

47. Richard Weir, "Relic, Hazard or Landmark? Old Refinery's Pros and Cons," *The New York Times,* 16 Jan. 2000, Sec. 14, p. 10.

48. New York City Department of City Planning, *The New Waterfront Revitalization Program,* as approved by the City Council October 13, 1999.

49. Brooklyn Bridge Facts, History and Information, 5 Dec. 2004, http://www.endex.com/gf/buildings/bbridge/bbridgefacts.htm.

50. New York City Department of Transportation, Bridges Information, 4 Dec. 2004, http://www.nyc.gov/himl/dot/html/motorist/bridges.html.

51. Tom Buckley, "The Eighth Bridge," *The New Yorker,* 14 Jan. 1991, Vol. 66, p. 48ff.

52. William Kornblum, *At Sea in the City,* Algonquin Books of Chapel Hill, Chapel Hill, N.C., 2002, p. 129.

53. Peter Hellman, "An Urban Edge of Water; the Lower Manhattan Shore Is More a Place to Play Than Work These Days," *The New York Times,* 13 May 2001, Sec. 14, p. 1.

54. Kevin Bone, ed., *The New York Waterfront: Evolution and Building Culture of the Port and Harbor,* The Monacelli Press, New York, 1997.

55. The National Park Service, Statue of Liberty and Ellis Island, Statue of Liberty, 4 Dec. 2004, http://www.nps.gov/stli/prod02.htm.

56 Meeting with Thomas DeMaria, Executive Director, Waterfront Commission, New York City, January 22, 2002.

57. The National Park Service, Ellis Island. 4 Dec. 2004, http://www.nps.gov/elis/.

Chapter 2

1. Meeting by author with Captain Kenneth Kelleher, Commanding Officer, NYC Police Department Harbor Unit, January 14, 2002.

2. "Peace Across the Hudson," *The New York Times,* Editorial, 6 June 2000.

3. Jamison W. Doig, *Empire on the Hudson: Entrepreneurial Vision and Political Power at the Port Authority,* Columbia University Press, New York, 2001.

4. *Ibid.,* p. 102.

5. *Ibid.,* p. 160.

6. Port Authority of New York and New Jersey, *Building a 21st-Century Port,* October 2000, p. 8.

7. Ron Marsico, "P.A. to Cut $2 Billion in Projects," *The Star-Ledger,* (Newark, N.J.), 14 November 2002.

8. Ronald Smothers, "Governors End Port Au-

thority Rift That Blocked Billions in Projects," *The New York Times*, 2 June 2000.

9. Ronald Smothers, "Port Authority Rift Revealed States' Competitive Instincts," *The New York Times*, 6 June 2000, Sec. B, p. 2.

10. "End of a Stalemate," *The Record* (Bergen County, N.J.), 5 June 2000, p. 12.

11. Joseph J. Seebode and Thomas J. Shea, III, "Synergy in Port Development and Environmental Protection Within the New York/New Jersey Harbor Estuary," Talk given by Joseph Seebode, 2002.

12. Meeting by author with Mr. Brian Maher, Chairman, Maher Terminals, Inc., March 18, 2002.

13. "Malcolm McClain Dies at 87; His Initiation of Container Shipping Revolutionized Maritime Trade," *The Star-Ledger*, (Newark, N.J.), 27 May 2001, p. 27.

14. Eric Lipton, "New York Hums Again, With Asian Trade," *The New York Times*, 22 Nov. 2004.

15. Meeting with Brad Winfree, Director of Warehouse and Logistics, Howland Hook Terminal, December 14, 2004.

16. Meeting by author with Commander Daniel Ronan, Director of Waterways Management, U.S. Coast Guard, in Staten Island, N.Y., on April 17, 2002.

17. "Breaking the Ice," *The New York Times*, 15 Feb. 1992, p. 1.

18. "Schumer Wants X-rays of All Import Boxes," *Journal of Commerce*, 17–23 Dec. 2001, p. 8.

19. Tom Brokaw, "Security of New York Harbor," NBC News broadcast, 15 Sept. 2004.

20. U.S. Coast Guard, "Qualship 21 Initiative," 11 July 2002, http://www.uscg.mil/hq/gm/psc/qualship/qualship.htm

21. George James, "Is the Coast Clear?," *The New York Times*, 26 May 2002, Sec. 14, p. 1.

22. Sherman, Ted, "Harbor Security Tightens Against Nuclear Threat," *The Star-Ledger* (Newark, N.J.), 2 Dec. 2001, p. 1.

23. Ted Sherman, "Security Stays Tight in Harbor; Shipping Restrictions Updated as Officials Fear a Dirty Bomb," *The Star-Ledger* (Newark, N.J.), December 5, 2001, p. 3.

24. Ted Sherman, "Coast Guard Ill-equipped for Its Massive Mission: Antiquated Fleet, Lack of Staff Hinder Anti-terror Effort," *The Star-Ledger* (Newark, N.J.), 24 Dec. 2001, p. 1.

25. Marion J. Klawonn, *Cradle of the Corps. A History of the New York District U.S. Army Corps of Engineers*, U.S. Army Corps of Engineers, 1977.

26. *Ibid.*

27. *Ibid.*

28. Meeting by author with Joseph J. Seebode, Harbor Program Manager, U.S. Army Corps of Engineers, July 23, 2002.

29. Fred, Powledge, "How to Clean a Harbor," *Bioscience*, June 1998. Vol. 48, p. 436.

30. "Harbor dredging to begin," *The Star-Ledger* (Newark, N.J.), 27 August 2002.

31. David Rogers, "Head of Corps of Engineers is Forced Out After Criticising Budget Cut for Agency," *Wall Street Journal*, 7 March 2002, Vol. 239, Issue 46, p. A16.

32. "A Chance to Reshape the Corps," *The New York Times* (Editorial), 18 March 2002, Vol. 151, Sec. A, p. 24.

33. Michael Krieger, *Where Rails Meet the Sea: America's Connection Between Ships and Trains*, Michael Friedman Publishing Group, New York, 1998, p. 29.

34. *Ibid.*, p. 50.

35. Edward Hungerford, *Men of Erie*, Random House, New York, 1946, p. 300.

36. Krieger, op. cit., p. 51.

37. Al Frank, "Giuliani's Rail Cargo Plan Gets Panned; Consultant Says Digging Channels Is Significantly Cheaper," *The Star-Ledger* (Newark, N.J.), 9 Dec. 1998, p. 47.

38. "Study Backs Freight-train Tunnel in New York Harbor," *The New York Times*, 4 Aug. 2000, Sec. B, p. 4.

39. Roberta E. Weisbrod, "Moving Freight on the Water," *Gotham Gazette*, 4 Dec. 2004, http//www.gothamgazette.com/waterfront/sep.01.shtml.

40. Meeting by author with Capt. W. W. Sherwood, president, N.Y. Sandy Hook Pilots Association and Capt. Richard J. Schoenlank president, United N.J. Sandy Hook Pilots Association, May 28, 2002.

41. Tom Cunliffe, *Pilots. Volume 1. Pilot Schooners of North America and Great Britain*, Wooden Boat Publications, Brooklin, Me., 2001.

42. Tom Feeney, "Captain's Final Voyage; One of Harbor's Dwindling Breed Retires," *The Star-Ledger* (Newark, N.J.), 28 Apr. 2002, sec. 1, p. 1.

43. Bob Reiss, "Last of the Family Tugs," *Double Take*, 4 Dec. 2004, http://www.doubletakemagazine.org/features/html/reiss/index.php.

44. Telephone discussion with Captain Brian A. McAllister, President, McAllister Towing Company, April 1, 2002.

45. Meeting with Captain Thomas Brown in Staten Island, July 29, 2002.

46. Josh Leventhal, *Tugs: the World's Hardest Working Boats*, Black Dog & Leventhal Publishers, New York, 1999.

47. Congressman Vito Fossella, Press Release, 15 Mar. 1999, "New Federal Regulations May Save Staten Island Boat Company." 4 Dec. 2004. http://www.house.gov/fossella/pr031599_tug.htm.

48. Raymond J. Baxter and Arthur G. Adams, *Railroad Ferries of the Hudson and Stories of a Deckhand*, Fordham University Press, New York, 1999, p. 18.

49. *Ibid.*, p. 242.

50. Joe Malinconico, "Ferry Operator Hits Choppy Waters," *The Star-Ledger* (Newark, N.J.), 23 Oct. 2004, p. 11.

51. Meeting by author with Alan Ohmsted, New York Center, October 24, 2002.

52. Personal Communication. Carter Craft, "Regional Ferry Coalition Forming," E-Mail, carter@waterwire.net, November 24, 2004.

Chapter 3

1. Ephesus. 5 Dec. 2004, http://www.turizm. net/cities/ephesus.

2. Rick Steve's Travel News: Ostia Antica. 4 Dec. 2004, http://www.ricksteves.com/news/0202/ostia.htm.

3. Mort J. Richardson, *The Dynamics of Dredging*, Placer Management Corporation, Irvine, Calif., 2001.

4. Jeremy Pearce, "Stirring the Waters," *New York Times*, 24 Aug. 2003, Sec. 14, p. 1f.

5. Associated Press, "Harbor Dredging to Begin," *The Star-Ledger* (Newark, N.J.), 27 Aug. 2002.

6. Personal Communication. Vance Barr, Coastal Resources Specialist, New York Department of State, 9 Feb. 2004.

7. John Waldman, *Heartbeats in the Muck*, The Lyons Press, New York, 1999, p. 39.

8. New York–New Jersey Harbor Estuary Program Habitat Workgroup, *2001 Status Report*, April 2001.

9. Meeting held with Mario P. DelVicario, EPA, Region 2, April 10, 2002.

10. Clean Ocean Action, "Contaminated Sediments Update," http://www.cleanoceanaction.org/NewsLetters/1997/Nov97/ContSed.html.

11. Kirk Johnson, "New York Harbor on a Hard Drive," *The New York Times*, June 3, 2002, p. 1.

12. A.M. Neyer, "Shoal Area Once Relegated New York to Lesser Status," *Ocean Navigator*, No. 63, September/October 1994, p. 25.

13. U.S. Works Progress Administration, *Study of Tides and Currents*, 1940.

14. "Tides," Columbia Encyclopedia, 6th Edition, 2000.

15. William Kornblum, *At Sea in the City*, Algonquin Books of Chapel Hill, Chapel Hill, .NC, 2002, p. 166

16. National Canal Museum, "Morris Canal," 4 Dec. 2004, http://www.canals.org/morris.htm.

17. Peter Kaminsky, "If You Land It, Is It Safe?," *The New York Times*, 23 Oct. 2002, Sec. F, p. 8.

18. Chelsea Piers, 4 Dec. 2004, http://www.chelseapiers.com.

19. "The Operation Sail 2000," *Sea History*, Winter 1997–98, Vol. 83, p. 30.

20. Andrew C. Revkin, "A Crowded, Uneasy Mix in Hudson and Harbor," *The New York Times*, 6 Sept. 1998.

21. "Increase in Traffic in the NY Harbor Causing Concerns Among Some Boaters." Eyewitness News. 4 Dec. 2004, http://abclocal.go.com/wabc/news/WABC_080202_boattraffic.html.

22. Gowanus Canal Community Development Corporation. Website: gowanus.org.

23. Metropolitan Waterfront Alliance. Website: waterwire.net.

24. Conversation with Mr. Carter Craft, Director, Metropolitan Waterfront Alliance, June 10, 2004.

Chapter 4

1. Marion J. Klawonn, *Cradle of the Corps: A History of the New York District U.S. Army Corps of Engineers*, U.S. Army Corps of Engineers, New York, June 1977, p. 166.

2. A.M. Neyer, "Shoal Area Once Relegated New York to Lesser Status," *Ocean Navigator*, No. 63, September/October 1994.

3. Al Frank, "It's a Close Call for the Regina; Huge Container Ship Barely Makes It into Port," *The Star-Ledger* (Newark, N.J.), 24 July 1998.

4. Marion J. Klawonn, *Cradle of the Corps: A History of the New York District U.S. Army Corps of Engineers*, U.S. Army Corps of Engineers, New York, June 1977, p. 74.

5. *Ibid.*, p. 69.

6. Edward T. O'Donnell, *Ship Ablaze. The Tragedy of the Steamboat General Slocum*, Broadway Books, New York, 2003.

7. Claude Rust, *The Burning of the General Slocum*, Elsevier/Nelson Books, New York, 1981.

8. An Historical Overview of Passenger Ship Disasters and Casualties, 4 Dec. 2004, http://www.webandwire.com/passengershipsafetyhistory.htm.

9. "Mayor Asks for Reinspection of Steamers," *The New York Times*, 19 June 1904, Sec. 1, p. 1.

10. "Reinspection," *The New York Times*, 23 June 1904, Sec. 8, p. 2.

11. "New York Harbor Patrolled by Customs Authorities in Search of License Violations," *The New York Times*, 29 June 1908, Sec. 3, p. 4.

12. "New York Port Marine Police to Keep Watch on Excursion Steamers," *The New York Times*, 2 July 1909, Sec. 16, p. 2.

13. Eric Hamberger, *The Historical Atlas of New York City*, Henry Holt and Company, New York, 1994.

14. "Munitions Explosions Shake New York," *The New York Times*, 30 July 1916, p. 1.

15. "Munitions Explosions Cause Loss of $20,000,000," *The New York Times*, 31 July 1916, p. 1.

16. Jules Witcover, *Sabotage at Black Tom: Imperial Germany's Secret War in America, 1914.* Algonquin Books of Chapel Hill, Chapel Hill, N.C., 1989.

17. New York State Historical Society, Port in a Storm: The Port of New York in World War II, 4 Jan. 2003, http://www.nysm.nysed.gov/research_collections/research/history/hisportofnewyork.html.

18. *Ibid.*, p. 1.

19. Elliot Willensky, *When Brooklyn Was the World 1920–1957*, Harmony Books, New York, 1986, p. 208.

20. *Ibid.*, p. 29.

21. Michael Gannon, *Operation Drumbeat: The Dramatic True Story of Germany's First U-Boat Attacks Along the American Coast in World War II*, Harper and Row, New York, 1990.

22. Richard Grudens, "A Mysterious End for the Majestic Normandie," *World War II*, 2 July 2002, Vol. 17, Issue 2.

23. Meeting with Cdr. Ronan of the Coast Guard, April 17, 2002.

24. "River Rescuers," *The Tribeca Tribune*, March 2002, pp. 22–23.

25. Andrew C. Rivken, "Old Savior of the Waterfront is Pressed Back in Service," *The New York Times*, 23 Sept. 2001.

26. John Snyder, "Ferries Speed to the Rescue after WTC Attack," *Marine Log*, Oct. 2001.

27. "A Shining Light in our Darkest Hour," *Professional Mariner*, December–January 2002.

28. "U.S. Navy Comfort Ship Cares for a City in Need," *New York Harbor Watch*, 12 Oct. 2001.

29. *Ibid.*

30. "In the Wake of September 11 Waterfront Evacuation, Calls Are Heard for Better Access to the Water," *The Battery Park Broadsheet*, 15–30 Nov. 2001.

31. Aaron Brown, "CNN Presents," 8 P.M., 11 Dec. 2004.

Chapter 5

1. "Port Authority Agrees to Let Piers Be Used for Brooklyn Bridge Park," *The New York Times*, 11 Feb. 2000.

2. Andrew C. Revkin, "Strides Seen in New York Harbor Cleanup," *The New York Times*, 15 June 1995.

3. Liberty State Park, "History of Liberty State Park," 15 Dec. 2002, http://www.libertystatepark.com/history.htm.

4. New York City Department of City Planning, *The New Waterfront Revitalization Program*, 13 Oct. 1999.

5. Frank T. Kryza, *The Power of Light*, McGraw-Hill, New York, 2003.

6. "Port Authority Hopes to Dig Up New Dredging Technology," *The Star-Ledger* (Newark, N.J.), 27 Dec. 2000, p. 31.

7. Al Frank, "It's a Close Call for the Regina; Huge Container Ship Barely Makes It into Port," *The Star-Ledger* (Newark, N.J.), 24 July 1998.

8. Tina Rosenberg, "Globalization: the Free-Trade Fix," *The New York Times*, 18 Aug. 2002, Sec. 6, p. 28.

9. Meeting with Joseph Seebode, Corps of Engineers, July 23, 2002

10. Meeting with Captain Sherwood, Sandy Hook Pilots, May 28, 2002.

11. Roberta E. Weisbrod, "Moving Freight on Water," *Gotham Gazette*, 4 Dec. 2004, http://www.gothamgazette.com/waterfront/sep.01.shtml.

12. "75 Years Late: The Harbor Freight Tunnel," Mobilizing the Region. 11 Oct. 2002, http://www.tstc.org/bulletin/19961220/mtr10904.htm.

13. Representative Jerrold Nadler, "Rail Freight Tunnel Gets Two Key Endorsement Letters," Press Release, 21 Oct. 2002.

14. Jerrold Nadler and Michael R. Long, "Make Brooklyn a World-Class Seaport," Op-ed, *The New York Times*, 13 Apr. 1996.

15. Port Authority of New York and New Jersey, *Building a 21st Century Port*, p. 25.

16. Ernst G. Frankel, *Port Planning and Development*, John Wiley and Sons, New York, 1987.

17. Peter Tirschwell, "It Isn't About In-Bond," *Journal of Commerce*, 17–23 Dec. 2001, p. 4.

Bibliography

Albion, Robert Greenhalgh. *The Rise of the New York Port.* New York: Charles Scribner and Sons, 1970.

Armbruster, William. "NY Harbor Seeks to Add 481 Dockworkers." *Journal of Commerce*, 5 May 2000.

Associated Press. "Harbor Dredging to Begin," *The Star-Ledger* (Newark, N.J.), 27 Aug. 2002.

Banfield, Edward C. *Political Influence.* The Free Press of Glencoe, 1961.

Barr, Vance. Personal Communication. Coastal Resources Specialist, New York Department of State, 9 Feb. 2004.

Baxter, Raymond J., and Adams, Arthur G. *Railroad Ferries of the Hudson and Stories of a Deckhand.* New York: Fordham University Press, 1999.

Blair, Jayson. "The Millennium Arrives in the Harbor by Sail and Steam." *The New York Times*, 29 June 2000, p. B1.

Bone, Kevin, ed. *The New York Waterfront: Evolution and Building Culture of the Port and Harbor.* New York: Monacelli, 1997.

"Breaking the Ice." *The New York Times*, 15 Feb. 1992, p.1.

Breen, Ann, and Ruth C. Thaler-Carter. *Keeping Waterfronts Distinctive: Choosing the Right Mix.* The Waterfront Press, 1990.

Brokaw, Tom. "Security of New York Harbor." NBC News Broadcast, 15 Sept. 2004.

Brooklyn Bridge Facts, History and Information, 5 Dec. 2004. http://www.endex.com/gf/buildings/bbridge/bbridgefacts.htm.

Brooklyn Navy Yard Development Corporation. Brooklyn Navy Yard, 5 Dec. 2004. http://www.brooklynnavyyard.org/main.html.

Brown, Aaron. "CNN Presents." 8 P.M., 11 Dec. 2004.

Brown, Thomas. Author Interview. Staten Island, New York, July 29, 2002.

Brozan, Nadine. "Sugar Relics Are Reborn on Each Side of the Hudson." *The New York Times*, 15 Mar. 2002, sec. B, p. 4.

Buckley, Tom. "The Eighth Bridge." *The New Yorker*, 14 Jan. 1991, Vol. 66, p. 48ff.

Buttenwieser, Ann L. *Manhattan Water-Bound.* New York University Press, 1987.

Capuzzo, Jill P. "Hitting Ground Zero Running." *The New York Times*, 27 Jan. 2002.

"Cash for the Channels. Millions Expended on New York's Harbor." *The Telegram*, 6 Mar. 1890.

Chambers, Steve. "Gold Coast Hits Pay Dirt." *The Star-Ledger* (Newark, N.J.), 30 Aug. 2004, p. 11.

"A Chance to Reshape the Corps." *The New York Times*, Editorial, 18 Mar. 2002, Vol. 151, sec. A, p. 24.

Chelsea Piers, 3 Dec. 2004. http://www.chelseapiers.com.

Christian, Nichole M. "A Landlubber Whose Mind Is on the Harbor." *The New York Times*, 4 Oct. 2002.

Clean Ocean Action, "Contaminated Sediments Update," http://www.cleanoceanaction.org/NewsLetters/1997/Nov97/ContSed.html.

Coastlines, "Reducing Contamination in New York Harbor Sediments; Cleaning Up Our Act," 4 Dec. 2004. http://www.epa.gov/owow/estuaries/coastlines/spring98/nyharbor.html.

Coleman, Steven J. Telephone Conversation. February 13, 2002.

Collins, Glenn. "Historians Weigh Attack's Impact on New York City." *The New York Times*, 6 Oct. 2001.

Coppola, John. "Fulton Ferry and the Brooklyn Navy Yard." 3 Dec. 2004. http://www.myc.org/Harbor%20Tour/History/Fulton_Ferry_Navy_Yard.htm.

Craft, Carter. Personal Communication. 10 June 2004; 24 November 2004.

Cretan, N. Nick. Telephone Conversation. March 22, 2002.

Cunliffe, Tom. *Pilots. Volume 1. Pilot Schooners of North America and Great Britain*. Brooklin, ME: Wooden Boat Publications, 2001.

Day, Andrew, "Swill Seeking." *Civilization*, April/May 1999, Vol. 6, Issue 2, p. 24.

DelVicario, Mario P., and Robert Nyman. Environmental Protection Agency, Region 2. Author Interview. New York, April 10, 2002.

DeMaria, Thomas, and David B. Greenfield. Waterfront Commission of New York Harbor. Author Interview. New York, January 22, 2002.

"Do All the Dredging Now." *The Star-Ledger* (Newark, N.J.), Editorial, 23 Jan. 2002, p. 10.

Doig, Jamison W. *Empire on the Hudson: Entrepreneurial Vision and Political Power at the Port Authority*. New York: Columbia University Press, 2001.

"Dream and Reality on the Hudson." *The New York Times*, Editorial, 21 Feb. 1998.

Dredged Material Management Plan, New York–New Jersey Harbor Marine Resource Advisory Council Bulletin, Vol. VIII, No. 2, 4 Dec. 2004. http://www.msrc.sunysb.edu/MRAC/pages/Bv8n2s03.html

"Dropping the Hook New York Style." *Ocean Navigator*, No. 88, March/April 1998.

Duffy, Francis J., and William H. Miller, *The New York Harbor Book*. Falmouth, ME: TBW Books, 1986.

Dunlap, David W. "Plans for the Neglected East River Shoreline." *The New York Times*, 1 Aug. 2002, sec. B, p. 1.

"End of a Stalemate." *The Record* (Bergen County, N.J.), 5 June 2000, p. 12.

Environmental Protection Agency. "Dredged Material Management Program." 4 Dec. 2004. http://www.epa.gov/region2/water/dredge/intro.htm.

Ephesus. 5 Dec. 2004. http://www.turizm.net/cities/ephesus.

"Erie Canal." *National Canal Museum*, 4 Dec. 2004. http://www.canals.org/erie.htm.

Feeney, Tom. "Captain's Final Voyage; One of Harbor's Dwindling Breed Retires." *The Star-Ledger* (Newark, N.J.), 28 Apr. 2002, sec. 1, p. 1.

Fort Tilden History. "Nazi U-Boats Attack New York Shipping!" 5 Dec. 2004. http://www.geocities.com/fort_tilden/uboats.html.

"For 2 ships: Goodbye, New York. Hello, Bayonne." *New York Times*, 4 Jan. 2004, Travel Section, p. 3.

Fossella, Congressman Vito. Press Release, March 15, 1999. "New Federal Regulations May Save Staten Island Boat Company." 4 Dec. 2004. http://www.house.gov/fossella/pr031599_tug.htm.

Frank, Al. "Giuliani's Rail Cargo Plan Gets Panned; Consultant Says Digging Channels Is Significantly Cheaper." *The Star-Ledger* (Newark, N.J.), 9 Dec. 1998, p. 47.

_____. "It's a Close Call for the Regina; Huge Container Ship Barely Makes It into Port." *The Star Ledger* (Newark, N.J.), 24 July 1998.

_____. "PA Looks to Deepen Kill Van Kull Even Further; Hearing to Be Held on Dredge Blasting." *The Star-Ledger* (Newark, N.J.), 22 January 2002.

_____. "Port Gets $120M for Channel Dredging; Deeper Cargo Ships Would Gain Entry." *The Star-Ledger* (Newark, N.J.), 23 Feb. 2002.

_____. "River Dance; Around-the-Clock Choreography of Tugboats Maneuvering Great Ships Goes Largely Unnoticed in the General Hubbub of New York Harbor, the Region's Center of Commerce." *The Star-Ledger* (Newark, N.J.), 5 July 1998, p. 1.

_____. "Whitman Asks Gore to Intercede in Dredge Rift." *The Star-Ledger* (Newark, N.J.), 14 April 2000.

"Fresh Kills: Landfill to Landscape." Community District 2, Northern Subarea. 3 Dec. 2004. http://www.ci.nyc.ny.us/html/dcp/html/fkl/ada/about/1_3.html.

Fried, Joseph P. "A Nineteenth Century Pier, A 21-st-Century Vision." *The New York Times*, 13 June 2004, Metro sec., p. 48.

Friedman, Andrew. "So Near and Yet So Far (and so Overrun with Rats)." *The New York Times*, 1 Apr. 2001, sec. L, p. 6.

Gannon, Michael. *Operation Drumbeat: The Dramatic True Story of Germany's First U-Boat Attacks Along the American Coast in World War II*. New York: Harper and Row, 1990.

"Governor's Island." *Columbia Encyclopedia*, April 23, 2003. 6th edition, New York: Columbia University Press, 2001.

Gowanus Canal, "City Activates Gowanus Canal Flushing Tunnel." 6 Dec. 2004. http://www.ci.myc.ny.us/html/dep/html/news/gowanus.html.

Gowanus Canal Community Development Corporation." Gowanus Canal Revitalization Program." 6 Dec. 2004. http://www.gowanus.org/gowproject.htm.

Greater Astoria Historical Society. "History Topics: Bridges Hell Gate Bridge." 4 Dec. 2004. www.astorialic.org/topics/transportation/hellgate.shtm

_____. "History Topics: Queensboro Bridge." 4 Dec. 2004. http://www.astorialic.org/topics/transportation/qbridge.shtm.

_____. "The LIC-Astoria Story." 3 Dec. 2004. http://www.astorialic.org/story/story.htm.

Grudens, Richard. "A Mysterious End for the Majestic Normandie." *World War II*, 2 July 2002, Vol. 17, Issue 2.

Hamberger, Eric. *The Historical Atlas of New York City*. New York: Henry Holt, 1994.

Harlem River and Spuyten Duyvil Improvement Association. *Report on Original and Present Condition of the Improvement*, 1893.

Hellman, Peter. "An Urban Edge of Water; the Lower Manhattan Shore Is More a Place to Play Than Work These Days." *The New York Times*, 13 May 2001, sec. 14, p. 1.

Herszenhorn, David M. "New Jersey, Proud Owner, To Raise Flag on Ellis Island." *The New York Times*, 4 July 1998, sec. B, p. 2.

"An Historical Overview of Passenger Ship Disasters and Casualties." 4 Dec. 2004. www.webandwire.com/passengershipsafetyhistory.htm.

Holusha, John. "Making Way for Bigger Ships." *The New York Times*, 5 Aug. 2001, sec. R, p. 1.

Hungerford, Edward. *Men of Erie*. New York: Random House, 1946.

"In the Wake of September 11 Waterfront Evacuation, Calls Are Heard for Better Access to the Water," *The Battery Park Broadsheet*, 15–30 Nov. 2001.

"Increase in Traffic in the NY Harbor Causing Concerns Among Some Boaters." Eyewitness News. 4 Dec. 2004. http://abclocal.go.com/wabc/news/WABC_080202_boattraffic.html.

Jackson, Nancy Beth. "Close-Knit Waterfront Enclave in Bronx." *The New York Times*, 14 April 2002, sec. L, p. 5.

James, George. "Is the Coast Clear?" *The New York Times*, 26 May 2002, sec. 14, p. 1.

Johnson, Harry, and Frederick S. Lightfoot. *Maritime New York in Old Photographs*. New York: Dover, 1980.

Johnson, Kirk. "Dumping Ends at Great Kills, Symbol of Throw-Away Era." *The New York Times*, 18 Mar. 2001, p. 1f.

_____. "New York Harbor on a Hard Drive." *The New York Times*, 3 June 2002, p. 1.

Jones, Stuart E., R. F. Sisson, and Davis S. Boyer. "Here's New York Harbor." *The National Geographic Magazine*, December 1954, p. 773f.

Kaminsky, Peter. "If You Land It, Is It Safe?" *The New York Times*, 23 Oct. 2002, sec. F, p. 8.

Kannapell, Andrea. "On the Waterfront; Developers' Glittering Dreams Are Alive Again Along the Hudson." *The New York Times*, 15 Feb. 1998.

Kelleher, Kenneth. Commanding Officer, New York City Police Department Harbor Unit. Author Interview. Brooklyn Army Terminal, Brooklyn, New York, January 14, 2002.

Kime, Patricia, and Seena Simon. "Coast Guard Plunges into Security Role." *Air Force Times*, 24 Sept. 2001, Vol. 62, Issue 9, p. 28.

Kinetz, Erika. "Envisioning a Day When Ferries Abound on City Waters." *The New York Times*, 22 July 2001.

Klawonn, Marion J. *Cradle of the Corps. A History of the New York District U.S. Army Corps of Engineers*. New York: U.S. Army Corps of Engineers, 1977.

Kornblum, William. *At Sea in the City*. Chapel Hill, NC: Algonquin Books 2002.

Krieger, Michael. *Where Rails Meet the Sea; America's Connection Between Ships and Trains*. New York: Michael Friedman, 1998.

Kryza, Frank T. *The Power of Light*. New York: McGraw-Hill, 2003.

Lang, Steven, and Peter H. Spectre. *On The Hawser: A Tugboat Album*. Camden, ME: Down East, 1980.

Lentz, Philip. "PA Harbors Plans to Up Port Traffic; Fast Digging Will Aid Economy." *Crain's New York Business*, 16 July 2001.

Leventhal, Josh. *Tugs: the World's Hardest Working Boats*. New York: Black Dog & Leventhal, 1999.

Liberty Landing Marina. 3 Dec. 2004. http://www.libertylandingmarina.com.

Liberty State Park Home Page. 4 Dec. 2004. http://www.libertystatepark.com.

Liberty State Park. Central Railroad Terminal. 4 Dec. 2004. http://www.libertystatepark.com/crrnj.htm.

_____. "History of Liberty State Park." 15 Dec. 2002, http://www.libertystatepark.com/history.htm.

Lippincott, E.E. "Sounding a Death Knell for a Long-forsaken Waterway." *The New York Times*, 10 Feb. 2002.

Lipton, Eric. "New York Hums Again, With Asian Trade." *The New York Times*, 22 November 2004.

Lisberg, Adam. "New Plan Would Dredge Port Channels All in One Stage; PA Still Needs Federal OK, Funding for Project." *The Record* (Bergen County, N.J.), 27 July 2001.

Lukas, Paul. "On Wings of Commerce." *Fortune*, 22 Mar. 2004, p. 109.

Maher, Brian. Maher Terminals, Inc. Author Interview. Jersey City, New Jersey, March 18, 2002.

Mahler, Jonathan. "Once Sprucer Gowanus Canal Aspires to Beauty Now." *The New York Times*, 8 June 2001.

Malinconico, Joe. "Ferry Operator Hits Choppy Waters." *The Star-Ledger* (Newark, N.J.), 23 Oct. 2004, p. 11.

Mansen, Mike, John Trubia, and Bob Haigney. New York City Police Department Harbor Unit. Author Interview. New York Harbor Police Patrol Boat, January 24, 2002.

The Maritime Association. 8 Dec. 2004. http://www.nymaritime.org.

Maritime Command Museum. World War II Convoys. 4 Dec. 2004. http://www.pspmembers.com/marcommuseum/convoys.html.

Marsico, Ron. "PA to Cut $2 Billion in Projects." *The Star-Ledger* (Newark, N.J.), 14 Nov. 2002.

Martin, Douglas. "New York Tug Strike Deals a Blow to a Shrinking Business." *The New York Times*, 8 June 1988, sec. B, p. 1.

Maynard, Daniel S. Manager Government and Community Relations, Port Authority of New York and New Jersey. Telephone Conversation. March 6, 2002.

"Mayor Asks for Reinspection of Steamers." *The New York Times*, 19 June 1904, sec.1, p. 1.

McAllister, Brian A. President, McAllister Towing Company, Inc. Telephone Conversion. April 1, 2002.

Metropolitan Waterfront Alliance. Website: waterwire.net.

Miller, Davis Neal. Brooklyn Navy Yard. 3 Dec. 2004. http://www.brooklyn.net/neighborhoods/navy_yard_01.html.

Moran, Eugene F. Sr. . *Famous Harbors of the World.* New York: Random House, 1953.

"Munitions Explosions Cause Loss of $ 20,000,000." *The New York Times*, 31 July 1916, p. 1.

"Munitions Explosions Shake New York." *The New York Times*, 30 July 1916, p. 1.

Museum of the City of New York, Research Department. Shipping Piers and Docks file. Notes. No date.

Nadler, Representative Jerrold. "Rail Freight Tunnel Gets Two Key Endorsement Letters." Press Release, 21 Oct. 2002.

National Canal Museum. "Morris Canal." 4 Dec. 2004. http://www.canals.org/morris.htm.

The National Park Service, Ellis Island. 4 Dec. 2004. http://www.nps.gov/elis.

The National Park Service, Statue of Liberty and Ellis Island, Statue of Liberty. 4 Dec. 2004. http://www.nps.gov/stli/prod02.htm.

Natural Resources Protective Association. "New York City Comprehensive Waterfront Plan.' 2 Dec. 2004. http://www.nrpa.com/waterfront.htm.

"New Attention from City Hall." Gotham Gazette.com. 3 Dec. 2004. http://www.gothamgazette.com/waterfront.

Newman, Andy. "Life Returns to a Fouled Creek." *The New York Times*, 12 Nov. 1999, sec. B, p. 1.

Newtown Creek Alliance. "History of Newtown Creek." 3 Dec. 2004. http://www.newtowncreek.org/history.html.

_____. "Sources of Pollution." 3 Dec. 2004. http://www.newtowncreek.org/pollution.html.

Newtown Creek Virtual Tour@OLDNYC.com. 3 Dec. 2004. http:www.oldnyc.com/newtown_creek/lic_lirr/lic_lirr_1.html.

New York City. Department of City Planning. *The New Waterfront Revitalization Program* as approved by the City Council. 13 Oct. 1999.

_____. Department of Transportation. Bridges Information. 4 Dec. 2004. http://www.nyc.gov/html/dot/html/motorist/bridges.html.

_____. _____. Macombs Dam Bridge over Harlem River. 3 Dec. 2004. http://www.nyc.gov/html/dot/html/bridges/bridges/macombs.html.

_____. Parks Department. *Improvement of Great Kills Harbor.* 1937.

"New York Harbor Patrolled by Customs Authorities in Search of License Violations." *The New York Times*, 29 June 1908, sec. 3, p. 4.

New York Naval Shipyard. 3 Dec. 2004. http://www.fas.org/man/company/shipyard/new_york.htm.

New York–New Jersey Harbor Estuary Program Habitat Workgroup. *2001 Status Report.* April 2001.

New York–New Jersey Harbor Estuary Program. *Final Comprehensive Conservation and Management Plan*, March 1996.

_____. *Harbor Health/Human Health.* 2001.

"New York Port Marine Police to Keep Watch on Excursion Steamers." *The New York Times*, 2 July 1909, sec. 16, p. 2.

New York Department of State. "Coastal Issues: NY Harbor Navigation Study." 4 Dec. 2004. http://www.dos.state.ny.us/cstl/harbor.html.

New York State Historical Society. "Port in a Storm: The Port of New York in World War II. 4 Jan. 2003. http://www.nysm.nysed.gov/hisportofnewyork.html.

The New York Times, Editorial, 1 Feb. 1893, p. 4, Col. 2.

Neyer, A.M. "Shoal Area Once Relegated New York to Lesser Status." *Ocean Navigator*, No. 63, September/October 1994, p. 25.

_____. "Taming Hell Gate Was Decades-Long Task." *Ocean Navigator*, No, 60, March/April 1994, p. 38.

Nugent, Meg. "East River Grounding Shakes Up 50 Aboard Ferry." *The Star-Ledger* (Newark, N.J.), 11 June 1999.

O'Donnell, Edward T. *Ship Ablaze. The Tragedy of the Steamboat General Slocum.* New York: Broadway Books, 2003.

Ohmsted, Alan. Head, Ferries, Department of Transportation, Department of Planning, New York City. Author Interview. New York, October 24, 2002.

"An Old Idea for the Waterfront, Pared Down, Still Provokes Passions." *The New York Times*, 3 Mar. 2002, p. 33.

Olson, Mancur, Jr. *The Logic of Collective Action.* New York: Schocken Books, 1965.

"The Operation Sail 2000." *Sea History*, Winter 1997–98, Vol. 83, p. 30.

"Peace Across the Hudson." *The New York Times*, Editorial, 6 June 2000.

Pearce, Jeremy. "Stirring the Waters." *New York Times*, 24 Aug. 2003, sec. 14, p. 1f.

Perry, John. *American Ferryboats.* New York: Wilfred Funk, 1957.

"Port Authority Agrees to Let Piers Be Used for Brooklyn Bridge Park." *The New York Times*, 11 Feb. 2000.

Port Authority Hopes to Dig Up New Dredging Technology." *The Star-Ledger* (Newark, N.J.), 27 Dec. 2000, p. 31.

Port Authority of New York and New Jersey. "About the Port Authority." 4 Dec. 2004. http://www.panynj.com.

_____. *Building a 21st Century Port*, October 2002.

_____. *Portviews*, January 2002, Vol. 1, No. 2.

_____. "Port Authority Receives Approval to Begin $1.8 Billion Program to Deepen NY-NJ Port Channels to 50 Feet." Press Release, 3 Dec. 2004. http://www.panynj.gov/pr/pressrelease.php3?id=244.

Powledge, Fred. "How to Clean a Harbor." *Bioscience*, June 1998, Vol. 48, p. 436.

Regalbuto, Captain Anthony. Chief of Port Security, U.S. Coast Guard, *Port Security, Testimony before House Sub-committee on Coast Guard and Marine Transportation*, 13 Mar. 2002.

"Reinspection." *The New York Times*, Editorial, 23 June 1904, sec. 8, p. 2.

Reiss, Bob. "Last of the Family Tugs." *Double Take*, 4 Dec. 2004. http://www.doubletakemagazine.org/features/html/reiss/index.php.

Revkin, Andrew C. "A Crowded, Uneasy Mix in Hudson and Harbor." *The New York Times*, 6 Sept. 1998.

_____. "Flushing Out the Foul and the Frustration. A New Vista for a Dead-end Canal." *The New York Times*, 1 Feb. 1998. sec. M, p. 1.

_____. "In Harbor, a Vanishing Era." *The New York Times*, 3 Jan. 1999, Metro sec. p. 23f.

_____. "Old Savior of the Waterfront Is Pressed Back in Service." *The New York Times*, 23 Sept. 2001.

_____. "Strides Seen in New York Harbor Cleanup." *The New York Times*, 15 June 1995.

Richardson, Mort J. *The Dynamics of Dredging.* Placer Management Corporation, 2001.

Rick Steve's Travel News: Ostia Antica. 4 Dec. 2004. http://www.ricksteves.com/news/0202/ostia.htm.

"River Rescuers." *The Tribeca Tribune*, March 2002, pp. 22–23.

Robinson, Bill. "Ripe for Development: New York Harbor; The New York Harbor Festival Shows Greater New York Waters—A Fine Area for Boating Activity, but Sadly Undeveloped." *Yachting*, October 1984, p. 41.

Rogers, David. "Head of Corps of Engineers is Forced Out After Criticizing Budget Cuts for Agency." *Wall Street Journal*, 7 Mar. 2002, Vol. 239, Issue 46, p. 16.

Ronan, Daniel. Director of Waterways Management, U.S. Coast Guard. Author Interview. Staten Island, New York, April 17, 2002.

Roosevelt Island Operating Corporation of New York State: History, 3 Dec. 2004. http://www.rioc.com/history.html.

"Roosevelt Island Report: A Cry for Independence and a Recommendation to Make Its Only Bridge an Immovable Object." *The New York Times*, 14 Jan. 2001, sec. 14, p. 7.

Rosenberg, Tina. "Globalization: The Free-Trade Fix." *The New York Times*, 18 Aug. 2002, sec. 6, p. 28.

Rust, Claude. *The Burning of the General Slocum.* New York: Elsevier/Nelson, 1981.

Schoenlank, Richard J. United New Jersey Sandy Hook Pilots. Author Interview. Staten Island, New York, May 28, 2002.

"Schumer Wants X-rays of All Import Boxes." *Journal of Commerce*, 17–23 Dec. 2001, p. 8.

Seebode, Joseph J. Harbor Program Manager, U.S. Army Corps of Engineers. Author Interview. New York, July 23, 2002.

_____, and Shea, Thomas J. III. "Synergy in Port Development and Environmental Protection Within the New York/New Jersey Harbor Estuary." Talk given by Joseph J. Seebode, 2002.

"75 Years Late: The Harbor Freight Tunnel." Mobilizing the Region. 11 Oct. 2002. http://www.tstc.org/bulletin/19961220/mtr10904.htm.

Shaw, David W. "Dredging New York Harbor." *Offshore*, October 1997.

Sherman, Ted. "Coast Guard Ill-equipped for Its Massive Mission; Antiquated Fleet, Lack of Staff Hinder Anti-terror Effort." *The Star-Ledger* (Newark, N.J.), 24 Dec. 2001, p. 1.

_____. "Harbor Security Tightens Against Nuclear Threat." *The Star-Ledger* (Newark, N.J.), 2 Dec. 2001, p. 1.

_____. "Security Stays Tight in Harbor; Shipping Restrictions Up-dated as Officials Fear a Dirty Bomb." *The Star-Ledger* (Newark, N.J.), December 5, 2001, p. 3.

Sherwood, W.W. President, New York Sandy Hook Pilots. Author Interview. Staten Island, New York, May 28, 2002.

"A Shining Light in Our Darkest Hour." *Professional Mariner*, December–January 2002.

Smith, Jean R. Managing Director, The Seamens Church Institute. Author Interview. Port Newark, New Jersey, January 15, 2002.

Smothers, Ronald. "As Port Authority Stalls, Ex-governors Urge Talks." *The New York Times*, 15 April 2000.

_____. "Big Obstacle to Dredging Posed by Little Larvae." *The New York Times*, 10 Mar. 2002, p. 44.

_____. "Governors End Port Authority Rift That Blocked Billions in Projects." *The New York Times*, 2 June 2000.

_____. "McGreevey's Port Nominee Faces Two-party Scrutiny." *The New York Times*, 24 Feb. 2002, p. 26.

_____. "Port Authority Rift Revealed States' Competitive Instincts." *The New York Times*, 6 June 2000, sec. B, p. 2.

_____. "The Rapidly Sinking Spirit of a Harbor Dredging Pact; Environmentalists and Port Interests Clash." *The New York Times*, 23 Jan. 2000.

Snyder-Grenier, Ellen M. *Brooklyn: an Illustrated History*. Philadelphia: Temple University Press, 1996, p. 152.

Snyder, John. "Ferries Speed to the Rescue after WTC Attack." *Marine Log*, Oct. 2001.

Strumsky, Steve. "A Walk Along the Water Is Not a Simple Matter." *The New York Times*, 13 Jan. 2002, sec. 14, p. 1.

"Study Backs Freight-train Tunnel in New York Harbor." *The New York Times*, 4 Aug. 2000, sec. B, p. 4.

Sullivan, Bill. "Putting New Jersey's Shore Back on the Map." *The Star-Ledger* (Newark, N.J.), 26 Jan. 2003, sec. 11, Pg. 1.

Sullivan, John. "From Here to There." *The New York Times*, 4 Nov. 2001.

Tirschwell, Peter. "It Isn't About In-bond." *Journal of Commerce*, 17–23 Dec. 2001, p.4.

_____. and Joseph A. Bonney. Journal of Commerce. Author Interview. Newark, New Jersey, March 28, 2002.

"A Trip Back in Time, to Welfare Island." *The New York Times*, 22 Feb. 1998, sec. 14, p. 12.

United States. Coast Guard. "Qualship 21 Initiative." 11 July 2002. http://www.uscg.mil/hq/g-m/psc/qualship/qualship.htm.

_____. Congress. House Committee on Public Works. *Waste Disposal in Coastal Waters of New York Harbor*, 1970.

_____. Senate. Committee on Commerce, Science and Transportation. *The Port and Maritime Security Act: Hearing on S. 1214*. Testimony of Stephen E. Flynn, Ph.D., Senior Fellow, National Security Studies, Council on Foreign Relations, 19 Feb. 2002.

_____. _____. _____. Oceans, Atmosphere and Fisheries subcommittee. *Hearing on the Role of the Coast Guard and NOAA in Maritime Security*. Testimony of Richard M. Larrabee, Director, Port Commerce Division, Port Authority of New York and New Jersey, 11 Oct. 2001.

"U.S. Navy Comfort Ship Cares for a City in Need." *New York Harbor Watch*, 12 Oct. 2001.

_____. Works Progress Administration. *Study of Tides and Currents*, 1940.

"Views." *The New York Times*, Sept. 2001.

Virtual Circle Line. Queensboro Bridge and Roosevelt Island Tram. 4 Dec. 2004. http://www.telescreen.org/circleline/index24.html.

Waldman, John. *Heartbeats in the Muck*. New York: The Lyons Press, 1999.

_____. "Public Parks, Recreational Access, and the Post-industrial Harbor of New York." Gothamgazette.com. 2 Dec. 2004.

Warner, Susan. "Lots of Work West of the Hudson." *The New York Times*, 26 Jan. 2003, sec. 14, p. 1.

"Waterfront," *Gothamgazette.com*, 5 Dec. 2004. http//www.gothamgazette.com/waterfront/apr.01.shtml.

Waterfront Commission of New York Harbor, *Annual Reports*, 1956–2000.

Weir, Richard. "Relic, Hazard or Landmark? Old Refinery's Pros and Cons." *The New York Times*, 16 Jan. 2000, sec. 14, p. 10.

Weisbrod, Roberta E. "Moving Freight on the Water." *Gotham Gazette*, 4 Dec. 2004. http://www.gothamgazette.com/waterfront/sep.01.shtml.

Werstein, Irving. *The General Slocum Incident: Story of an Ill-fated Ship*, New York: John Day, 1965.

White, Norval. *New York: A Physical History*. New York: Macmillan, 1987.

Wikipedia. "Kill Van Kull." 3 Dec. 2004. http://en.wikipedia.org/wiki/Kill_Van_Kull.

Willensky, Elliot. *When Brooklyn Was the World, 1920–1957*. New York: Harmony Books, 1986.

Winchell, Matthew. Assistant Hd. Ferries, Department of Transportation, Department of Planning. Author Interview. New York, October 24, 2002.

Witcover, Jules. *Sabotage at Black Tom: Imperial Germany's Secret War in America, 1914*, Chapel Hill, NC: Algonquin Books, 1989.

Woods, William. Head, Waterfront Development, New York City, City Planning Department. Author Interview. New York, September 13, 2002.

Younger, William Lee. *Old Brooklyn in Early Photographs*. New York: Dover, 1978.

Index